ADDICTION COUNSELING COMPETENCIES

The Knowledge, Skills, and Attitudes of Professional Practice

Technical Assistance Publication (TAP) Series

21

U.S. Department of Health and Human Services
Substance Abuse and Mental Health Services Administration
Center for Substance Abuse Treatment

1 Choke Cherry Road
Rockville, MD 20857

Acknowledgments

A number of people deserve recognition for their tireless and dedicated work on this document. The publication was originally conceived and written by the National Addiction Technology Transfer Center (ATTC) Curriculum Committee. The Committee, one of six national committees designed to serve the ATTC Network, comprises representatives from several ATTC Regional Centers and the ATTC National Office. This group was responsible for the original 1998 publication and for the 2000 draft on which this updated edition is based (see page v). A second Committee convened in 2005 to update and finalize the current document (see page vi). Karl D. White, Ed.D., and Catherine D. Nugent, M.S., served as the Center for Substance Abuse Treatment (CSAT) ATTC Project Officers. Christina Currier served as the CSAT Government Project Officer. This publication was produced by JBS International, Inc. (JBS), under the Knowledge Application Program (KAP) contract number 270-04-7049.

Disclaimer

The views, opinions, and content of this publication are those of the authors and do not necessarily reflect the views, opinions, or policies of SAMHSA or HHS.

Public Domain Notice

All materials appearing in this volume except those taken directly from copyrighted sources are in the public domain and may be reproduced or copied without permission from SAMHSA or the authors. Citation of the source is appreciated. However, this publication may not be reproduced or distributed for a fee without the specific, written authorization of the Office of Communications, SAMHSA, HHS.

Electronic Access and Printed Copies

This publication may be ordered or downloaded from SAMHSA's Publications Ordering Web page at http://store.samhsa.gov. Or, please call SAMHSA at 1-877-SAMHSA-7 (1-877-726-4727) (English and Español).

Recommended Citation

Center for Substance Abuse Treatment. *Addiction Counseling Competencies: The Knowledge, Skills, and Attitudes of Professional Practice*. Technical Assistance Publication (TAP) Series 21. HHS Publication No. (SMA) 15-4171. Rockville, MD: Substance Abuse and Mental Health Services Administration, 2006.

Originating Office

Quality Improvement and Workforce Development Branch, Division of Services Improvement, Center for Substance Abuse Treatment, Substance Abuse and Mental Health Services Administration, 1 Choke Cherry Road, Rockville, MD 20857.

HHS Publication No. (SMA) 15-4171
First Printed 2006
Revised 2007, 2008, 2009, 2011, 2012, 2013, 2014, and 2015

Contents

Curriculum Committees v
    1998 National ATTC Curriculum Committee v
    2005 Update Committee vi

Foreword vii

Introduction 1

Section 1: Transdisciplinary Foundations 5
    I. Understanding Addiction 7
    II. Treatment Knowledge 13
    III. Application to Practice 19
    IV. Professional Readiness 27

Section 2: Practice Dimensions 35
    I. Clinical Evaluation 37
    II. Treatment Planning 53
    III. Referral 67
    IV. Service Coordination 77
    V. Counseling 99
    VI. Client, Family, and Community Education 131
    VII. Documentation 141
    VIII. Professional and Ethical Responsibilities 151

Section 3: Additional Resources 161
    Cultural Competency 162
    Internet Resources 163
    Attitudes Bibliography 164
    Recovery Bibliography 166

Section 4: Appendices 169
    A. Glossary 171
    B. The Competencies: A Complete List 177
    C. National Validation Study: Defining and Measuring the Competence
       of Addiction Counselors 189
    D. Complete Bibliography 197
    E. Other Contributors 225

CURRICULUM COMMITTEES

1998 NATIONAL ATTC CURRICULUM COMMITTEE

Affiliations indicated below are those at the time of the work.

David A. Deitch, Ph.D. (Chair)
Pacific Southwest ATTC
University of California San Diego
La Jolla, California

G.E. Carrier, Ph.D.
Representing the Texas ATTC
Alvin Community College
Alvin, Texas

Steven L. Gallon, Ph.D.
Northwest Frontier ATTC
Oregon Health and Science University
Salem, Oregon

Paula K. Horvatich, Ph.D.
Mid-Atlantic ATTC
Virginia Commonwealth University
Richmond, Virginia

Mary Beth Johnson, M.S.W.
ATTC National Office
University of Missouri–Kansas City
Kansas City, Missouri

Hendi Crosby Kowal, M.P.H.
DC/Delaware ATTC
Danya International, Inc.
Silver Spring, Maryland

Linda Nicholas
Great Lakes ATTC
University of Illinois–Chicago
Jane Addams School of Social Work
Chicago, Illinois

Alan M. Parsons, M.S.W., ACSW
Northeastern States ATTC
State University of New York at Albany
Albany, New York

Nancy Roget, M.S., MFT, LADC
Mountain West ATTC
University of Nevada–Reno
Reno, Nevada

Susanne R. Rohrer, RN, M.B.A.
Center for Substance Abuse Treatment
Substance Abuse and Mental Health
    Services Administration
Washington, D.C.

Anne Helene Skinstad, Psy.D.
Prairielands ATTC
University of Iowa
Iowa City, Iowa

Patricia L. Stilen, LCSW, CADAC
Mid-America ATTC
University of Missouri–Kansas City
Kansas City, Missouri

Susan A. Storti, RN, M.A.
ATTC of New England
Brown University
Providence, Rhode Island

Elleen M. Yancey, Ph.D.
Southeast ATTC
Morehouse School of Medicine
Atlanta, Georgia

2005 Update Committee

Paula K. Horvatich, Ph.D. (Chair)
Mid-Atlantic ATTC
Virginia Commonwealth University
Richmond, Virginia

Carol Davidson, M.S.W., CDP
Evergreen Treatment Services
Seattle, Washington

Steven L. Gallon, Ph.D.
Northwest Frontier ATTC
Office of Alcohol and Drug Abuse Programs
Salem, Oregon

Michael Hoge, Ph.D.
Annapolis Coalition
Yale University
New Haven, Connecticut

James Holder, M.A., LPC-S, MAC
National Association for Alcohol and
  Drug Addiction Counselors
McLeod Behavioral Health
Florence, South Carolina

Mary Beth Johnson, M.S.W.
ATTC National Office
University of Missouri–Kansas City
Kansas City, Missouri

Linda Kaplan, M.A.
National Association for Children
  of Alcoholics
Rockville, Maryland

**Captain Florentino (Tino)
  Merced-Galindez, M.S.N., RN**
Center for Substance Abuse Prevention
Substance Abuse and Mental Health
  Services Administration
Rockville, Maryland

Randolph Muck, M.Ed.
Center for Substance Abuse Treatment
Substance Abuse and Mental Health
  Services Administration
Rockville, Maryland

Paul D. Nagy, M.S., LCAS, LPC, CCS
Duke Addictions Program
Duke University Medical Center
Durham, North Carolina

Nancy Roget, M.S., MFT, LADC
Mountain West ATTC
University of Nevada–Reno
Reno, Nevada

Gerard J. Schmidt, M.A., LPC, MAC
NAADAC–The Association for Addiction
  Professionals
Valley HealthCare System
Morgantown, West Virginia

Michael Shafer, Ph.D.
Pacific Southwest ATTC
Tucson, Arizona

James L. Sorensen, Ph.D.
San Francisco General Hospital
University of California–San Francisco
San Francisco, California

Patricia L. Stilen, LCSW, CADAC
Mid-America ATTC
University of Missouri–Kansas City
Kansas City, Missouri

Deborah Stone, Ph.D.
Center for Mental Health Services
Substance Abuse and Mental Health
  Services Administration
Rockville, Maryland

Pamela Waters, M.Ed., CAPP
Southern Coast ATTC
Florida Certification Board
Tallahassee, Florida

Foreword

Counselors who treat people with substance use disorders do life-changing work on a daily basis, amid difficult circumstances that include staff shortages, high turnover, low salaries, and scant program funding. Counselors come to this important work by various paths and with vastly different skills and experience. The diversity of backgrounds and types of preparation can be a strength, provided there is a common foundation from which counselors work. This publication addresses the following questions: What professional standards should guide substance abuse treatment counselors? What is an appropriate scope of practice for the field? Which competencies are associated with positive outcomes? What knowledge, skills, and attitudes (KSAs) should all substance abuse treatment professionals have in common?

Workforce development is essential to the field of substance use disorder treatment. The Substance Abuse and Mental Health Services Administration (SAMHSA) has included workforce development in its Matrix of Priority Programs. A major focus of this workforce development strategy is improving the competencies of professionals in the field. This updated edition of Technical Assistance Publication (TAP) 21: *Addiction Counseling Competencies: The Knowledge, Skills, and Attitudes of Professional Practice (The Competencies)* is a key component of that strategy.

In 1998, in cooperation with its Addiction Technology Transfer Center (ATTC) Network, SAMHSA published TAP 21, a comprehensive list of 123 competencies that substance abuse treatment counselors should master to do their work effectively. TAP 21 has been used to develop and evaluate addiction counseling curricula, advise students, and assess counseling proficiencies.

The overarching competencies in this updated version of TAP 21 remain largely unchanged from the original TAP 21. The KSAs have been changed from those in the 1998 edition when necessary, in light of new thinking in the field. The competencies and the KSAs in practice dimensions that address clinical evaluation and treatment planning have been revised to reflect changes in the field. The competencies are defined by sublists of the KSAs needed to master each competency. Bibliographies have been supplemented with new publications through 2005. The format has been improved to make the information more accessible and useful.

SAMHSA's TAP series provides a flexible format for the timely transfer of important technical information to the substance abuse treatment field. This updated version of TAP 21 exemplifies the flexibility of the TAP format. We are grateful to the members of the ATTC Network and staff and to all those who participated in the validation and updating of these competency lists.

Pamela S. Hyde, J.D.
Administrator
Substance Abuse and Mental Health Services Administration

Daryl W. Kade, M.A.
Acting Director
Center for Substance Abuse Treatment
Substance Abuse and Mental Health Services Administration

INTRODUCTION

In 1998, the Substance Abuse and Mental Health Services Administration (SAMHSA) and the Center for Substance Abuse Treatment (CSAT) published *Addiction Counseling Competencies: The Knowledge, Skills, and Attitudes of Professional Practice (The Competencies)* as Technical Assistance Publication (TAP) 21. Developed by the National Curriculum Committee of the Addiction Technology Transfer Center (ATTC) Network, TAP 21 identifies 123 competencies that are essential to the effective practice of counseling for psychoactive substance use disorders. TAP 21 also presents the knowledge, skills, and attitudes (KSAs) counselors need to become fully proficient in each competency.

TAP 21 has been widely distributed by SAMHSA's Public Engagement Platform (PEP) and the ATTC Network. It has become a benchmark by which curricula are developed and educational programs and professional standards are measured for the field of substance abuse treatment in the United States. In addition, it has been translated into several languages.

Because the ATTC Network is committed to technology transfer, after the initial publication of TAP 21, the National Curriculum Committee began exploring ways to enhance the document for future printings. Successful technology transfer requires more than presenting good information. It entails transmitting scientific knowledge in a way that makes it understandable, feasible to implement in a real-world setting, and supportable at a systematic level—in other words, getting the right information across in a way that makes it useable. The National Curriculum Committee examined how best to package and present TAP 21 to help people learn key elements and adopt new strategies. The result was a revision of TAP 21—a process that was begun in 2000, was completed in 2005, and resulted in the current publication.

HISTORY OF *THE COMPETENCIES*

In 1993 CSAT created a multidisciplinary network of 11 ATTC Regional Centers geographically dispersed across the United States and in Puerto Rico and the U.S. Virgin Islands. Since its inception, the ATTC Network has collaborated with diverse international, national, State, regional, and local partners from multiple disciplines to recruit qualified addiction treatment practitioners and enhance academic preparation and professional development opportunities in the substance abuse treatment field.

The National Curriculum Committee, composed of ATTC Directors, was established at the Network's inaugural meeting. The committee's initial charge was to collect and evaluate existing addiction educational and professional development curricula and establish future priorities for ATTC curriculum development. This effort led to researching existing practice and professional literature and defining an extensive list of addiction practice competencies determined to be essential to effective counseling for substance use disorders. These initial competencies would serve as benchmarks to guide future ATTC curriculum design, development, and evaluation.

In addition to its own work, the National Curriculum Committee reviewed and incorporated other publications on the work of addiction counselors.[1] In 1995 the committee's work resulted in the ATTC publication *Addiction Counselor Competencies*. Subsequent to this publication, the ATTCs conducted a national survey to validate the competencies (see appendix C). Results supported virtually all of the competencies as being essential to the professional practice of addiction counseling.

In 1996, the International Certification and Reciprocity Consortium (ICRC) convened a national leadership group to evaluate the need for model addiction counselor training. After careful deliberation, the group concluded that much of the work to define such a curriculum standard had already been accomplished by the ATTC National Curriculum Committee and the ICRC in the National Curriculum Committee's *Addiction Counselor Competencies* and the ICRC's 1996 *Role Delineation Study*,[2] respectively.

Soon after, CSAT agreed to fund a collaborative effort to finalize a document that could be used as a national standard. CSAT convened a panel—The National Steering Committee for Addiction Counseling Standards (NSC)—that comprised representatives from five national educational, certification, and professional associations. The NSC was successful in achieving unanimous endorsement of the *Addiction Counselor Competencies*—a milestone in the addiction counseling field.

Based on this foundation, the National Curriculum Committee began to delineate the KSAs that undergird each competency statement. Input was solicited from a number of key national organizations and selected field reviewers. In 1998 CSAT published the results of this ground-breaking work as TAP 21 (*The Competencies*).

After TAP 21 was published, the National Curriculum Committee systematically conducted focus groups and a national survey to elicit feedback from the field about the impact of TAP 21. Although feedback was uniformly positive and thousands of copies of TAP 21 were disseminated through SAMHSA's PEP and the ATTC Network, refinements were needed to improve the utility of the publication and enhance its effect in both the addiction practice and educational systems.

Feedback obtained from the survey and the focus groups indicated a need for additional information to help the field incorporate the competencies into daily practice. Feedback also suggested that there was no need to change the competencies. The most common suggestions were to refine the 1998 publication by presenting the content in a more user-friendly fashion and linking it to professional literature and specific applications. The National Curriculum Committee revised TAP 21 in 2000 based on the feedback of dedicated addiction practice and education professionals; however, this revision was never published.

A new Update Committee was convened in 2005 to update the revised 2000 edition with literature published between 2000 and 2005. The Update Committee consisted of some of the original members from the National Curriculum Committee; representatives from NAADAC—The Association for Addiction Professionals, CSAT, the Center for Mental Health Services, the Center for Substance Abuse Prevention, the National Association for Children of Alcoholics, and the Annapolis Coalition; treatment providers; and experts in addiction research. The current updated edition retains all of the feedback-based improvements of the 2000 revised version and adds relevant literature

---

[1] Birch and Davis Corporation (1986). *Development of Model Professional Standards for Counselor Credentialing*. Dubuque, IA: Kendall/Hunt Publishing.

[2] International Certification and Reciprocity Consortium (ICRC)/Alcohol and Other Drug Abuse (1991). *Role Delineation Study for Alcohol and Other Drug Abuse Counselors*. Raleigh, NC: ICRC.

Introduction

published after 2000. In addition, the competencies and KSAs of several practice dimensions, in particular those that address clinical evaluation and treatment planning, were rewritten to reflect current best practices.

WHAT YOU WILL FIND INSIDE

The Model

When creating *The Competencies*, the National Curriculum Committee recognized a need to emphasize three characteristics of competency: knowledge, skills, and attitudes. Many hours were spent conceptualizing a differentiated model when designing TAP 21—a model that could address general KSAs necessary for all practitioners dealing with substance use disorders while explaining the more specific needs of professional substance abuse treatment counselors.

The first section of the model addresses the generic KSAs. This section contains the transdisciplinary foundations, comprising four discrete building blocks: understanding addiction, treatment knowledge, application to practice, and professional readiness. The term "transdisciplinary" was selected to describe the knowledge and skills needed by all disciplines (e.g., medicine, social work, pastoral guidance, corrections, social welfare) that deal directly with individuals with substance use disorders.

The second section of the model specifically addresses the professional practice needs, or practice dimensions, of addiction counselors. Each practice dimension includes a set of competencies, and, within each competency, the KSAs necessary for effective addiction counseling are outlined. Many additional competencies may be desirable for counselors in specific settings. Education and experience affect the depth of the individual counselor's knowledge and skills; not all counselors will be experienced and proficient in all the competencies discussed. The National Curriculum Committee's goal for the future is to help ensure that every addiction counselor possesses, to an appropriate degree, each competency listed, regardless of setting or treatment model.

The relationship of the components in the competencies model is conceptualized as a hub with eight spokes (see figure 1). The hub contains the four transdisciplinary foundations that are central to the work of all addiction professionals. The eight spokes are the practice dimensions, each containing the competencies the addiction counselor should attain to master each practice dimension.

FIGURE 1. COMPONENTS IN THE COMPETENCIES MODEL

3

Addiction Counseling Competencies

Recommended Readings
Journal articles, book chapters, and other critical literature for each transdisciplinary foundation and practice dimension have been reviewed and included in this document. Moreover, separate bibliographies on attitudes and recovery have been added, as have lists of Internet and cultural competency resources. These can be found in section 3.

Appendices
Appendices include a glossary (appendix A), a complete list of the competencies (appendix B), a summary of the results of the Committee's National Validation Study of *The Competencies* (appendix C), a complete bibliography with a detailed overview of the methodology used for literature searches (appendix D), and a list of people who acted as field reviewers or provided research assistance (appendix E).

Companion Volume—TAP 21-A
As a companion to this volume on counselor competencies, CSAT is publishing TAP 21-A, *Competencies for Substance Abuse Treatment Clinical Supervisors*, which discusses the qualities and abilities integral to supervising substance abuse treatment clinicians.

USES OF *THE COMPETENCIES*
Since its inception, *The Competencies* has been improving addiction counseling and addiction counselor education across the country in a number of ways. The most common reported applications have been in curriculum/course evaluation and design for higher education; personal professional development; student advising, supervision, and assessment; assessment of competent practices; design of professional development and continuing education programs; and certification standards/exams. Examples of how *The Competencies* is being used are given on the following pages:

Montana	24
Illinois	31
Nebraska	40
New York	44
Missouri	45
Texas	48
Puerto Rico	56
International Applications	59
New England	72
Idaho, Oregon, and Washington	74
Nevada	85
Texas	88
Florida	89
Virginia	91
Northeast	93
Idaho	103
Washington	112
California	116
Oregon and Wisconsin	135
Iowa	137
Georgia	143
Alaska, Hawaii, Idaho, Oregon, and Washington	155

Section 1:
Introduction to the Transdisciplinary Foundations

The Transdisciplinary Foundations

Addiction professionals work in a broad variety of disciplines but share an understanding of the addictive process that goes beyond the narrow confines of any one specialty. Specific proficiencies, skills, levels of involvement with clients, and scope of practice vary widely among specializations. At their base, however, all addiction-focused disciplines are built on four common **foundations**.

This section focuses on four sets of **competencies** that are transdisciplinary in that they underlie the work not just of counselors but of all addiction professionals. The four areas of knowledge identified here serve as prerequisites to the development of competency in any of the addiction-focused disciplines.

The Four Transdisciplinary Foundations

I. Understanding Addiction
II. Treatment Knowledge
III. Application to Practice
IV. Professional Readiness

Regardless of professional identity or discipline, each treatment provider must have a basic understanding of addiction that includes knowledge of current models and theories, appreciation of the multiple contexts within which substance use occurs, and awareness of the effects of psychoactive drug use. Each professional must be knowledgeable about the continuum of care and the social contexts affecting the treatment and recovery process.

Each addiction specialist must be able to identify a variety of helping strategies that can be tailored to meet the needs of individual clients. Each professional must be prepared to adapt to an ever-changing set of challenges and constraints.

Although specific skills and applications vary across disciplines, the attitudinal components tend to remain constant. The development of effective practice in addiction counseling depends on the presence of attitudes reflecting openness to alternative approaches, appreciation of diversity, and willingness to change.

The following **knowledge** and **attitudes** are prerequisite to the development of competency in the professional treatment of substance use disorders. Such **knowledge** and **attitudes** form the basis of understanding on which discipline-specific proficiencies are built.

Transdisciplinary Foundation I

Understanding Addiction

TF I. Understanding Addiction

Competency 1:
Understand a variety of models and theories of addiction and other problems related to substance use.

Knowledge
- Terms and concepts related to theory, etiology, research, and practice.
- Scientific and theoretical basis of model from medicine, psychology, sociology, religious studies, and other disciplines.
- Criteria and methods for evaluating models and theories.
- Appropriate applications of models.
- How to access addiction-related literature from multiple disciplines.

Attitudes
- Openness to information that may differ from personally held views.
- Appreciation of the complexity inherent in understanding addiction.
- Valuing of diverse concepts, models, and theories.
- Willingness to form personal concepts through critical thinking.

Competency 2:
Recognize the social, political, economic, and cultural context within which addiction and substance abuse exist, including risk and resiliency factors that characterize individuals and groups and their living environments.

Knowledge
- Basic concepts of social, political, economic, and cultural systems and their impact on drug-taking activity.
- The history of licit and illicit drug use.
- Research reports and other literature identifying risk and resiliency factors for substance use.
- Statistical information regarding the incidence and prevalence of substance use disorders in the general population and major demographic groups.

Attitudes
- Recognition of the importance of contextual variables.
- Appreciation for differences between and within cultures.

COMPETENCY 3:

Describe the behavioral, psychological, physical health, and social effects of psychoactive substances on the person using and significant others.

KNOWLEDGE

- Fundamental concepts of pharmacological properties and effects of all psychoactive substances.
- The continuum of drug use, such as initiation, intoxication, harmful use, abuse, dependence, withdrawal, craving, relapse, and recovery.
- Behavioral, psychological, social, and health effects of psychoactive substances.
- The effects of chronic substance use on clients, significant others, and communities within a social, political, cultural, and economic context.
- The varying courses of addiction.
- The relationship between infectious diseases and substance use.

ATTITUDES

- Sensitivity to multiple influences in the developmental course of addiction.
- Interest in scientific research findings.

COMPETENCY 4:

Recognize the potential for substance use disorders to mimic a variety of medical and mental health conditions and the potential for medical and mental health conditions to coexist with addiction and substance abuse.

KNOWLEDGE

- Normal human growth and development.
- Symptoms of substance use disorders that are similar to those of other medical and/or mental health conditions and how these disorders interact.
- The medical and mental health conditions that most commonly exist with addiction and substance use disorders.
- Methods for differentiating substance use disorders from other medical or mental health conditions.

ATTITUDES

- Willingness to reserve judgment until completion of a thorough clinical evaluation.
- Willingness to work with people who might display and/or have mental health conditions.
- Willingness to refer for treating conditions outside one's expertise.
- Appreciation of the contribution of multiple disciplines to the evaluation process.

Bibliography

Members of the National ATTC Curriculum Committee reviewed the bibliography from the first printing of ***The Competencies***. Following previously established guidelines, the Committee reviewed and linked each reference with a specific transdisciplinary foundation. Primarily textbooks are referenced in this section; however, such texts are not mutually exclusive of the practice dimensions.

TF I. Understanding Addiction

Akers, R.L. (1992). *Drugs, Alcohol, and Society: Social Structure, Process, and Policy*. Monterey, CA: Brooks/Cole.

Baer, J.S., Marlatt, G.A., & McMahon, R.J. (Eds.) (1993). *Addictive Behaviors Across the Life Span*. Newbury Park, CA: Sage Publications.

Bennett, L.A., Reiss, D., et al. (1987). *The Alcoholic Family*. New York: Basic Books.

Blevins, G.A., Dana, R.Q., & Lewis, J.A. (1994). *Substance Abuse Counseling: An Individual Approach* (2nd ed.). Pacific Grove, CA: Brooks/Cole.

Cohen, W.E., Holstein, M.E., & Inaba, D.S. (1997). *Uppers, Downers, All Arounders: Physical and Mental Effects of Psychoactive Drugs* (3rd ed.). Ashland, OR: CNS Publications.

Collins, R.L., Leonard, K.E., & Searles, J.S. (Eds.) (1990). *Alcohol and the Family: Research and Clinical Perspectives*. New York: Guilford Press.

Curtis, O. (1998). *Chemical Dependency: A Family Affair*. Pacific Grove, CA: Brooks/Cole.

Epstein, E.E., & McCrady, B.S. (Eds.) (1999). *Addictions: A Comprehensive Guidebook*. New York: Oxford University Press.

Fisher, G.L., & Harrison, T.C. (2004). *Substance Abuse: Information for School Counselors, Social Workers, Therapists, and Counselors*. Boston: Allyn & Bacon.

Gullotta, T.P., Adams, G.R., & Montemayor, R. (Eds.) (1994). *Substance Misuse in Adolescence*. Thousand Oaks, CA: Sage Publications.

Jaffe, J. (Ed.) (1995). *Encyclopedia of Drugs and Alcohol*. New York: Macmillan.

Jonnes, J. (1999). *Hep-Cats, Narcs, and Pipe Dreams: A History of America's Romance With Illegal Drugs*. Baltimore: Johns Hopkins University Press.

Kinney, J. (2003). *Loosening the Grip: A Handbook of Alcohol Information* (7th ed.). New York: McGraw-Hill.

Lawson, A.W., Lawson, G.W., & Rivers, P.C. (1996). *Essentials of Chemical Dependency Counseling* (2nd ed.). Gaithersburg, MD: Aspen Publishers.

Lawson, G.W., & Lawson, A.W. (1992). *Adolescent Substance Abuse: Etiology, Treatment, and Prevention*. Gaithersburg, MD: Aspen Publishers.

Lewis, J.A., Dana, R.Q., & Blevins, G.A. (2001). *Substance Abuse Counseling* (3rd ed.). Pacific Grove, CA: Brooks/Cole.

Lowinson, J.H., Ruiz, P., et al. (Eds.) (1997). *Substance Abuse: A Comprehensive Textbook* (3rd ed.). Baltimore: Lippincott Williams & Wilkins.

McKim, W.A. (2002). *Drugs and Behavior: An Introduction to Behavioral Pharmacology* (5th ed.). Upper Saddle River, NJ: Prentice Hall.

Miller, G. (2004). *Learning the Language of Addiction Counseling* (2nd ed.). Hoboken, NJ: John Wiley & Sons.

Musto, D.F. (1999). *The American Disease: Origins of Narcotic Control* (3rd ed.). New York: Oxford University Press.

Nathan, P.E., & Gorman, J.M. (Eds.) (2002). *A Guide to Treatments That Work* (2nd ed.). New York: Oxford University Press.

Pita, D.D. (2004). *Addictions Counseling: A Practical and Comprehensive Guide to Counseling People With Addictions*. New York: Crossroad Publishing.

Rutzky, J. (1998). *Coyote Speaks: Creative Strategies for Psychotherapists Treating Alcoholics and Addicts*. Northvale, NJ: Jason Aronson.

Thombs, D.L. (1999). *Introduction to Addictive Behaviors* (2nd ed.). New York: Guilford Press.

Venturelli, P. (Ed.) (1994). *Drug Use in America: Social, Cultural, and Political Perspectives*. Boston: Jones and Bartlett Publishers.

Wallen, J. (1993). *Addiction in Human Development: Developmental Perspectives on Addiction and Recovery*. New York: Haworth Press.

White, W.L. (1998). *Slaying the Dragon: The History of Addiction Treatment and Recovery in America*. Bloomington, IL: Chestnut Health Systems.

Transdisciplinary Foundation II

TREATMENT KNOWLEDGE

TF II. Treatment Knowledge

Competency 5:
Describe the philosophies, practices, policies, and outcomes of the most generally accepted and scientifically supported models of treatment, recovery, relapse prevention, and continuing care for addiction and other substance-related problems.

Knowledge

- Generally accepted models, such as but not limited to:
    - pharmacotherapy
    - mutual help and self-help
    - behavioral self-control training
    - mental health
    - self-regulating community
    - psychotherapeutic
    - relapse prevention.
- The philosophy, practices, policies, and outcomes of the most generally accepted therapeutic models.
- Alternative therapeutic models that demonstrate potential.

Attitudes

- Acceptance of the validity of a variety of approaches and models.
- Openness to new, evidence-based treatment approaches, including pharmacological interventions.

Competency 6:
Recognize the importance of family, social networks, and community systems in the treatment and recovery process.

Knowledge

- The role of family, social networks, and community systems as assets or obstacles in treatment and recovery processes.
- Methods for incorporating family and social dynamics in treatment and recovery processes.

Attitudes

- Appreciation for the significance and complementary nature of various systems in facilitating treatment and recovery.

Competency 7:

Understand the importance of research and outcome data and their application in clinical practice.

Knowledge

- Research methods in the social and behavioral sciences.
- Sources of research literature relevant to the prevention and treatment of addiction.
- Specific research on epidemiology, etiology, and treatment efficacy.
- Benefits and limitations of research.

Attitudes

- Recognition of the importance of scientific research to the delivery of addiction treatment.
- Openness to new information.

Competency 8:

Understand the value of an interdisciplinary approach to addiction treatment.

Knowledge

- Roles and contributions of multiple disciplines to treatment efficacy.
- Terms and concepts necessary to communicate effectively across disciplines.
- The importance of communication with other disciplines.

Attitudes

- Desire to collaborate.
- Respect for the contribution of multiple disciplines to the recovery process.
- Commitment to professionalism.

BIBLIOGRAPHY

Members of the National ATTC Curriculum Committee reviewed the bibliography from the first printing of ***The Competencies***. Following previously established guidelines, the Committee reviewed and linked each reference with a specific transdisciplinary foundation. Primarily textbooks are referenced in this section; however, such texts are not mutually exclusive of the practice dimensions.

TF II. Treatment Knowledge

Benshoff, J.J., & Janikowski, T.P. (2000). *The Rehabilitation Model of Substance Abuse Counseling*. Pacific Grove, CA: Brooks/Cole.

Berg, I.K., & Miller, S.D. (1992). *Working With the Problem Drinker: A Solution-Focused Approach*. New York: W.W. Norton.

Brown, S. (Ed.) (1995). *Treating Alcoholism*. San Francisco: Jossey-Bass.

Donigian, J., & Malnati, R. (1996). *Systemic Group Therapy: A Triadic Model*. Pacific Grove, CA: Brooks/Cole.

Greenlick, M., Lamb, S., & McCarty, D. (Eds.) (1998). *Bridging the Gap Between Practice and Research: Forging Partnerships With Community-Based Drug and Alcohol Treatment*. Washington, DC: National Academy Press.

Heather, N., & Miller, W.R. (Eds.) (1998). *Treating Addictive Behaviors* (2nd ed.). New York: Plenum Press.

Institute of Medicine (1990). *Broadening the Base of Treatment for Alcohol Problems*. Washington, DC: National Academy Press.

L'Abate, L., Farrar, J.L., & Serritella, D. (1991). *Handbook of Differential Treatments for Addictions*. Boston: Allyn & Bacon.

Lawson, A.W., & Lawson, G.W. (1998). *Alcoholism and the Family: A Guide to Treatment and Prevention* (2nd ed.). Gaithersburg, MD: Aspen Publishers.

Miller, W.R., & Rollnick, S. (1991). *Motivational Interviewing: Preparing People To Change Addictive Behavior*. New York: Guilford Press.

Nowinski, J. (1990). *Substance Abuse in Adolescents and Young Adults: A Guide to Treatment*. New York: W.W. Norton.

Stevens, P., & Smith, R.L. (2004). *Substance Abuse Counseling: Theory and Practice* (3rd ed.). Old Tappan, NJ: Prentice Hall.

Transdisciplinary Foundation III

APPLICATION TO PRACTICE

TF III. Application to Practice

Competency 9:
Understand the established diagnostic criteria for substance use disorders, and describe treatment modalities and placement criteria within the continuum of care.

Knowledge

- Established diagnostic criteria, including but not limited to current *Diagnostic and Statistical Manual of Mental Disorders (DSM)* standards and current *International Classification of Diseases* (ICD) standards.
- Established placement criteria developed by various States and professional organizations.
- Strengths and limitations of various diagnostic and placement criteria.
- Continuum of treatment services and activities.

Attitudes

- Openness to a variety of treatment services based on client need.
- Recognition of the value of research findings.

Competency 10:
Describe a variety of helping strategies for reducing the negative effects of substance use, abuse, and dependence.

Knowledge

- A variety of helping strategies, including but not limited to:
  - evaluation methods and tools
  - stage-appropriate interventions
  - motivational interviewing
  - involvement of family and significant others
  - mutual-help and self-help programs
  - coerced and voluntary care models
  - brief and longer term interventions.

Attitudes

- Openness to various approaches to recovery.
- Appreciation that different approaches work for different people.

COMPETENCY 11:
Tailor helping strategies and treatment modalities to the client's stage of dependence, change, or recovery.

KNOWLEDGE
- Strategies appropriate to the various stages of dependence, change, and recovery.

ATTITUDES
- Flexibility in choice of treatment modalities.
- Respect for the client's racial, cultural, economic, and sociopolitical backgrounds.

COMPETENCY 12:
Provide treatment services appropriate to the personal and cultural identity and language of the client.

KNOWLEDGE
- Various cultural norms, values, beliefs, and behaviors.
- Cultural differences in verbal and nonverbal communication.
- Resources to develop individualized treatment plans.

ATTITUDES
- Respect for individual differences within cultures.
- Respect for differences between cultures.

COMPETENCY 13:
Adapt practice to the range of treatment settings and modalities.

KNOWLEDGE
- The strengths and limitations of available treatment settings and modalities.
- How to access and make referrals to available treatment settings and modalities.

ATTITUDES
- Flexibility and creativity in practice application.

TF III. Application to Practice

COMPETENCY 14:
Be familiar with medical and pharmacological resources in the treatment of substance use disorders.

KNOWLEDGE

- Current literature regarding medical and pharmacological interventions.
- Assets and liabilities of medical and pharmacological interventions.
- Health practitioners in the community who are knowledgeable about addiction and addiction treatment.
- The role that medical problems and complications can play in the intervention and treatment of addiction.

ATTITUDES

- Open and flexible with respect to the potential risks and benefits of pharmacotherapies to the treatment and recovery process.

COMPETENCY 15:
Understand the variety of insurance and health maintenance options available and the importance of helping clients access those benefits.

KNOWLEDGE

- Existing public and private payment plans including treatment orientation and coverage options.
- Methods for gaining access to available payment plans.
- Policies and procedures used by available payment plans.
- Key personnel, roles, and positions within plans used by the client population.

ATTITUDES

- Willingness to cooperate with payment providers.
- Willingness to explore treatment alternatives.
- Interest in promoting the most cost-effective, high-quality care.

Addiction Counseling Competencies

COMPETENCY 16:
Recognize that crisis may indicate an underlying substance use disorder and may be a window of opportunity for change.

KNOWLEDGE

- The features of crisis, which may include but are not limited to:
  - family disruption
  - social and legal consequences
  - physical and psychological
  - panic states
  - physical dysfunction.
- Substance use screening and assessment methods.
- Prevention and intervention principles and methods.
- Principles of crisis case management.
- Posttraumatic stress characteristics.
- Critical incident debriefing methods.
- Available resources for assistance in the management of crisis situations.

ATTITUDES

- Willingness to respond and follow through in crisis situations.
- Willingness to consult when necessary.

COMPETENCY 17:
Understand the need for and the use of methods for measuring treatment outcome.

KNOWLEDGE

- Treatment outcome research literature.
- Scientific process in applied research.
- Appropriate measures of outcome.
- Methods for measuring the multiple variables of treatment outcome.

ATTITUDES

- Recognition of the importance of collecting and reporting on outcome data.
- Interest in integrating research findings into ongoing treatment design.

USES OF *THE COMPETENCIES*

The Competencies has been used in a number of different ways in Montana. It was incorporated into the Montana certification and oral exam process. In higher education settings at colleges and universities, *The Competencies* has been used to define behavioral expectations and objectives for addiction counseling courses. Clinically, it has been used to establish "employment competencies" for counselors working in a hospital-based setting with clients who abuse substances. These employment competencies were also modified for use by substance abuse counseling programs on the Crow Indian Reservation and the Rocky Boy Indian Reservation.

BIBLIOGRAPHY

Members of the National ATTC Curriculum Committee reviewed the bibliography from the first printing of ***The Competencies***. Following previously established guidelines, the Committee reviewed and linked each reference with a specific transdisciplinary foundation. Primarily textbooks are referenced in this section; however, such texts are not mutually exclusive of the practice dimensions.

TF III. Application to Practice

American Psychiatric Association (1994). *Diagnostic and Statistical Manual of Mental Disorders* (4th ed.). Washington, DC: American Psychiatric Association.

Bennett, L.A., Reiss, D., et al. (1987). *The Alcoholic Family*. New York: Basic Books.

Berg, I.K., & Miller, S.D. (1992). *Working With the Problem Drinker: A Solution-Focused Approach*. New York: W.W. Norton.

Brown, S. (Ed.) (1995). *Treating Alcoholism*. San Francisco: Jossey-Bass.

Cavanaugh, E.R., Ginzburg, H.M., et al. (1989). *Drug Abuse Treatment: A National Study of Effectiveness*. Chapel Hill, NC: University of North Carolina Press.

Chiauzzi, E.J. (1991). *Preventing Relapse in the Addictions: A Biopsychosocial Approach*. New York: Pergamon.

Deitch, D., & Solit, R. (1993). Training of drug abuse treatment personnel in therapeutic community methodology. *Psychotherapy*, 30(2):305-316.

Donigian, J., & Malnati, R. (1997). *Systemic Group Therapy: A Triadic Model*. Pacific Cove, CA: Brooks/Cole.

Ettore, E. (1992). *Women and Substance Use*. New Brunswick, NJ: Rutgers University Press.

Evans, K., & Sullivan, J.M. (2001). *Dual Diagnosis: Counseling the Mentally Ill Substance Abuser* (2nd ed.). New York: Guilford Press.

Flores, P.J. (1997). *Group Psychotherapy With Addicted Populations: An Integration of Twelve-Step and Psychodynamic Theory* (2nd ed.). New York: Haworth Press.

Galanter, M. (1993). *Network Therapy for Alcohol and Drug Abuse*. New York: Guilford Press.

Institute of Medicine (1990). *Treating Drug Problems, Volume 1: The Report*. Washington, DC: National Academy Press.

Levin, J.D. (1995). *Introduction to Alcoholism Counseling: A Bio-Psycho-Social Approach* (2nd ed.). New York: Taylor & Francis.

Lewis, J.A. (Ed.) (1994). *Addictions: Concepts and Strategies for Treatment*. Gaithersburg, MD: Aspen Publishers.

McCrady, B.S., & Miller, W.R. (Eds.) (1993). *Research on Alcoholics Anonymous: Opportunities and Alternatives*. New Brunswick, NJ: Rutgers Center of Alcohol Studies.

McLellan, A.T., Woody, G.E., et al. (1988). Is the counselor an "active ingredient" in substance abuse rehabilitation? An examination of treatment success among four counselors. *Journal of Nervous and Mental Disease*, 176:430-432.

Meyers, R.J., & Smith, J.E. (1995). *Clinical Guide to Alcohol Treatment: The Community Reinforcement Approach*. New York: Guilford Press.

Miller, N.S., Gold, M.S., & Smith, D.E. (Eds.) (1997). *Manual of Therapeutics for Addictions*. New York: Wiley-Liss.

Miller, W.R., & Heather, N. (Eds.) (1998). *Treating Addictive Behaviors: Processes of Change* (2nd ed.). New York: Plenum Press.

Moos, R.H., Finney, J.W., & Cronkite, R.C. (1990). *Alcoholism Treatment: Context, Process, and Outcome*. New York: Oxford University Press.

Murphy, L.L., & Impara, J.C. (Eds.) (1996). *Buros Desk Reference: Assessment of Substance Abuse*. Lincoln, NE: Buros Institute of Mental Measurements.

Najavits, L.M., & Weiss, R.D. (1994). Variations in therapist effectiveness in the treatment of patients with substance use disorder: An empirical review. *Addictions*, 89:679-688.

Prochaska, J.O., DiClemente, C.C., & Norcross, J.C. (1992). In search of how people change: Applications to addictive behaviors. *American Psychologist*, 47:1102-1114.

Rutzky, J. (1998). *Coyote Speaks: Creative Strategies for Psychotherapists Treating Alcoholics and Addicts*. Northvale, NJ: Jason Aronson.

Vannicelli, M. (1992). *Removing the Roadblocks: Group Psychotherapy With Substance Abusers and Family Members*. New York: Guilford Press.

Washton, A.M. (1995). *Psychotherapy and Substance Abuse: A Practitioner's Handbook*. New York: Guilford Press.

Zweben, J.E. (Ed.) (1990). Understanding and preventing relapse. *Journal of Psychoactive Drugs*, 22(2).

Transdisciplinary Foundation IV

PROFESSIONAL READINESS

TF IV. Professional Readiness

Competency 18:
Understand diverse cultures, and incorporate the relevant needs of culturally diverse groups, as well as people with disabilities, into clinical practice.

Knowledge

- Information and resources regarding racial and ethnic cultures, lifestyles, gender, and age as well as relevant needs of people with disabilities.
- The unique influence the client's culture, lifestyle, gender, and other relevant factors may have on behavior.
- The relationship between substance use and diverse cultures, values, and lifestyles.
- Assessment and intervention methods that are appropriate to culture and gender.
- Counseling methods relevant to the needs of culturally diverse groups and people with disabilities.
- The Americans with Disabilities Act and other legislation related to human, civil, and clients' rights.

Attitudes

- Willingness to explore and identify one's own cultural values.
- Acceptance of other cultural values as valid for other individuals.

Competency 19:
Understand the importance of self-awareness in one's personal, professional, and cultural life.

Knowledge

- Personal and professional strengths and limitations.
- Cultural, ethnic, or gender biases.

Attitudes

- Openness to constructive supervision.
- Willingness to grow and change personally and professionally.

Competency 20:

Understand the addiction professional's obligations to adhere to ethical and behavioral standards of conduct in the helping relationship.

Knowledge

- The features of crisis, which may include but are not limited to:
  - family disruption
  - social and legal consequences
  - physical and psychological panic states
  - physical dysfunction.
- Substance use screening and assessment methods.
- Intervention principles and methods.
- Principles of crisis case management.
- Posttraumatic stress characteristics.
- Critical incident debriefing methods.
- Available resources for assistance in the management of crisis situations.

Attitudes

- Willingness to conduct oneself in accordance with the highest ethical standards.
- Willingness to comply with regulatory and professional expectations.

Competency 21:

Understand the importance of ongoing supervision and continuing education in the delivery of client services.

Knowledge

- Benefits of self-assessment and clinical supervision to professional growth and development.
- The value of consultation to enhance personal and professional growth.
- Resources available for continuing education.
- Supervision principles and methods.

Attitudes

- Commitment to continuing professional education.
- Willingness to engage in a supervisory relationship.

COMPETENCY 22:
Understand the obligation of the addiction professional to participate in prevention and treatment activities.

KNOWLEDGE

- Research-based prevention models and strategies.
- The relationship between prevention and treatment.
- Environmental strategies and prevention campaigns.
- Benefits of working with community coalitions.

ATTITUDES

- Appreciation of the inherent value of prevention.
- Openness to research-based prevention strategies.

COMPETENCY 23:
Understand and apply setting-specific policies and procedures for handling crisis or dangerous situations, including safety measures for clients and staff.

KNOWLEDGE

- Setting-specific policies and procedures.
- What constitutes a crisis or danger to the client and/or others.
- The range of appropriate responses to a crisis or dangerous situation.
- Universal precautions.
- Legal implications of crisis response.
- Exceptions to confidentiality rules in crisis or dangerous situations.

ATTITUDES

- Understanding of the potential seriousness of crisis situations.
- Awareness for the need for caution and self-control in the face of crisis or danger.
- Willingness to request help in potentially dangerous situations.

USES OF *THE COMPETENCIES*

The Board of Directors of the Illinois Alcohol and Other Drug Abuse Professional Certification Association has endorsed and will be incorporating the knowledge, skills, and attitudes provided in *The Competencies* into all of its models for Certified Alcohol and Other Drug Abuse Counselors. The 22 training programs in Illinois that will be implementing these models are supportive of this change.

A recently developed certificate for people who are employed in support positions for alcohol and drug abuse treatment programs is based on *The Competencies*. This credential completes a career path for alcohol and drug abuse treatment professionals in Illinois that will take them from support staff to master's level.

BIBLIOGRAPHY

Members of the National ATTC Curriculum Committee reviewed the bibliography from the first printing of *The Competencies*. Following previously established guidelines, the Committee reviewed and linked each reference with a specific transdisciplinary foundation. Primarily textbooks are referenced in this section; however, such texts are not mutually exclusive of the practice dimensions.

TF IV. Professional Readiness

Atkinson, D.R., Morten, G., & Sue, D.W. (1997). *Counseling American Minorities*. New York: McGraw-Hill.

Bell, P. (2002). *Chemical Dependency and the African American: Counseling and Prevention Strategies* (2nd ed.). Center City, MN: Hazelden.

Bepko, C. (Ed.) (1992). *Feminism and Addiction*. New York: Haworth Press.

Berg, I.K., & Miller, S.D. (1992). *Working With the Problem Drinker: A Solution-Focused Approach*. New York: W.W. Norton.

Bissell, L., & Royce, J.E. (1994). *Ethics for Addiction Professionals* (2nd ed.). Center City, MN: Hazelden.

Cushner, K., & Brislin, R.W. (1997). *Improving Intercultural Interactions—Modules for Cross-Cultural Training Programs*. Thousand Oaks, CA: Sage Publications.

Delgado, M. (Ed.) (1998). *Alcohol Use/Abuse Among Latinos: Issues and Examples of Culturally Competent Services*. New York: Haworth Press.

Delgado, M., Segal, B., & Lopex, R. (Eds.) (1999). *Conducting Drug Abuse Research With Minority Populations: Advances and Issues*. New York: Haworth Press.

Ettore, E. (1992). *Women and Substance Use*. New Brunswick, NJ: Rutgers University Press.

Feld, B.C. (1999). *Bad Kids: Race and the Transformation of the Juvenile Court*. New York: Oxford University Press.

Gardenswartz, L., & Rowe, A. (1994). *The Managing Diversity Survival Guide: A Complete Collection of Checklists, Activities, and Tips* (book and disk). Chicago: Irwin Professional Publishing.

Gomberg, E.S.L., & Nirenberg, T.D. (Eds.) (1993). *Women and Substance Abuse*. Norwood, NJ: Ablex Publishing.

Gordon, J.U. (Ed.) (1994). *Managing Multiculturalism in Substance Abuse Services*. Thousand Oaks, CA: Sage Publications.

Hawkins, J.D., & Catalano, R.F. (1992). *Communities That Care: Action for Drug Abuse Prevention*. San Francisco: Jossey-Bass.

Heinemann, A. (Ed.) (1993). *Substance Abuse and Physical Disability*. New York: Haworth Press.

Herring, R.D. (1999). *Counseling Native American Indians and Alaska Natives: Strategies for Helping Professionals*. Thousand Oaks, CA: Sage Publications.

Hogan, J.A., Gabrielson, K.R., et al. (2003). *Substance Abuse Prevention: The Intersection of Science and Practice*. Boston: Allyn & Bacon.

Imhof, J. (1991). Countertransference issues in alcoholism and drug addiction. *Psychiatric Annals*, 21:292-306.

Ivey, A.E., Simek-Morgan, L., et al. (2001). *Theories of Counseling and Psychotherapy: A Multicultural Perspective* (5th ed.). Boston: Allyn & Bacon.

Ja, D., & Aoki, B. (1993). Substance abuse treatment: Cultural barriers in the Asian-American community. *Journal of Psychoactive Drugs*, 25(1):61-71.

Jandt, F.E. (Ed.) (2003). *Intercultural Communication: A Global Reader*. Thousand Oaks, CA: Sage Publications.

Lipton, H., & Lee, P. (1998). *Drugs and the Elderly: Clinical, Social, and Policy Perspectives*. Stanford, CA: Stanford University Press.

Lowinson, J.H., Ruiz, P., et al. (Eds.) (1997). *Substance Abuse: A Comprehensive Textbook* (3rd ed.). Baltimore: Lippincott Williams & Wilkins.

Maracle, B. (1994). *Crazywater: Native Voices on Addiction and Recovery*. New York: Penguin Books.

Miller, G. (2004). *Learning the Language of Addiction Counseling* (2nd ed.). Hoboken, NJ: John Wiley & Sons.

Pagani-Tousignant, C. (1992). *Breaking the Rules: Counseling Ethnic Minorities*. Minneapolis, MN: Johnson Institute.

Paniagua, F.A. (2005). *Assessing and Treating Culturally Diverse Clients: A Practical Guide* (3rd ed.). Thousand Oaks, CA: Sage Publications.

Paul, J.P., Stall, R., & Bloomfield, K.A. (1991). Gay and alcoholic: Epidemiologic and clinical issues. *Alcohol Health and Research World*, 15:151-160.

Pedersen, P.B. (1997). *Culture-Centered Counseling Interventions: Striving for Accuracy*. Thousand Oaks, CA: Sage Publications.

Pedersen, P.B. (1997). *Decisional Dialogues in a Cultural Context: Structured Exercises*. Thousand Oaks, CA: Sage Publications.

Pedersen, P.B., Draguns, J.G., et al. (Eds.) (2002). *Counseling Across Cultures* (5th ed.). Thousand Oaks: Sage Publications.

Perkinson, R.R. (1997). *Chemical Dependency Counseling: A Practical Guide*. Thousand Oaks, CA: Sage Publications.

Pope-Davis, D.B., & Coleman, H.L.K. (1997). *Multicultural Counseling Competencies, Assessment, Education and Training, and Supervision*. Thousand Oaks, CA: Sage Publications.

Singelis, T.M. (Ed.) (1998). *Teaching About Culture, Ethnicity, and Diversity: Exercises and Planned Activities*. Thousand Oaks, CA: Sage Publications.

Storti, S.A. (1997). *Alcohol, Disabilities, and Rehabilitation*. San Diego, CA: Singular Publishing Group.

Sue, D.W., & Sue, D. (2002). *Counseling the Culturally Different: Theory and Practice* (4th ed.). New York: John Wiley & Sons.

Trimble, J.E., Bolek, C.S., & Niemcryk, S.J. (Eds.) (1992). *Ethnic and Multicultural Drug Abuse: Perspectives on Current Research*. New York: Harrington Park Press.

Weinstein, D.L. (Ed.) (1993). *Lesbians and Gay Men: Chemical Dependency Treatment Issues*. New York: Haworth Press.

Williams, R., & Gorski, T.T. (1997). *Relapse Prevention Counseling for African Americans: A Culturally Specific Model*. Independence, MO: Herald House/Independence Press.

Williams, R., & Gorski, T.T. (1997). *Relapse Warning Signs for African Americans: A Culturally Specific Model*. Independence, MO: Herald House/Independence Press.

Section 2:

Introduction to the Practice Dimensions

The Practice Dimensions

Professional practice for addiction counselors is based on eight **practice dimensions**, each of which is necessary for effective performance of the counseling role. Several of the **practice dimensions** are subdivided into **elements**. The dimensions identified, along with the **competencies** that support them, form the heart of this section of *The Competencies*.

The Eight Practice Dimensions of Addiction Counseling

I. Clinical Evaluation
   – Screening
   – Assessment
II. Treatment Planning
III. Referral
IV. Service Coordination
   – Implementing the Treatment Plan
   – Consulting
   – Continuing Assessment and Treatment Planning
V. Counseling
   – Individual Counseling
   – Group Counseling
   – Counseling Families, Couples, and Significant Others
VI. Client, Family, and Community Education
VII. Documentation
VIII. Professional and Ethical Responsibilities

A counselor's success in carrying out a **practice dimension** depends on his or her ability to attain the **competencies** underlying that component. Each **competency**, in turn, depends on its own set of knowledge, skills, and attitudes. For an addiction counselor to be truly effective, he or she should possess the knowledge, skills, and attitudes associated with each competency that are consistent with the counselor's training and professional responsibilities.

Practice Dimension I

CLINICAL EVALUATION

PD I. Clinical Evaluation

Elements:
- Screening
- Assessment

Definition: The systematic approach to screening and assessment of individuals thought to have a substance use disorder, being considered for admission to addiction-related services, or presenting in a crisis situation.

Element: Screening

Screening is the process by which the counselor, the client, and available significant others review the current situation, symptoms, and other available information to determine the most appropriate initial course of action, given the client's needs and characteristics and the available resources within the community.

Competency 24:
Establish rapport, including management of a crisis situation and determination of need for additional professional assistance.

Knowledge
- Importance and purpose of rapport building.
- Rapport-building methods and issues.
- The range of human emotions and feelings.
- What constitutes a crisis.
- Steps in crisis prevention and management.
- Situations and conditions for which additional professional assistance may be necessary.
- Available sources of assistance.

Skills
- Demonstrating effective verbal and nonverbal communication in establishing rapport.
- Accurately identifying the client's beliefs and frame of reference.
- Reflecting the client's feelings and message.
- Recognizing and defusing volatile or dangerous situations.
- Demonstrating empathy, respect, and genuineness.

Attitudes
- Recognition of personal biases, values, and beliefs and their effect on communication and the treatment process.
- Willingness to establish rapport.

Competency 25:

Gather data systematically from the client and other available collateral sources, using screening instruments and other methods that are sensitive to age, developmental level, culture, and gender. At a minimum, data should include current and historic substance use; health, mental health, and substance-related treatment histories; mental and functional statuses; and current social, environmental, and/or economic constraints.

Knowledge

- Validated screening instruments for substance use and mental status, including their purpose, application, and limitations.
- Concepts of reliability and validity as they apply to screening instruments.
- How to interpret the results of screening.
- How to gather and use information from collateral sources.
- How age, developmental level, culture, and gender affect patterns and history of use.
- How age, developmental level, culture, and gender affect communication.
- Client mental status—presenting features and relationship to substance use disorders and psychiatric conditions.
- How to apply confidentiality rules and regulations.

Skills

- Administering and scoring screening instruments.
- Screening for physical and mental health status.
- Facilitating information sharing and data collection from a variety of sources.
- Communicating effectively in emotionally charged situations.
- Writing accurately, concisely, and legibly.

Attitudes

- Appreciation of the value of the data-gathering process.

Uses of *The Competencies*

In Nebraska, *The Competencies* is used as a resource for instructors teaching core classes preparing students for State certification. It also is used as supplemental reading for students in these courses and other continuing education programs sponsored by the Prairielands ATTC.

COMPETENCY 26:

Screen for psychoactive substance toxicity, intoxication, and withdrawal symptoms; aggression or danger to others; potential for self-inflicted harm or suicide; and co-occurring mental disorders.

KNOWLEDGE

- Symptoms of intoxication, withdrawal, and toxicity for all psychoactive substances, alone and in interaction with one another.
- Physical, pharmacological, and psychological implications of psychoactive substance use.
- Effects of chronic psychoactive substance use or intoxication on cognitive abilities.
- Available resources for help with drug reactions, withdrawal, and violent behavior.
- When to refer for toxicity screening or additional professional help.
- Basic concepts of toxicity screening options, limitations, and legal implications.
- Toxicology reporting language and the meaning of toxicology reports.
- Relationship between psychoactive substance use and violence.
- Basic diagnostic criteria for suicide risk, danger to others, withdrawal syndromes, and major psychiatric conditions.
- Mental and physical conditions that mimic drug intoxication, toxicity, and withdrawal.
- Legal requirements concerning suicide and violence potential and mandatory reporting for abuse and neglect.

SKILLS

- Eliciting pertinent information from the client and relevant others.
- Intervening appropriately with a client who may be intoxicated.
- Assessing suicide and/or violence potential using an approved risk-assessment tool.
- Assessing risks of abuse and neglect of children and others.
- Preventing and managing crises in collaboration with health, mental health, and public safety professionals.

ATTITUDES

- Willingness to be respectful toward the client in his or her presenting state.
- Appreciation of the importance of empathy in the face of feelings of anger, hopelessness, or suicidal or violent thoughts and feelings.
- Appreciation of the importance of legal and administrative obligations.

COMPETENCY 27:
Assist the client in identifying the effect of substance use on his or her current life problems and the effects of continued harmful use or abuse.

KNOWLEDGE

- The progression and characteristics of substance use disorders.
- The effects of psychoactive substances on behavior, thinking, feelings, health status, and relationships.
- Denial and other defense mechanisms in client resistance.

SKILLS

- Establishing a therapeutic relationship.
- Demonstrating effective communication and interviewing skills.
- Determining and confirming with the client the effects of substance use on life problems.
- Assessing client readiness to address substance use issues.
- Interpreting the client's perception of his or her experiences.

ATTITUDES

- Respect for the client's perception of his or her experiences.

COMPETENCY 28:
Determine the client's readiness for treatment and change as well as the needs of others involved in the current situation.

KNOWLEDGE

- Current validated instruments for assessing readiness to change.
- Treatment options.
- Stages of readiness.
- Stages-of-change models.
- The role of family and significant others in supporting or hindering change.

SKILLS

- Assessing client readiness for treatment.
- Assessing extrinsic and intrinsic motivators.
- Assessing the needs of family members including children for appropriate levels of care and providing support; recommending followup services.

ATTITUDES

Acceptance of nonreadiness as a stage of change.

- Appreciation that motivation is not a prerequisite for treatment.
- Recognition of the importance of the client's self-assessment.

PD I. Clinical Evaluation

COMPETENCY 29:
Review the treatment options that are appropriate for the client's needs, characteristics, goals, and financial resources.

KNOWLEDGE

- Treatment options and their philosophies and characteristics.
- Relationship among client needs, available treatment options, and other community resources.

SKILLS

- Eliciting and determining relevant client characteristics, needs, and goals.
- Making appropriate recommendations for treatment and use of other available community resources.
- Collaborating with the client to determine the best course of action.

ATTITUDES

- Recognition of one's own treatment biases.
- Appreciation of various treatment approaches.
- Willingness to link client with a variety of helping resources.

COMPETENCY 30:
Apply accepted criteria for diagnosis of substance use disorders in making treatment recommendations.

KNOWLEDGE

- The continuum of care and the available range of treatment modalities.
- Current *Diagnostic and Statistical Manual of Mental Disorders* (DSM) or other accepted criteria for substance use disorders, including strengths and limitations of such criteria.
- Use of commonly accepted criteria for client placement into levels of care.
- Multiaxis diagnostic criteria.

SKILLS

- Using current DSM or other accepted diagnostic standards.
- Using appropriate placement criteria.
- Obtaining information necessary to develop a diagnostic impression.

ATTITUDES

- Recognition of personal and professional limitations of practice, based on knowledge and training.
- Willingness to base treatment recommendations on the client's best interest and preferences.

Addiction Counseling Competencies

Uses of *The Competencies*

The Office of Alcoholism and Substance Abuse Services uses the International Certification and Reciprocity Consortium/Alcohol and Other Drug Abuse, Inc.'s examination for Alcohol and Other Drug Abuse Counselors as the standard of minimum competence for counselors seeking a credential in New York State. This examination is based on the 12 Core Functions of alcoholism and substance abuse counselors, which are consistent with the practice dimensions and competencies outlined in ***The Competencies***.

Competency 31:

Construct with the client and appropriate others an initial action plan based on client needs, client preferences, and resources available.

Knowledge

- Appropriate content and format of the initial action plan.
- The client's needs and preferences.
- Available resources for admission or referral.

Skills

- Developing the action plan in collaboration with the client and appropriate others.
- Documenting the action plan.
- Contracting with the client concerning the initial action plan.

Attitudes

- Willingness to work collaboratively with the client and others.

Competency 32:

Based on the initial action plan, take specific steps to initiate an admission or referral and ensure followthrough.

Knowledge

- Admission and referral protocols.
- Resources for referral.
- Ethical standards regarding referrals.
- Appropriate documentation.
- How to apply confidentiality rules and regulations.
- Clients' rights to privacy.

Skills

- Communicating clearly and appropriately.
- Networking and advocating with service providers.
- Negotiating and advocating client admissions to appropriate treatment resources.
- Facilitating client followthrough.
- Documenting accurately and appropriately.

Attitudes

- Willingness to renegotiate.

USES OF *THE COMPETENCIES*

The Competencies is being used in a series of scale validation studies by Alicia Wendler of the Mid-America ATTC and Tamera Murdock and Johanna Nilsson of the University of Missouri–Kansas City to develop the Addiction Counseling Self-Efficacy Scale (ACSES). The 32-item ACSES assesses addiction counselors' perceptions of their self-efficacy for addiction counseling skills and includes five subscales:

- Executing specific addiction counseling skills
- Assessment, treatment planning, and referral skills
- Working with various co-occurring mental disorders
- Group counseling skills
- Basic counseling microskills.

The researchers reported adequate internal consistency of the scale with a sample of 451 addiction counselors. Preliminary validity evidence for the scale was determined through two exploratory factor analyses, and the scale was found to be sensitive to counselor experience and degree levels.

Addiction Counseling Competencies

Element: Assessment

Assessment is an ongoing process through which the counselor collaborates with the client and others to gather and interpret information necessary for planning treatment and evaluating client progress.

COMPETENCY 33:

Select and use a comprehensive assessment process that is sensitive to age, gender, racial and ethnic culture, and disabilities that includes but is not limited to:
- History of alcohol and drug use
- Physical health, mental health, and addiction treatment histories
- Family issues
- Work history and career issues
- History of criminality
- Psychological, emotional, and worldview concerns
- Current status of physical health, mental health, and substance use
- Spiritual concerns of the client
- Education and basic life skills
- Socioeconomic characteristics, lifestyle, and current legal status
- Use of community resources
- Treatment readiness
- Level of cognitive and behavioral functioning.

KNOWLEDGE

- Basic concepts of test validity and reliability.
- Current validated assessment instruments and protocols.
- Appropriate use and limitations of standardized instruments.
- The range of life areas to be assessed in a comprehensive assessment.
- How age, developmental level, cognitive and behavioral functioning, racial and ethnic culture, gender, and disabilities can influence the validity and appropriateness of assessment instruments and interview protocols.

SKILLS

- Selecting and administering appropriate assessment instruments and protocols within the counselor's scope of practice.
- Introducing and explaining the purpose of assessment.
- Addressing client perceptions and providing appropriate explanations of issues being discussed.
- Conducting comprehensive assessment interviews and collecting information from collateral sources.

ATTITUDES

- Respect for the limits of assessment instruments and one's ability to interpret them.
- Willingness to refer for additional specialized assessment.

COMPETENCY 34:
Analyze and interpret the data to determine treatment recommendations.

KNOWLEDGE

- Appropriate scoring methodology for assessment instruments.
- How to analyze and interpret assessment results.
- The range of available treatment options.

SKILLS

- Scoring assessment tools.
- Interpreting data relevant to the client.
- Using results to identify client needs and appropriate treatment options.
- Communicating recommendations to the client and appropriate service providers.

ATTITUDES

- Respect for the value of assessment in determining appropriate treatment plans.

COMPETENCY 35:
Seek appropriate supervision and consultation.

KNOWLEDGE

- The counselor's role, responsibilities, and scope of practice.
- The limits of the counselor's training and education.
- The supervisor's role and how supervision can contribute to quality assurance and improvement of clinical skills.
- Available consultation services and roles of consultants.
- The multidisciplinary assessment approach.

SKILLS

- Recognizing the need for review by or assistance from a supervisor.
- Recognizing when consultation is appropriate.
- Providing appropriate documentation.
- Communicating oral and written information clearly.
- Incorporating information from supervision and consultation into assessment findings.

ATTITUDES

- Commitment to professionalism.
- Acceptance of one's own personal and professional limitations.
- Willingness to continue learning and improving clinical skills.

Addiction Counseling Competencies

Competency 36:
Document assessment findings and treatment recommendations.

Knowledge

- Agency-specific protocols and procedures.
- Appropriate terminology and abbreviations.
- Legal implications of actions and documentation.
- How to apply confidentiality rules and regulations and clients' rights to privacy.

Skills

- Providing clear, concise, and legible documentation.
- Incorporating information from various sources.
- Preparing and clearly presenting, in oral and written form, assessment findings to the client and other professionals within the bounds of confidentiality rules and regulations.

Attitudes

- Recognition of the value of accurate documentation.

Uses of *The Competencies*

The Competencies has been used as a training standard for the Licensed Chemical Dependency Counselor credential in Texas. The competencies were infused not only into academic course work, but also into three levels of supervised work experience. A companion evaluation tool was developed to monitor mastery of the competencies.

In addition, a number of colleges and universities across Texas have infused the knowledge, skills, and attitudes from *The Competencies* into their addiction counseling coursework and curricula. Many have changed course descriptions, learning outcomes, and course objectives.

Bibliography

PD I. Clinical Evaluation: Screening

Allen, J.P., & Litten, R.Z. (1998). Screening instruments and biochemical screening tests. In A.W. Graham, T.K. Schultz, & B.B. Wilford (Eds.) *Principles of Addiction Medicine* (2nd ed.). Chevy Chase, MD: American Society of Addiction Medicine, 263-271.

American Psychiatric Association (1994). *Diagnostic and Statistical Manual of Mental Disorders* (4th ed.). Washington, DC: American Psychiatric Press.

Anton, R.F., Litten, R.Z., & Allen, J.P. (1995). Biological assessment of alcohol consumption. In J.P. Allen & M. Columbus (Eds.) *Assessing Alcohol Problems: A Guide for Clinicians and Researchers*. NIAAA Treatment Handbook Series, No. 4. Bethesda, MD: National Institute on Alcohol Abuse and Alcoholism, 31-39.

Ball, S.A., & Kosten, T.A. (1998). Diagnostic classification systems. In A.W. Graham, T.K. Schultz, & B.B. Wilford (Eds.) *Principles of Addiction Medicine* (2nd ed.). Chevy Chase, MD: American Society of Addiction Medicine, 279-290.

Bradley, K.A., Boyd-Wickizer, B.A., et al. (1998). Alcohol screening questionnaires in women: A critical review. *JAMA*, 280(2):166-171.

Cherpital, C.J. (1998). Differences in performance of screening instruments for problem drinking among Blacks, Whites, and Hispanics in an emergency room population. *Journal of Studies on Alcohol*, July:420-426.

Connors, G.J. (1995). Screening for alcohol problems. In J.P. Allen & M. Columbus (Eds.) *Assessing Alcohol Problems: A Guide for Clinicians and Researchers*. NIAAA Treatment Handbook Series, No. 4. Bethesda, MD: National Institute on Alcohol Abuse and Alcoholism, 17-29.

Cooney, N.L., Zweben, A., & Fleming, M.F. (2002). Screening for alcohol problems and at-risk drinking in health-care settings. In R.K. Hester & W.R. Miller (Eds.) *Handbook of Alcoholism Treatment Approaches* (3rd ed.). Boston: Allyn & Bacon, 45-60.

Finn, P. (1994). Addressing the needs of cultural minorities in drug treatment. *Journal of Substance Abuse Treatment*, 11(4):325-337.

Hser, Y. (1995). A referral system that matches drug users to treatment programs: Existing research and relevant issues. *Journal of Drug Issues*, 25(1):209-224.

Knight, J.R., Sherritt, L., et al. (2002). Validity of the CRAFFT substance abuse screening test among adolescent clinic patients. *Archives of Pediatrics and Adolescent Medicine*, 156(6):607-614.

Knight, J.R., Sherritt, L., et al. (2003). Validity of brief alcohol screening tests among adolescents: A comparison of the AUDIT, POSIT, CAGE, and CRAFFT. *Alcohol, Clinical and Experimental Research*, 27(1):67-73.

Maisto, S.A., & McKay, J.R. (1995). Diagnosis. In J.P. Allen & M. Columbus (Eds.) *Assessing Alcohol Problems: A Guide for Clinicians and Researchers*. NIAAA Treatment Handbook Series, No. 4. Bethesda, MD: National Institute on Alcohol Abuse and Alcoholism, 41-54.

Maisto, S.A., & Saitz, R. (2003). Alcohol use disorders: Screening and diagnosis. *American Journal on Addictions*, 12:S12-S25.

Mee-Lee, D., Miller, M.M., & Shulman, G.D. (1996). *Patient Placement Criteria for the Treatment of Substance-Related Disorders* (2nd ed.). Chevy Chase, MD: American Society of Addiction Medicine.

Miller, W.R., & Rollnick, S. (1991). *Motivational Interviewing: Preparing People To Change Addictive Behavior*. New York: Guilford Press.

Prochaska, J.O., DiClemente, C.C., & Norcross, J.C. (1992). In search of how people change: Applications to the addictive behaviors. *American Psychologist*, 47:1102-1114.

Rydz, D., Shevell, M.I., et al. (2005). Developmental screening. *Journal of Child Neurology*, 20(1):4-21.

Schafer, J., & Cherpitel, C.J. (1998). Differential item functioning of the CAGE, TWEAK, BMAST, and AUDIT by gender and ethnicity. *Contemporary Drug Problems*, 25(2):399-409.

Schorling, J.B., & Buchsbaum, D.G. (1997). Screening for alcohol and drug abuse. *Medical Clinics of North America*, 81(4):845-865.

Zimmerman, M., Sheeran, T., et al. (2004). Screening for psychiatric disorders in outpatients with DSM-IV substance use disorders. *Journal of Substance Abuse Treatment*, 26(3):181-188.

PD I. Clinical Evaluation: Assessment

Adesso, V.J., Cisler, R.A., et al. (2004). Substance abuse. In M. Hersen (Ed.) *Psychological Assessment in Clinical Practice: A Pragmatic Guide*. New York: Brunner-Routledge, 147-173.

Albanese, M., & Khantzian, E. (2001). The difficult-to-treat patient with substance abuse. In M.J. Dewan & R.W. Pies (Eds.) *The Difficult-to-Treat Psychiatric Patient*. Arlington, VA: American Psychiatric Publishing, Inc., 273-298.

Annis, H.M., Sobell, L.C., et al. (1996). Drinking-related assessment instruments: Cross-cultural studies. *Substance Use & Misuse*, 31(11&12):1525-1546.

Armstrong, T.D., & Costello, E.J. (2002). Community studies on adolescent substance use, abuse or dependence and psychiatric comorbidity. *Journal of Consulting and Clinical Psychology*, 70(6):1224-1239.

Barker, S.B., Kerns, L.L., & Schnoll, S.H. (1996). Assessment of medical history, health status, intoxication, and withdrawal. In B.J. Rounsaville, F.M. Tims, et al. (Eds.) *Diagnostic Source Book on Drug Abuse Research and Treatment*. Rockville, MD: National Institute on Drug Abuse, 35-48.

Carey, K.B. (2002). Clinically useful assessments: Substance use and comorbid psychiatric disorders. *Behaviour Research & Therapy*, 40:1345.

Carey, K.B., & Correia, C.J. (1998). Severe mental illness and addictions: Assessment considerations. *Addictive Behaviors*, 23(6):735-748.

Carroll, K.M., & Rounsaville, B.J. (2002). On beyond urine: Clinically useful assessment instruments in the treatment of drug dependence. *Behaviour Research & Therapy*, 40:1329.

Center for Substance Abuse Prevention (1993). *Maternal Substance Use Assessment Methods Reference Manual: A Review of Screening and Clinical Assessment Instruments for Examining Maternal Use of Alcohol, Tobacco and Other Drugs*. CSAP Special Report 13. Rockville, MD: Substance Abuse and Mental Health Services Administration.

Dennis, M.L., Dawud-Noursi, S., et al. (2003). The need for developing and evaluating adolescent treatment models. In S.J. Stevens & H.R. Morral (Eds.) *Adolescent Substance Abuse Treatment in the United States*. New York: Haworth Press, 3-35.

Dennis, M.L., & Stevens, S.J. (2003). Maltreatment issues and outcomes of adolescents enrolled in substance abuse treatment. *Child Maltreatment*, 8(1):3-6.

DiNitto, D.M., & Crisp, C. (2002). Addictions and women with major psychiatric disorders. In S.L.A. Straussner & S. Brown (Eds.) *The Handbook of Treatment for Women*. San Francisco: Jossey-Bass, 423-450.

Donovan, D.M. (1995). Assessments to aid in the treatment planning process. In J.P. Allen & M. Columbus (Eds.) *Assessing Alcohol Problems: A Guide for Clinicians and Researchers*. NIAAA Treatment Handbook Series 4. Bethesda, MD: National Institute on Alcohol Abuse and Alcoholism, 75-122.

Donovan, D.M. (1999). Assessment strategies and measures in addictive behaviors. In B.S. McCrady & E.E. Epstein (Eds.) *Addictions: A Comprehensive Guidebook*. New York: Oxford University Press, 187-215.

Donovan, D.M., & Marlatt, G.A. (Eds.) (2005). *Assessment of Addictive Behaviors* (2nd ed.). New York: Guilford Press.

Fleming, M.F. (2002). Identification and treatment of alcohol use disorders in older adults. In A.M. Gurnack, R. Atkinson, & N. Osgood (Eds.) *Treating Alcohol and Drug Abuse in the Elderly*. New York: Springer Publishing, 85-108.

Garito, P.J. (2002). Assessing and treating psychiatric comorbidity in chemically dependent analysis. In D. O'Connell, E. Beyer, et al. (Eds.) *Managing the Dually Diagnosed Patient: Current Issues and Clinical Approaches* (2nd ed). New York: Haworth Press, 153-185.

Gavetti, M.F., & Constantine, M.G. (2001). Assessment and treatment of alcoholism in older adults: Considerations for mental health clinicians. *Journal of Psychiatry in Independent Practice*, 2(3):61-71.

Graham, K., Brett, P.J., & Bois, C. (1995). Treatment entry and engagement: A study of the process at assessment/referral centers. *Journal of Contemporary Drug Problems*, 22(1):61-104.

Guthmann, D., & Sandberg, K. (1998). Assessing substance abuse problems in deaf and hard of hearing individuals. *American Annals of the Deaf*, 143(1):14-19.

Hyams, G., Cartwright, A., & Spratley, T. (1996). Engagement in alcohol treatment: The client's experience of, and satisfaction with, the assessment interview. *Addiction Research*, 4(2):105-123.

Kaminer, Y. (2004). Dually diagnosed teens: Challenges for assessment and treatment. *Counselor*, 5(2):62-68.

Knight, D.K., & Simpson, D.D. (1999). Family assessment. In P.J. Ott, R.E. Tarter, & R.T. Ammerman (Eds.) *Sourcebook on Substance Abuse: Etiology, Epidemiology, Assessment, and Treatment*. Boston: Allyn & Bacon, 236-247.

Kramer, K.L., Robbins, J.M., et al. (2003). Detection and outcomes of substance use disorders in adolescents seeking mental health treatment. *Journal of the American Academy of Child and Adolescent Psychiatry*, 42(11):1318-1326.

Lewis, J.A. (2005). Assessment, diagnosis, and treatment planning. In R.H. Coombs (Ed.) *Addiction Counseling Review: Preparing for Comprehensive, Certification, and Licensing Examinations*. Mahwah, NJ: Lawrence Erlbaum Associates, 357-379.

Meyers, K., Hagan, T.A., et al. (1999). Critical issues in adolescent substance use assessment. *Drug and Alcohol Dependence*, 55(3):235-246.

National Institute on Drug Abuse (NIDA) (1994). *Assessing Drug Abuse Among Adolescents and Adults: Standardized Instruments*. Clinical Report Series. Rockville, MD: NIDA.

Oslin, D.W., & Holden, R. (2002). Recognition and assessment of alcohol and drug dependence in the elderly. In A.M. Gurnack, R. Atkinson, & N. Osgood (Eds.) *Treating Alcohol and Drug Abuse in the Elderly*. New York: Springer Publishing, 11-31.

Read, J.P., Bollinger, A.R., & Sharkansky, E. (2003). Assessment of comorbid substance use disorder and posttraumatic stress disorder. In P. Ouimette & P.J. Brown (Eds.) *Trauma and Substance Abuse: Causes, Consequences, and Treatment of Comorbid Disorders*. Washington, DC: American Psychological Association.

Rotgers, F. (2002). Clinically useful, research validated assessment of persons with alcohol problems. *Behaviour Research & Therapy*, 40:1425.

Schwartz, R.C., & Smith, S.D. (2003). Screening and assessing adolescent substance abuse: A primer for counselors. *Journal of Addictions & Offender Counseling*, 24:23-34.

Stasiewicz, P.R., & Bradizza, C.M. (2002). Alcohol use disorders. In M. Hersen & L.K. Porzelius (Eds.) *Diagnosis, Conceptualization, and Treatment Planning for Adults: A Step-by-Step Guide*. Mahwah, NJ: Lawrence Erlbaum Associates, 271-290.

Winters, K.C. (2001). Assessing adolescent substance use problems and other areas of functioning: State of the art. In P.M. Monti, S.M. Colby, & T.A. O'Leary (Eds.) *Adolescents, Alcohol, and Substance Abuse: Reaching Teens Through Brief Interventions*. New York: Guilford Press, 80-108.

Winters, K.C., Latimer, W.W., & Stinchfield, R. (2002). Clinical issues in the assessment of adolescent alcohol and other drug use. *Behaviour Research & Therapy*, 40(12):1443-1456.

PRACTICE DIMENSION II

TREATMENT PLANNING

PD II. Treatment Planning

Definition: *A collaborative process in which professionals and the client develop a written document that identifies important treatment goals; describes measurable, time-sensitive action steps toward achieving those goals with expected outcomes; and reflects a verbal agreement between a counselor and client.*

At a minimum an individualized treatment plan addresses the identified substance use disorder(s), as well as issues related to treatment progress, including relationships with family and significant others, potential mental conditions, employment, education, spirituality, health concerns, and social and legal needs.

Competency 37:
Use relevant assessment information to guide the treatment planning process.

Knowledge

- The role assessment plays in identifying client problems, resources, and barriers to treatment.
- Stages of change and readiness for treatment.
- The impact that the client and family systems have on treatment decisions and outcomes.
- Other sources of assessment information.

Skills

- Establishing treatment priorities based on all available assessment data.
- Interpreting assessment information considering the client's age, developmental level, treatment readiness, gender, and racial and ethnic culture.
- Using assessment information to individualize the client's treatment goals.

Attitudes

- Appreciation of the strengths and limitations of the assessment data.
- Recognition that assessment is an ongoing process throughout treatment.

Competency 38:
Explain assessment findings to the client and significant others.

Knowledge

- How to apply confidentiality rules and regulations.
- How to communicate assessment data in understandable terms.
- Factors affecting the client's comprehension of assessment data.
- Roles and expectations of significant others involved in treatment.

Skills

- Summarizing and synthesizing assessment results.
- Translating assessment information into treatment goals and objectives.
- Evaluating the client's comprehension of assessment feedback.
- Communicating with the client in a manner that is sensitive to the client's age, developmental level, gender, and racial and ethnic culture.
- Communicating assessment findings to interested parties within the bounds of confidentiality rules and regulations and practice standards.

Attitudes

- Recognition of how biases influence communication of assessment data and results.
- Recognition of the client's right and need to understand assessment results.
- Respect for the roles of others.

Uses of The Competencies

The former Caribbean Basin and Hispanic ATTC in Puerto Rico translated *The Competencies* into Spanish and had widely distributed it in Puerto Rico and the mainland. (The translation is posted on the CBHATTC Web site, http://www.attcnetwork.org/regcenters/productDocs/1/productpdf/Manuales/TAP21/TAP21.pdf.)

The curriculum of the Substance Abuse Graduate Program of the Universidad Central del Caribe was based on *The Competencies*.

The Competencies has been used as a resource for trainers teaching workshops such as Clinical Skills in Supervision, S.M.A.R.T., Treatment Planning, and Levels of Care in Substance Abuse.

Some community-based organizations have incorporated *The Competencies* into their inservice trainings.

The Comisión Certificadora de Profesionales en Substancias Sicoactivas of Puerto Rico (certification board) incorporated *The Competencies* into its certifications standards.

The Puerto Rico Drug Control Office used *The Competencies* to develop the Addiction Prevention Specialist Licensure standards in Puerto Rico.

PD II. Treatment Planning

COMPETENCY 39:
Provide the client and significant others with clarification and additional information as needed.

KNOWLEDGE

- Verbal and nonverbal communication styles.
- Methods to elicit feedback from the client and significant others.

SKILLS

- Eliciting and integrating feedback during the planning process.
- Working collaboratively with the client and significant others.
- Establishing a trusting relationship with the client and significant others.

ATTITUDES

- Willingness to communicate interactively with the client and significant others.
- Openness to client questions and input.

COMPETENCY 40:
Examine treatment options in collaboration with the client and significant others.

KNOWLEDGE

- Treatment interventions, client placement criteria, and outside referral options.
- Current research findings on various treatment models.
- Alternatives to treatment, including no treatment.

SKILLS

- Presenting the range of treatment options and settings available.
- Using assessment data to make treatment recommendations.
- Considering the client's needs and preferences when selecting treatment settings.
- Using the treatment planning process to foster collaborative relationships with the client and significant others.

ATTITUDES

- Willingness to negotiate treatment options with the client.
- Openness to a variety of approaches.
- Respect for the input of the client and significant others.

Competency 41:
Consider the readiness of the client and significant others to participate in treatment.

KNOWLEDGE

- Stages-of-change process.
- Methods of tailoring treatment strategies to match the client's motivational level.

SKILLS

- Assessing the client's stage of change.
- Developing strategies to address ambivalence.
- Eliciting the client's preferences.
- Promoting the client's readiness to engage in treatment.

ATTITUDES

- Respect for the client's values, goals, and readiness to change.
- Recognition and acceptance of behavioral change as a multistep process.

Competency 42:
Prioritize the client's needs in the order they will be addressed in treatment.

KNOWLEDGE

- Treatment sequencing and the continuum of care.
- Hierarchy-of-needs models.
- Holistic view of the client's biological, psychological, social, and spiritual needs and resources.

SKILLS

- Accessing referral resources necessary to address the client's needs.
- Using clinical judgment in prioritizing client problems.
- Assessing severity of client problems and prioritizing appropriately.

ATTITUDES

- Recognition and acceptance of the client as an active participant in prioritizing needs.
- Willingness to make referrals to address the client's needs.

COMPETENCY 43:
Formulate mutually agreed-on and measurable treatment goals and objectives.

KNOWLEDGE

- Use of goals and objectives to individualize treatment planning.
- Treatment needs of diverse populations.
- How to write specific and measurable goal and objective statements.

SKILLS

- Translating assessment information into measurable treatment goal and objective statements.
- Collaborating with the client to develop specific, measurable, and realistic goals and objectives.
- Engaging, contracting, and negotiating mutually agreeable goals with the client.
- Writing goal and objective statements in terms understandable to the client and significant others.

ATTITUDES

- Respect for the client's choice of treatment goals.
- Respect for the client's individual pace toward achieving goals.
- Acceptance of the client's readiness to change.
- Appreciation for incremental achievements in completing goals.

INTERNATIONAL APPLICATIONS OF *THE COMPETENCIES*

International applications of *The Competencies* are noteworthy. It was translated for use in the Czech Republic, Greece, Hungary, and Slovakia. A Spanish translation has been completed. Committee members have provided consultation on *The Competencies* in American Samoa, Bulgaria, the Commonwealth of the Northern Mariana Islands, the Federated States of Micronesia, Poland, the Republic of the Marshall Islands, the Republic of Palau, Italy, Slovenia, and the Territory of Guam. *The Competencies* also is being considered for trainings in Thailand by a Thai delegation through CSAT. In addition, the Web site created for the original version of *The Competencies* has been visited by individuals from 34 countries.

Addiction Counseling Competencies

COMPETENCY 44:
Identify appropriate strategies for each treatment goal.

KNOWLEDGE

- Intervention strategies, onsite services, and outside referral options.
- Client's interest in various treatment service options.
- Treatment strategies sensitive to diverse populations.

SKILLS

- Matching interventions to the client's needs and resources.
- Explaining strategies in terms understandable to the client and significant others.
- Identifying and making referrals to outside resources.

ATTITUDES

- Recognition that client retention improves when services are matched to the client's needs and resources.
- Appreciation for various treatment strategies.

COMPETENCY 45:
Coordinate treatment activities and community resources in a manner consistent with the client's diagnosis and existing placement criteria.

KNOWLEDGE

- Treatment strategies and community resources.
- Contributions of other professionals and mutual- or self-help support groups.
- Levels of care and existing placement criteria.
- The importance of the client's age, developmental and educational level, gender, and racial and ethnic culture in coordinating resources.

SKILLS

- Coordinating treatment activities and resources consistent with the client's needs and preferences.
- Communicating to the client and significant others the rationale behind treatment recommendations.

ATTITUDES

- Acceptance of a variety of treatment recommendations.
- Recognition of the importance of coordinating treatment activities.

Competency 46:

Develop with the client a mutually acceptable treatment plan and method for monitoring and evaluating progress.

Knowledge

- The relationship among problem statements, treatment goals, objectives, and intervention strategies.
- Short- and long-term treatment planning.
- Methods for evaluating treatment progress.

Skills

- Individualizing treatment plans that balance strengths and resources with problems and deficits.
- Negotiating and contracting a mutually agreeable plan.
- Writing a plan using positive, jargon-free, and proactive terms.
- Establishing criteria to evaluate progress.

Attitudes

- Sensitivity to the client's age, developmental and educational level, gender, and racial and ethnic culture.
- Appreciation for measurable criteria of client progress.
- Willingness to negotiate a plan.

Addiction Counseling Competencies

COMPETENCY 47:
Inform the client of confidentiality rights, program procedures that safeguard them, and the exceptions imposed by regulations.

KNOWLEDGE
- Federal, State, and agency confidentiality rules and regulations, requirements, and policies.
- Resources for legal consultation.

SKILLS
- Communicating the roles of various interested parties and support systems.
- Explaining clients' rights and responsibilities and applicable confidentiality rules and regulations.
- Responding to questions and providing clarification as needed.
- Referring to appropriate legal authority.

ATTITUDES
- Respect for clients' confidentiality rights.
- Commitment to professionalism.
- Recognition of the importance of professional collaboration within the bounds of confidentiality.

COMPETENCY 48:
Reassess the treatment plan at regular intervals or when indicated by changing circumstances.

KNOWLEDGE
- How to evaluate the client's response to treatment.
- When and how to revise the treatment plan.

SKILLS
- Assessing the client's response to treatment.
- Modifying the treatment plan based on review of the client's response to treatment and/or changing circumstances.
- Negotiating changes to the plan with the client and significant others.

ATTITUDES
- Recognition of the value of client input in revising the treatment plan.
- Openness to critically examine one's work.
- Respect for the input of the client and significant others.
- Willingness to learn from clinical supervision and modify practice accordingly.

BIBLIOGRAPHY

PD II. Treatment Planning

Adams, N., & Grieder, D.M. (2005). *Treatment Planning for Person-Centered Care: The Road to Mental Health and Addiction Recovery*. Burlington, MA: Elsevier Academic Press.

Allen, J.P., & Mattson, M.E. (1993). Psychometric instruments to assist in alcoholism treatment planning. *Journal of Substance Abuse Treatment*, 10(3):289-296.

Anderson, A.J. (1999). Comparative impact evaluation of two therapeutic programs for mentally ill chemical abusers. *International Journal of Psychosocial Rehabilitation*, 4:11-26.

Appelbaum, P.S., & Gutheil, T.G. (1982). Clinical aspects of treatment refusal. *Comprehensive Psychiatry*, 23(6):560-566.

Argeriou, M., & Daley, M. (1998). An examination of racial and ethnic differences within a sample of Hispanic, White (non-Hispanic), and African American Medicaid-eligible pregnant substance abusers: The MOTHERS Project. *Journal of Substance Abuse Treatment*, 14(5):489-498.

Barber, J.P., Luborsky, L., et al. (1999). Therapeutic alliance as a predictor of outcome in treatment of cocaine dependence. *Psychotherapy Research*, 9(1):54-73.

Barber, J.P., Luborsky, L., et al. (2001). Therapeutic alliance as a predictor of outcome in retention in the National Institute on Drug Abuse collaborative cocaine treatment study. *Journal of Consulting and Clinical Psychology*, 69(1):119-124.

Borkman, T.J. (1998). Is recovery planning any different from treatment planning? *Journal of Substance Abuse Treatment*, 15(1):37-42.

Cacciola, J.S., Koppenhaver, J.M., et al. (1999). Test-retest reliability of the lifetime items on the Addiction Severity Index. *Psychological Assessment*, 11(1):86-93.

Carise, D., Gurel, O., et al. (2005). Getting patients the services they need using a computer-assisted system for patient assessment and referral—CASPAR. *Drug and Alcohol Dependence*, 80(2):177-189.

Crevecoeur, D., Finnerty, B., & Rawson, R. (2004). Los Angeles County Evaluation System (LACES): Bringing accountability to alcohol and drug abuse treatment through a collaboration between providers, payers, and researchers. *Journal of Drug Issues*, 32(1):881-892.

DiClemente, C.C., & Scott, C.W. (1997). Stages of change: Interactions with treatment compliance and involvement. In L.S. Onken, J.D. Blaine, & J.J. Boren (Eds.) *Beyond the Therapeutic Alliance: Keeping the Drug-Dependent Individual in Treatment*. NIDA Research Monograph No. 165. Rockville, MD: National Institute on Drug Abuse, 131-156.

Drake, R.E., & Mueser, K.T. (2000). Psychosocial approaches to dual diagnosis. *Schizophrenia Bulletin*, 26(1):105-118.

Drake, R.E., Mueser, K.T., et al. (2004). A review of treatments for people with severe mental illnesses and co-occurring disorders. *Psychiatric Rehabilitation Journal*, 27(4):360-374.

Harkness, A.R., & Lilienfeld, S.O. (1997). Individual differences science for treatment planning: Personality traits. *Psychological Assessment*, 9(4):349-360.

Hser, Y.-I., Polinsky, M.L., et al. (1999). Matching client's needs with drug treatment services. *Journal of Substance Abuse Treatment*, 16(4):299-305.

Huitt, W.G. (2004). Maslow's hierarchy of needs. *Educational Psychology Interactive*. Valdosta, GA: Valdosta State University.

Jensen, J. (1992). Treatment planning in the 90's: Part 1. *Addiction and Recovery*, 12(7):48-50.

Jensen, J. (1993). Treatment planning in the 90's: Part 2. *Addiction and Recovery*, 13(3):50-52.

Joe, G.W., Simpson, D.D., & Broome, K.M. (1998). Effects of readiness for drug abuse treatment on client retention and assessment of process. *Addiction*, 93(8):1177-1190.

Johnson, S.L. (2004). *Therapist's Guide to Clinical Intervention* (2nd ed.). San Diego, CA: Elsevier, Inc.

Joint Commission on Accreditation of Healthcare Organizations (JCAHO) (2002). *A Practical Guide to Documentation in Behavioral Health Care* (2nd ed.). Oakbrook Terrace, IL: JCAHO.

Kadden, R.M., & Skerker, P.M. (1999). Treatment decision making and goal setting. In B.S. McCrady & E.E. Epstein (Eds.) *Addictions: A Comprehensive Guidebook*. New York: Oxford University Press, 216-231.

Kosten, T.R., Rounsaville, B.J., & Kleber, H.D. (1987). Multidimensionality and prediction and treatment outcome in opioid addicts: 2.5-year follow-up. *Comprehensive Psychiatry*, 28(1):3-13.

Lordan, E.J., Kelley, J.M., et al. (1997). Treatment placement decisions: How substance abuse professionals assess and place clients. *Evaluation and Program Planning*, 20(2):137-149.

Luborsky, L., Crits-Christoph, P., et al. (1986). Do therapists vary much in their success? Findings from four outcome studies. *American Journal of Orthopsychiatry*, 56(4):501-512.

Luborsky, L., Diguer, L., et al. (1996). Factors in outcomes of short-term dynamic psychotherapy for chronic vs. nonchronic major depression. *Journal of Psychotherapy Practice and Research*, 5(2):152-159.

Makover, R.B. (2004). *Treatment Planning for Psychotherapists: A Practical Guide to Better Outcomes*. Arlington, VA: American Psychiatric Publishing, Inc.

McLellan, A.T., Carise, D., & Kleber, H.D. (2003). Can the national addiction treatment infrastructure support the public's demand for quality care? *Journal of Substance Abuse Treatment*, 25(2):117-121.

McLellan, A.T., Grissom, G.R., et al. (1993). Private substance abuse treatments: Are some programs more effective than others? *Journal of Substance Abuse Treatment*, 10(3):243-254.

McLellan, A.T., Grissom, G.R., et al. (1997). Problem-service "matching" in addiction treatment: A prospective study in 4 programs. *Archives of General Psychiatry*, 54(8):730-735.

McLellan, A.T., Hagan, T.A., et al. (1999). Does clinical case management improve outpatient addiction treatment? *Drug & Alcohol Dependence*, 55(1-2):91-103.

McLellan, A.T., Kushner, H., et al. (1992). The fifth edition of the Addiction Severity Index. *Journal of Substance Abuse Treatment*, 9(3):199-213.

McLellan, A.T., Luborsky, L., et al. (1980). An improved diagnostic evaluation instrument for substance abuse patients: The Addiction Severity Index. *Journal of Nervous and Mental Disease*, 168(1):26-33.

McLellan, A.T., Luborsky, L., et al. (1985). New data from the Addiction Severity Index: Reliability and validity in three centers. *Journal of Nervous and Mental Disease*, 173(7):412-423.

McLellan, A.T., & McKay, J.R. (1998). Components of successful treatment programs: Lessons from the research literature. In A.W. Graham, T.K. Schultz, & B.B. Wilford (Eds.) *Principles of Addiction Medicine* (2nd ed.). Chevy Chase, MD: American Society of Addiction Medicine, 327-343.

Mee-Lee, D. (1998). Use of patient placement criteria in the selection of treatment. In A.W. Graham, T.K. Schultz, & B.B. Wilford (Eds.) *Principles of Addiction Medicine* (2nd ed.). Chevy Chase, MD: American Society of Addiction Medicine, 363-370.

National Institute on Drug Abuse (NIDA) (1999). *Principles of Drug Addiction Treatment: A Research-Based Guide*. NIH Publication No. 00-4180. Rockville, MD: NIDA.

Perkinson, R.R. (1997). *Chemical Dependency Counseling: A Practical Guide*. Thousand Oaks, CA: Sage Publications.

Prochaska, J.O., & DiClemente, C.C. (1982). Transtheoretical therapy: Toward a more integrative model of change. *Psychotherapy: Theory, Research, and Practice*, 19:276-288.

Prochaska, J.O., & DiClemente, C.C. (1986). Toward a comprehensive model of change. In W.R. Miller & N. Heather (Eds.) *Treating Addictive Behaviors: Processes of Change*. New York: Plenum Press, 3-27.

Roget, N., & Johnson, M. (1995). *Pre- and Post-Treatment Planning in the Substance Abuse Treatment Case Management Process*. Carson City, NV: Nevada Bureau of Alcohol and Drug Abuse.

Rollnick, S. (1998). Readiness, importance, and confidence: Critical conditions of change in treatment. In W.R. Miller & N. Heather (Eds.) *Treating Addictive Behaviors* (2nd ed.). New York: Plenum Press, 49-60.

Sanchez-Craig, M., & Wilkinson, D.A. (1997). Guidelines for advising on treatment goals. In S. Harrison & V. Carver (Eds.) *Alcohol and Drug Problems: A Practical Guide for Counselors* (2nd ed.). Toronto, Canada: Addiction Research Foundation, 125-139.

Schuckit, M.A. (1999). Goals of treatment. In M. Galanter & H.D. Kleber (Eds.) *American Psychiatric Press Textbook of Substance Abuse Treatment* (2nd ed.). Washington, DC: American Psychiatric Press, 89-95.

Schultz, J.E., & Parran, T., Jr. (1998). Principles of identification and intervention. In A.W. Graham, T.K. Schultz, & B.B. Wilford (Eds.) *Principles of Addiction Medicine* (2nd ed.). Chevy Chase, MD: American Society of Addiction Medicine, 249-261.

Semlitz, L. (2001). Treatment planning and case management. In T.W. Estroff (Ed.) *Manual of Adolescent Substance Abuse Treatment*. Arlington, VA: American Psychiatric Publishing, Inc.

Sobell, M.B., & Sobell, L.C. (1999). Stepped care for alcohol problems: An efficient method for planning and delivering clinical services. In J.A. Tucker, D.M. Donovan, & G.A. Marlatt (Eds.) *Changing Addictive Behavior: Bridging Clinical and Public Health Strategies*. New York: Guilford Press, 331-343.

Soden, T., & Murray, R. (1997). Motivational interviewing techniques. In S. Harrison & V. Carver (Eds.) *Alcohol and Drug Problems: A Practical Guide for Counselors* (2nd ed.). Toronto, Canada: Addiction Research Foundation, 19-59.

Sylvestre, D.L., Loftis, J.M., et al. (2004). Co-occurring hepatitis C, substance use, and psychiatric illness: Treatment issues and developing integrated models of care. *Journal of Urban Health*, 81(4):719-734.

Tickle-Degnen, L. (1998). Communication with clients about treatment outcomes: The use of meta-analytic evidence in collaborative treatment planning. *American Journal of Occupational Therapy*, 52(7):526-530.

Tickle-Degnen, L. (1998). Using research evidence in planning treatment for the individual client. *Canadian Journal of Occupational Therapy*, 65(3):152-159.

Waltman, D. (1995). Key ingredients to effective addictions treatment. *Journal of Substance Abuse Treatment*, 12(6):429-439.

Weed, L.L. (1968). Medical records that guide and teach. *New England Journal of Medicine*, 278:593-600.

Wiger, D.E., & Solberg, K.B. (2001). *Tracking Mental Health Outcomes: A Therapist's Guide to Measuring Client Progress, Analyzing Data, and Improving Your Practice*. New York: John Wiley & Sons.

Practice Dimension III

REFERRAL

PD III. Referral

Definition: *The process of facilitating the client's use of available support systems and community resources to meet needs identified in clinical evaluation or treatment planning.*

Competency 49:
Establish and maintain relationships with civic groups, agencies, other professionals, governmental entities, and the community at large to ensure appropriate referrals, identify service gaps, expand community resources, and help address unmet needs.

Knowledge

- The mission, function, resources, and quality of services offered by such entities as the following:
  - civic groups, community groups, and neighborhood organizations
  - health and allied healthcare systems (managed care)
  - employment and vocational rehabilitation services
  - cultural enhancement organizations
  - faith-based organizations
  - governmental entities
  - criminal justice systems
  - child welfare agencies
  - housing administrations
  - childcare facilities
  - crisis intervention programs
  - abused persons programs
  - mutual- and self-help groups
  - advocacy groups
  - other agencies.
- Community demographics.
- Community political and cultural systems.
- Criteria for receiving community services, including fee and funding structures.
- How to access community agencies and service providers.
- State and Federal legislative mandates and regulations.
- Confidentiality rules and regulations.
- Service gaps and appropriate ways of advocating for new resources.
- Effective communication styles.
- Community resources for both affected children and other household members.

Skills

- Networking and communicating.
- Using existing community resource directories including computer databases.
- Advocating for the client.
- Working with others as part of a team.

Attitudes

- Respect for interdisciplinary service delivery.
- Respect for both the client's needs and agency services.
- Respect for collaboration and cooperation.
- Appreciation of strengths-based principles that emphasize client autonomy and skills development.

Competency 50:

Continuously assess and evaluate referral resources to determine their appropriateness.

Knowledge

- The needs of the client population being served.
- How to access current information on the function, mission, and resources of community service providers.
- How to access current information on referral criteria and accreditation status of community service providers.
- How to access client satisfaction data about community service providers.

Skills

- Establishing and nurturing collaborative relationships with key contacts in community service organizations.
- Interpreting and using evaluation and client feedback data.
- Giving feedback to community resources regarding their service delivery.

Attitudes

- Respect for confidentiality rules and regulations.
- Willingness to advocate on behalf of the client.

COMPETENCY 51:

Differentiate between situations in which it is most appropriate for the client to self-refer to a resource and situations requiring counselor referral.

KNOWLEDGE

- Client motivation and ability to initiate and follow through with referrals.
- Factors in determining the optimal time to engage the client in the referral process.
- Clinical assessment methods.
- Empowerment techniques.
- Crisis prevention and intervention methods.

SKILLS

- Interpreting assessment and treatment planning materials to determine appropriateness of client or counselor referral.
- Assessing the client's readiness to participate in the referral process.
- Educating the client about appropriate referral processes.
- Motivating the client to take responsibility for referral and followup.
- Applying crisis prevention and intervention techniques.

ATTITUDES

- Respect for the client's ability to initiate and follow up with referral.
- Willingness to share decisionmaking power with the client.
- Respect for the goal of positive self-determination.
- Recognition of the counselor's responsibility to engage in client advocacy when needed.

Addiction Counseling Competencies

COMPETENCY 52:
Arrange referrals to other professionals, agencies, community programs, or appropriate resources to meet the client's needs.

KNOWLEDGE

- Comprehensive treatment planning.
- Methods of assessing the client's progress toward treatment goals.
- How to tailor resources to the client's treatment needs.
- How to access key resource persons in the community service provider network.
- Mission, function, and resources of appropriate community service providers.
- Referral protocols of selected service providers.
- Logistics necessary for client access and followthrough with referrals.
- Applicable confidentiality rules and regulations and protocols.
- Factors to consider when determining the appropriate time to engage a client in the referral process.

SKILLS

- Using oral and written communication for successful referrals.
- Using appropriate technology to access, collect, and forward necessary documentation.
- Conforming to all applicable confidentiality rules and regulations and protocols.
- Documenting the referral process accurately.
- Maintaining and nurturing relationships with key contacts in the community.
- Implementing followup activities with the client.

ATTITUDES

- Respect for the client and the client's needs and privacy rights.
- Respect for collaboration and cooperation.
- Respect for interdisciplinary, comprehensive approaches to meet the client's needs.

USES OF *THE COMPETENCIES*

In New England, *The Competencies* serves as the foundation of the nationally recognized ATTC-New England (NE) Distance Education program. *The Competencies* has been an outstanding and essential tool used in the development and delivery of more than 220 online presentations during the past 8 years. Instructors use *The Competencies* in all ATTC-NE trainings. In addition, the ATTC-NE training staff has designed a Web-based course (Core Functions of Addiction Counseling) that focuses entirely on *The Competencies*. This training has been delivered at least 10 times to participants from all sectors of the treatment field including counselors, physicians, correctional personnel, judiciary staff, those in the educational field, and government personnel. *The Competencies* continues to be a guiding force in course development, and the Web-based training is provided to participants from New England and other regions.

The Competencies was used in the development of a B.S. program in chemical dependency and addiction studies at Rhode Island College. It has been used in designing curriculum and developing course content.

Competency 53:

Explain in clear and specific language the necessity for and process of referral to increase the likelihood of client understanding and followthrough.

Knowledge

- How treatment planning and referral relate to the goals of recovery.
- How the client's defenses, abilities, personal preferences, cultural influences, personal resources, presentation, and appearance affect referral and followthrough.
- Comprehensive referral information and protocols.
- Terminology and structure used in referral settings.

Skills

- Using language and terms the client easily understands.
- Interpreting the treatment plan and how referral relates to progress.
- Engaging in effective communication about the referral process: negotiating, educating, personalizing risks and benefits, and contracting.

Attitudes

- Awareness of personal biases toward referral resources.

Competency 54:

Exchange relevant information with the agency or professional to whom the referral is being made in a manner consistent with confidentiality rules and regulations and generally accepted professional standards of care.

Knowledge

- Mission, function, and resources of the referral agency or professional.
- Protocols and documentation necessary to make the referral.
- Pertinent local, State, and Federal confidentiality rules and regulations; applicable clients' rights and responsibilities; client consent procedures; and other guiding principles for exchange of relevant information.
- Ethical standards of practice related to this exchange of information.

Skills

- Using oral and written communication for successful referrals.
- Using appropriate technology to access, collect, and forward relevant information needed by the agency or professional.
- Obtaining informed client consent and documentation needed for the exchange of relevant information.
- Reporting relevant information accurately and objectively.

Attitudes

- Commitment to professionalism.
- Respect for the importance of confidentiality rules and regulations and professional standards.
- Appreciation for the need to exchange relevant information with other professionals.

COMPETENCY 55:
Evaluate the outcome of the referral.

KNOWLEDGE
- Methods of assessing the client's progress toward treatment goals.
- Appropriate sources and techniques for evaluating referral outcomes.

SKILLS
- Using appropriate measurement processes and instruments.
- Collecting objective and subjective data on the referral process.

ATTITUDES
- Appreciation for the value of the evaluation process.
- Appreciation for the value of interagency collaboration.
- Appreciation for the value of interdisciplinary referral.

USES OF *THE COMPETENCIES*

In January 2001, a counselor performance assessment system was published by the Northwest Frontier (NF) ATTC based on *The Competencies*. Developed by a noted educational psychologist, the publication identifies a series of benchmarks that indicate a counselor's progress toward mastery of each competency for the developing, proficient, and exemplary clinician. Work is underway to add competencies for the entry-level counselor.

Another NFATTC publication based on *The Competencies* is called Proficiency Levels for Graduates of Academic Degree Programs. The document establishes proficiency targets for each knowledge, skill, and attitude included in *The Competencies* at the associate's, bachelor's, and master's levels.

In addition, NFATTC developed a 21-hour Clinical Supervision I course and a 14-hour Clinical Supervision II course based on *The Competencies*. The courses orient supervisors to *The Competencies*, introduce methods for assessing proficiency, and teach specific strategies for enhancing counselor knowledge, skills, and attitudes. Recent projects in treatment agencies in Idaho, Oregon, and Washington have looked at infusing *The Competencies* into the agencies' clinical supervision practices. *The Competencies* is used by each agency to develop specific learning plans for counselors. Idaho endorsed the NFATTC Clinical Supervision model and requires each treatment agency in the State system to use that model.

Bibliography

PD III. Referral

Humphreys, K., Wing, S., et al. (2004). Self-help organizations for alcohol and drug problems: Toward evidence-based practice and policy. *Journal of Substance Abuse Treatment*, 26(3):151-158, discussion 159-165.

Johnson, N.P., & Chappel, J.N. (1994). Using AA and other 12-Step programs more effectively. *Journal of Substance Abuse Treatment*, 11(2):137-142.

Lyter, S.C., & Lyter, L.L. (2000). Intervention with groups. In A.A. Abbott (Ed.) *Alcohol, Tobacco, and Other Drugs: Challenging Myths, Assessing Theories, Individualizing Interventions*. Washington, DC: National Association of Social Workers Press, 247-304.

McCaughrin, W.C., & Price, R.H. (1992). Effective outpatient drug treatment organizations: Program features and selection effects. *International Journal of the Addictions*, 27:1335-1358.

Moos, R.H., & Moos, B.S. (2004). Help-seeking careers: Connections between participation in professional treatment and Alcoholics Anonymous. *Journal of Substance Abuse Treatment*, 26(3):167.

Morehouse, E.R. (2000). Matching services and the needs of children of alcoholic parents: A spectrum of help. In S. Abbott (Ed.) *Children of Alcoholics: Selected Readings, Volume II*. Rockville, MD: National Association for Children of Alcoholics, 95-117.

Riordan, R.J., & Walsh, L. (1994). Guidelines for professional referral to Alcoholics Anonymous and other twelve step groups. *Journal of Counseling & Development*, 72:351-355.

Spencer, J.W. (1993). Making "suitable referrals": Social workers' construction and use of informal referral networks. *Sociological Perspectives*, 36(3):271-285.

Practice Dimension IV

SERVICE COORDINATION

PD IV. Service Coordination

Elements:
- Implementing the Treatment Plan
- Consulting
- Continuing Assessment and Treatment Planning

Definition: *The administrative, clinical, and evaluative activities that bring the client, treatment services, community agencies, and other resources together to focus on issues and needs identified in the treatment plan.*

Service coordination, which includes case management and client advocacy, establishes a framework of action to enable the client to achieve specified goals. It involves collaboration with the client and significant others, coordination of treatment and referral services, liaison activities with community resources and managed care systems, client advocacy, and ongoing evaluation of treatment progress and client needs.

Element: Implementing the Treatment Plan

Competency 56:
Initiate collaboration with the referral source.

Knowledge

- How to access and transmit information necessary for referral.
- Missions, functions, and resources of the community service network.
- Managed care and other systems affecting the client.
- Eligibility criteria for referral to community service providers.
- Appropriate confidentiality rules and regulations.
- Terminologies appropriate to the referral source.

Skills

- Using appropriate technology to access, collect, summarize, and transmit referral data about the client.
- Communicating respect and empathy for cultural and lifestyle differences.
- Demonstrating appropriate oral and written communication.
- Establishing trust and rapport with colleagues in the community.
- Assessing the level and intensity of client care needed.
- Being aware of the need to consult with professionals in other disciplines and specialties.

Attitudes

- Respect for contributions and needs of multiple disciplines to the treatment process.
- Confidence in using diverse systems and treatment approaches.
- Openmindedness to a variety of treatment approaches.
- Willingness to modify or adapt plans.

Competency 57:

Obtain, review, and interpret all relevant screening, assessment, and initial treatment planning information.

Knowledge

- Methods for obtaining relevant screening, assessment, and initial treatment planning information.
- How to interpret information for service coordination.
- Theories, concepts, and philosophies of screening and assessment tools.
- How to define long- and short-term goals of treatment.
- Biopsychosocial assessment methods.

Skills

- Using accurate, clear, and concise oral and written communication.
- Interpreting, prioritizing, and using client information.
- Soliciting comprehensive and accurate information from numerous sources, including the client.
- Using appropriate technology to document appropriate information.

Attitudes

- Appreciation for all sources and types of data and their possible treatment implications.
- Awareness of personal biases that may affect work with the client.
- Respect for the client's self-assessment and reporting.

Competency 58:
Confirm the client's eligibility for admission and continued readiness for treatment and change.

Knowledge

- Philosophies, policies, procedures, and admission protocols for community agencies.
- Eligibility criteria for referral to community service providers.
- Principles for tailoring treatment to client needs.
- Methods of assessing and documenting client change over time.
- Federal and State confidentiality rules and regulations and clients' privacy rights.

Skills

- Working with the client to select the most appropriate treatment.
- Accessing available funding resources.
- Using effective communication styles.
- Recognizing, documenting, and communicating client change.
- Involving family and significant others in the treatment planning process.
- Effectively interviewing and communicating with clients who have cognitive or psychiatric impairments.
- Accurately describing the client's signs and symptoms of cognitive or psychiatric impairment when consulting with medical and mental health professionals.

Attitudes

- Recognition of the importance of continued support, encouragement, and optimism.
- Willingness to accept the limitations of treatment.
- Appreciation for the goal of self-determination.
- Recognition of the importance of family and significant others to treatment planning.
- Appreciation for the need for continuing assessment and modifications to the treatment plan.

PD IV. Service Coordination

COMPETENCY 59:
Complete necessary administrative procedures for admission to treatment.

KNOWLEDGE

- Admission criteria and protocols.
- Documentation requirements and confidentiality rules and regulations.
- Appropriate Federal, State, and local regulations related to admission.
- Funding mechanisms, reimbursement protocols, and required documentation.
- Protocols required by managed care organizations.

SKILLS

- Demonstrating accurate, clear, and concise oral and written communication.
- Using language the client easily understands.
- Negotiating with diverse treatment systems.
- Advocating for services for the client.

ATTITUDES

- Acceptance of the necessity to deal with bureaucratic systems.
- Recognition of the importance of collaboration.
- Appreciation of strengths-based principles that emphasize client autonomy and skills development.

Competency 60:

Establish accurate treatment and recovery expectations with the client and involved significant others, including but not limited to:

- The nature of services
- Program goals
- Program procedures
- Rules regarding client conduct
- The schedule of treatment activities
- Costs of treatment
- Factors affecting duration of care
- Clients' rights and responsibilities
- The effect of treatment and recovery on significant others.

Knowledge

- Functions and resources provided by treatment services and managed care systems.
- Available community services.
- Effective communication styles.
- Clients' rights and responsibilities.
- Treatment schedule, timeframes, admission and discharge criteria, and costs.
- Rules and regulations of the treatment program.
- Roles and limitations of significant others in treatment.
- How to apply confidentiality rules and regulations and clients' privacy rights.

Skills

- Demonstrating clear and concise oral and written communication.
- Establishing appropriate boundaries with the client and significant others.

Attitudes

- Respect for the input of the client and significant others.

PD IV. Service Coordination

COMPETENCY 61:
Coordinate all treatment activities with services provided to the client by other resources.

KNOWLEDGE

- Methods for determining the client's progress in achieving treatment goals and objectives.
- Documentation and reporting methods used by community agencies.
- Service reimbursement issues and their effect on the treatment plan.
- Case presentation techniques and protocols.
- Applicable confidentiality rules and regulations.
- Terminology and methods used by community agencies.

SKILLS

- Delivering case presentations.
- Using appropriate technology to collect and interpret client treatment information from diverse sources.
- Demonstrating accurate, clear, and concise oral and written communication.
- Participating in interdisciplinary team building.
- Participating in negotiation, advocacy, conflict resolution, problemsolving, and mediation.

ATTITUDES

- Willingness to collaborate with community agencies and service providers.

USES OF *THE COMPETENCIES*

The Competencies is the foundation for addiction counseling coursework at the University of Nevada–Reno and the University of Nevada–Las Vegas. Both institutions offer an undergraduate minor and a graduate emphasis in addiction counseling with a number of courses developed directly from *The Competencies*. In addition, all instructors and students in these counseling programs are provided copies of the publication.

Element: Consulting

COMPETENCY 62:
Summarize the client's personal and cultural background, treatment plan, recovery progress, and problems inhibiting progress to ensure quality of care, gain feedback, and plan changes in the course of treatment.

KNOWLEDGE

- Methods for assessing the client's past and present biopsychosocial status.
- Methods for assessing social systems that may affect the client's progress in treatment.
- Methods for continuous assessment and modification of the treatment plan.
- Methods for assessing progress toward treatment goals.

SKILLS

- Demonstrating clear and concise oral and written communication.
- Synthesizing information and developing modified treatment goals and objectives.
- Soliciting and interpreting feedback related to the treatment plan.
- Prioritizing and documenting relevant client data.
- Observing and identifying problems that might impede progress.
- Soliciting client satisfaction feedback.

ATTITUDES

- Respect for the personal nature of the information shared by the client and significant others.
- Respect for interdisciplinary work.
- Appreciation for incremental progress in completing treatment goals.
- Recognition of relapse as an opportunity for positive change.

PD IV. Service Coordination

COMPETENCY 63:
Understand the terminology, procedures, and roles of other disciplines related to the treatment of substance use disorders.

KNOWLEDGE
- Functions and unique terminology of related disciplines.

SKILLS
- Demonstrating accurate, clear, and concise oral and written communication.
- Participating in interdisciplinary collaboration.
- Interpreting oral and written data from various sources.

ATTITUDES
- Confidence in asking questions and providing information across disciplines.

COMPETENCY 64:
Contribute as part of a multidisciplinary treatment team.

KNOWLEDGE
- Roles, responsibilities, and areas of expertise of other team members and professional disciplines.
- Confidentiality rules and regulations.
- Team dynamics and group process.

SKILLS
- Demonstrating clear and concise oral and written communication.
- Participating in problemsolving, decisionmaking, mediation, and advocacy.
- Communicating about confidentiality issues.
- Coordinating the client's treatment with representatives of multiple disciplines and external systems.
- Participating in team building and group process.

ATTITUDES
- Interest in cooperation and collaboration with diverse service providers.
- Respect and appreciation for other team members and their professional disciplines.
- Recognition of the need to consult with professionals in other disciplines and specialties.

Uses of *The Competencies*

Kathryn Miller, Ph.D., associate professor at San Antonio College, used *The Competencies* as the basis for the article "A Resource for Addiction Counseling: LCDCs in Texas" published in the *Texas Counseling Association Journal*. The article explains to graduate-level counselors the scope of chemical dependency counseling practice and encourages cooperation between counseling generalists and specialists.

Competency 65:
Apply confidentiality rules and regulations appropriately.

Knowledge

- Federal, State, and local confidentiality rules and regulations, especially as they apply to substance abuse treatment, health care, mental health care, child welfare, and criminal justice.
- How to apply confidentiality rules and regulations to documentation and sharing of client information.
- Ethical standards related to confidentiality rules and regulations.
- Clients' rights and responsibilities.
- How to apply confidentiality rules and regulations in emergency situations (medical/suicide prevention/mandatory reports of child abuse or neglect situations).

Skills

- Explaining and applying confidentiality rules and regulations.
- Obtaining informed consent.
- Communicating with the client, family and significant others, and other service providers within the boundaries of existing confidentiality rules and regulations.
- Communicating the need for client referral information in emergency situations and documenting these encounters.

Attitudes

- Recognition of the importance of confidentiality rules and regulations.
- Respect for a client's right to privacy.
- Recognition of the need to seek support or supervision in client health and safety emergency situations.

PD IV. Service Coordination

COMPETENCY 66:
Demonstrate respect and nonjudgmental attitudes toward clients in all contacts with community professionals and agencies.

KNOWLEDGE
- Behaviors appropriate to professional collaboration.
- Clients' rights and responsibilities.

SKILLS
- Establishing and maintaining nonjudgmental, respectful relationships with clients and service providers.
- Demonstrating clear, concise, accurate communication with other professionals or agencies.
- Applying confidentiality rules and regulations when communicating with agencies.
- Transferring client information to other service providers in a professional manner.
- Advocating with outside systems.

ATTITUDES
- Willingness to advocate on behalf of the client.
- Professional concern for the client.
- Commitment to professionalism.

USES OF *THE COMPETENCIES*

The Florida Certification Board (FCB) used the national standards for substance abuse counseling set forth in *The Competencies* to standardize the process of certification in the State of Florida and elevate the level of professionalism in the substance abuse treatment field. In 2003 FCB used this publication to develop Scopes of Professional Practice for three levels of addiction certification in Florida. To enhance the three Scopes of Practice, FCB expanded the educational requirements for certification. Using *The Competencies* to identify the specific educational content individuals would need to become certified according to the new Scopes of Practice, the educational components for certification were updated to include specific hours in each transdisciplinary foundation and practice dimension. Providers of continuing education for FCB are now required to detail the educational/training content on certificates to match the transdisciplinary foundations and practice dimensions.

Addiction Counseling Competencies

Element: Continuing Assessment and Treatment Planning

COMPETENCY 67:
Maintain ongoing contact with the client and involved significant others to ensure adherence to the treatment plan.

KNOWLEDGE

- Social, cultural, and family systems.
- Techniques to engage the client in treatment process.
- Outreach, followup, and continuing care techniques.
- Methods for determining the client's goals, treatment plan, and motivational level.
- Assessment mechanisms to measure the client's progress toward treatment objectives.

SKILLS

- Engaging the client, family, and significant others in the ongoing treatment process.
- Assessing client progress toward treatment goals.
- Helping the client maintain motivation to change.
- Assessing the comprehension level of the client, family, and significant others.
- Documenting the client's adherence to the treatment plan.
- Recognizing and addressing ambivalence and resistance.
- Implementing followup and continuing care protocols.

ATTITUDES

- Respect for client's efforts to achieve treatment goals.
- Appreciation for incremental progress in completing treatment goals.
- Respect for client's choice of treatment goals.
- Professional concern for the client, the family, and significant others.
- Recognition of the importance of continued support, encouragement, and optimism.
- Recognition of relapse as an opportunity for positive change.
- Appreciation of strengths-based principles that emphasize client autonomy and skills development.

PD IV. Service Coordination

COMPETENCY 68:
Understand and recognize stages of change and other signs of treatment progress.

KNOWLEDGE

- How to recognize incremental progress toward treatment goals.
- The client's cultural norms, biases, unique characteristics, and preferences for treatment.
- Generally accepted treatment outcome measures.
- Methods for evaluating treatment progress.
- Methods for assessing the client's motivation and adherence to treatment plans.
- Theories and principles of the stages of change and recovery.

SKILLS

- Identifying and documenting change.
- Assessing adherence to treatment plans.
- Applying treatment outcome measures.
- Communicating with people of other cultures.
- Reinforcing positive change.

ATTITUDES

- Appreciation for cultural issues that affect treatment progress.
- Respect for individual differences and readiness to change.
- Recognition of the importance of continued support, encouragement, and optimism.

USES OF *THE COMPETENCIES*

The Competencies has been used as a resource by instructors in developing online courses for Access ED, in presenting the Mid-Atlantic ATTC's Center for Online Courses, and for traditional classroom delivery tailored to counselors, case managers, and supervisors. In Virginia specifically, *The Competencies* guided the design of the Virginia Institute for Professional Addictions Counselor Training (VIPACT) curriculum, which provides the didactic hours required for the Virginia Certified Substance Abuse Counselor credential. This program has been delivered to nondegreed, as well as B.S.- and M.S.-prepared, counselors and case managers over the past 3 years. VIPACT was developed and continues to be delivered under a cooperative agreement between the Mid-Atlantic ATTC and the Virginia Department of Mental Health, Mental Retardation and Substance Abuse Services.

Competency 69:

Assess treatment and recovery progress, and, in consultation with the client and significant others, make appropriate changes to the treatment plan to ensure progress toward treatment goals.

Knowledge

- Continuum of care.
- Interviewing techniques.
- Stages in the treatment and recovery processes.
- Individual differences in the recovery process.
- Methods for evaluating treatment progress.
- Methods for reinvolving the client in the treatment planning process.

Skills

- Participating in conflict resolution, problemsolving, and mediation.
- Observing, recognizing, assessing, and documenting client progress.
- Eliciting the client's perspectives on progress.
- Demonstrating clear and concise oral and written communication.
- Interviewing individuals, groups, and families.
- Acquiring and prioritizing relevant treatment information.
- Assisting the client in maintaining motivation.
- Maintaining contact with the client, referral sources, and significant others.

Attitudes

- Willingness to be flexible.
- Respect for the client's right to self-determination.
- Appreciation of the role significant others play in the recovery process.
- Appreciation of individual differences in the recovery process.

PD IV. Service Coordination

COMPETENCY 70:
Describe and document the treatment process, progress, and outcome.

KNOWLEDGE
- Treatment modalities.
- Documentation of process, progress, and outcome.
- Factors affecting the client's success in treatment.
- Generally accepted outcome measures.
- Treatment planning.

SKILLS
- Demonstrating clear and concise oral and written communication.
- Observing and assessing client progress.
- Engaging the client in the treatment process.
- Applying progress and outcome measures.

ATTITUDES
- Appreciation of the importance of accurate documentation.
- Recognition of the importance of multidisciplinary treatment planning.

COMPETENCY 71:
Use accepted treatment outcome measures.

KNOWLEDGE
- Treatment outcome measures.
- Concepts of validity and reliability of outcome measures.

SKILLS
- Using outcome measures in the treatment planning process.

ATTITUDES
- Appreciation of the need to measure outcomes.

USES OF *THE COMPETENCIES*

The Northeast (Ne) ATTC instructs vendors and fellowship applicants to use *The Competencies* when designing and developing NeATTC-sponsored training curricula, educational products, and services. This activity helps agencies and individuals institutionalize the use of *The Competencies* as a tool in project planning and subsequent project activity.

Competency 72:
Conduct continuing care, relapse prevention, and discharge planning with the client and involved significant others.

Knowledge

- Treatment planning process.
- Continuum of care.
- Social and family systems available for continuing care.
- Community resources available for continuing care.
- Signs and symptoms of relapse.
- Relapse prevention strategies.
- Family and social systems theories.
- Discharge planning process.
- Confidentiality rules and regulations.

Skills

- Accessing information from referral sources.
- Demonstrating clear and concise oral and written communication.
- Assessing and documenting treatment progress.
- Participating in confrontation, conflict resolution, and problemsolving.
- Collaborating with referral sources.
- Engaging the client and significant others in the treatment process and continuing care.
- Assisting the client in developing a relapse prevention plan.

Attitudes

- Recognition of the importance of continued support, encouragement, and optimism.
- Appreciation of strengths-based principles that emphasize client autonomy and skills development.

PD IV. Service Coordination

COMPETENCY 73:
Document service coordination activities throughout the continuum of care.

KNOWLEDGE

- Documentation requirements, including but not limited to:
  - addiction counseling
  - other disciplines
  - funding sources
  - agencies and service providers.
- Service coordination role in the treatment process.

SKILLS

- Demonstrating clear and concise written communication.
- Using appropriate technology to report information in an accurate and timely manner within the bounds of confidentiality rules and regulations.

ATTITUDES

- Acceptance of documentation as an integral part of the treatment process.
- Willingness to use appropriate technology.

COMPETENCY 74:
Apply placement, continued stay, and discharge criteria for each modality on the continuum of care.

KNOWLEDGE

- Treatment planning along the continuum of care.
- Initial and ongoing placement criteria.
- Methods to assess current and ongoing client status.
- Stages of progress associated with treatment modalities.
- Appropriate discharge indicators.
- Managed care continuing care criteria and utilization review procedures.

SKILLS

- Observing and assessing client progress.
- Demonstrating clear and concise oral and written communication.
- Participating in conflict resolution, problemsolving, mediation, and negotiation.
- Tailoring treatment to meet client needs.
- Applying placement, continued stay, and discharge criteria.

ATTITUDES

- Confidence in the client's ability to progress within a continuum of care.
- Appreciation for the fair and objective use of placement, continued stay, and discharge criteria.

Bibliography

PD IV. Service Coordination

Bois, C., & Graham, K. (1997). Case management. In S. Harrison & V. Carver (Eds.) *Alcohol and Drug Problems: A Practical Guide for Counsellors* (2nd ed.). Toronto, Canada: Addiction Research Foundation, 61-76.

Bokos, P.J., Mejta, C.L., et al. (1993). A case management model for intravenous drug users. In J.A. Inciardi, R.M. Tims, & B.W. Fletcher (Eds.) *Innovative Approaches in the Treatment of Drug Abuse—Program Models and Strategies*. Westport, CT: Greenwood Press, 87-96.

Brindis, C., Pfeffer, R., & Wolfe, A. (1995). A case management program for chemically dependent clients with multiple needs. *Journal of Case Management*, 4:22-28.

Brindis, C.D., & Theidon, K.S. (1997). The role of case management in substance abuse treatment services for women and their children. *Journal of Psychoactive Drugs*, 29:79-88.

Brown, T.G., Seraganian, P., et al. (2002). Matching substance abuse aftercare treatment to client characteristics. *Addictive Behavior*, 27(4):585-604.

Center for Substance Abuse Treatment (1998). *Comprehensive Case Management for Substance Abuse Treatment*. Treatment Improvement Protocol (TIP) Series 27. DHHS Publication No. (SMA) 98-3222. Rockville, MD: Substance Abuse and Mental Health Services Administration.

Drake, R.E., & Noordsy, D.L. (1994). Case management for people with coexisting severe mental disorder and substance use disorder. *Psychiatric Annals*, 24:427-431.

Erickson, J.R., Chong, J., et al. (1995). Service linkages: Understanding what fosters and what deters from service coordination for homeless adult drug users. *Contemporary Drug Problems*, 22:343-362.

Galanter, M. (2002). Healing through social and spiritual affiliation. *Psychiatric Services*, 53(9):1072-1074.

Godley, S.H., Godley, M.D., et al. (1994). Case management services for adolescent substance abusers: A program description. *Journal of Substance Abuse Treatment*, 11(4):309-317.

Graham, K., Timney, C.B., et al. (1995). Continuity of care in addictions treatment: The role of advocacy and coordination in case management. *American Journal of Drug and Alcohol Abuse*, 21:433-451.

Grant, R.M., Ernst, C.C., et al. (1996). When case management isn't enough: A model of paraprofessional advocacy for drug- and alcohol-abusing mothers. *Journal of Case Management*, 5:3-11.

Grella, C.E., & Gilmore, J. (2002). Improving service delivery to the dually diagnosed in Los Angeles County. *Journal of Substance Abuse Treatment*, 23(2):115-122.

Gruber, K.J., & Fleetwood, T.W. (2004). In-home continuing care services for substance use affected families. *Substance Use & Misuse*, 39(9):1379-1403.

Hser, Y.-I., & Anglin, M.D. (2005). Drug treatment and aftercare programs. In R.H. Coombs (Ed.) *Addiction Counseling Review*. Mahwah, NJ: Lawrence Erlbaum Associates.

Legal Action Center (2003). *Confidentiality and Communication: A Guide to the Federal Drug and Alcohol Confidentiality Law and HIPAA*. New York: Legal Action Center.

Martin, S.S., & Inciardi, J.A. (1993). A case management treatment program for drug-involved prison releases. *Prison Journal*, 73:319-331.

McKay, J.R., Lynch, K.G., et al. (2005). Do patient characteristics and initial progress in treatment moderate the effectiveness of telephone-based continuing care for substance use disorders? *Addiction*, 100(2):216-226.

McKay, J.R., Lynch, K.G., et al. (2005). The effectiveness of telephone-based continuing care for alcohol and cocaine dependence: 24-month outcomes. *Archives of General Psychiatry*, 62(2):199-207.

McLellan, A.T., Hagan, R.A., et al. (1999). Does clinical case management improve outpatient addiction treatment? *Drug and Alcohol Dependence*, 55:91-103.

Mejta, C.L., Bokos, P.J., et al. (1997). Improving substance abuse treatment access and retention using a case management approach. *Journal of Drug Issues*, 27:329-340.

Rapp, R.C., Siegal, H.A., & Fisher, J.H. (1992). A strengths-based model of case management/advocacy: Adapting a mental health model to practice work with persons who have substance abuse problems. In R.S. Ashery (Ed.) *Progress and Issues in Case Management*. NIDA Research Monograph No. 127. DHHS Publication No. (ADM) 92-19467. Rockville, MD: National Institute on Drug Abuse, 79-91.

Ridley, M.S. (1994). Practical issues in the application of case management to substance abuse treatment. *Journal of Case Management*, 3:132-138.

Siegal, H.A. (2005). Case management. In R.H. Coombs (Ed.) *Addiction Counseling Review: Preparing for Comprehensive, Certification and Licensing Examinations*. Mahwah, NJ: Lawrence Erlbaum Associates, 381-399.

Siegal, H.A., Rapp, R.C., et al. (1995). The strengths perspective of case management: A promising inpatient substance abuse treatment enhancement. *Journal of Psychoactive Drugs*, 27:67-72.

Siegal, H.A., Rapp, R.C., et al. (1997). The role of case management in retaining clients in substance abuse treatment: An exploratory analysis. *Journal of Drug Issues*, 27:821-832.

Snyder, C.M., Kaempfer, S.H., & Reis, K. (1996). An interdisciplinary, interagency, primary care approach to case management of the dually diagnosed patient with HIV disease. *Journal of the Association of Nurses in AIDS Care*, 7(5):72-82.

Practice Dimension V

COUNSELING

PD V. Counseling

Elements:
- Individual Counseling
- Group Counseling
- Counseling, Families, Couples, and Significant Others

Definition: *A collaborative process that facilitates the client's progress toward mutually determined treatment goals and objectives.*

Counseling includes methods that are sensitive to individual client characteristics and to the influence of significant others, as well as the client's cultural and social context. Competence in counseling is built on an understanding of, appreciation of, and ability to appropriately use the contributions of various addiction counseling models as they apply to modalities of care for individuals, groups, families, couples, and significant others.

Element: Individual Counseling

Competency 75:
Establish a helping relationship with the client characterized by warmth, respect, genuineness, concreteness, and empathy.

Knowledge
- Theories, research, and evidence-based literature.
- Approaches to counseling that are person centered and have demonstrated effectiveness with substance use disorders.
- Definitions of warmth, respect, genuineness, concreteness, and empathy.
- The role of the counselor.
- Transference and countertransference.

Skills
- Active listening, including paraphrasing, reflecting, and summarizing.
- Conveying warmth, respect, and genuineness in a culturally appropriate manner.
- Validating.
- Demonstrating empathic understanding.
- Using power and authority appropriately in support of treatment goals.

Attitudes
- Respect for the client.
- Recognition of the importance of cooperation and collaboration with the client.
- Professional objectivity.

COMPETENCY 76:
Facilitate the client's engagement in the treatment and recovery process.

KNOWLEDGE
- Theory and research related to client motivation.
- Alternative theories and methods for motivating the client in a culturally appropriate manner.
- Theory, research, and evidence-based literature.
- Counseling strategies that promote and support successful client engagement.
- Stages-of-change models used in engagement and treatment strategies.

SKILLS
- Implementing appropriate engagement and interviewing approaches.
- Assessing the client's readiness for change.
- Using culturally appropriate counseling strategies.
- Assessing the client's responses to therapeutic interventions.

ATTITUDES
- Respect for the client's frame of reference and context.

COMPETENCY 77:
Work with the client to establish realistic, achievable goals consistent with achieving and maintaining recovery.

KNOWLEDGE
- Assessment and treatment planning.
- Stages of change and recovery.
- Strategies to support recovery.

SKILLS
- Formulating and documenting concise, descriptive, and measurable treatment outcome statements.
- Facilitating the client's ability to determine goals and formulate action plans.
- Knowing one's limitations with respect to the therapeutic relationship.

ATTITUDES
- Appreciation for the client's resources and preferences.
- Appreciation for individual differences in the treatment and recovery process.

USES OF *THE COMPETENCIES*
In Idaho, the State certification board and the Idaho Educators in Addiction Studies collaborated to establish a new entry-level counselor certification for the State. Educational requirements for certification were based on ***The Competencies***. To facilitate the process, college faculty members were trained in competency-based teaching methods to enhance student proficiency.

PD V. Counseling

COMPETENCY 78:
Promote client knowledge, skills, and attitudes that contribute to a positive change in substance use behaviors.

KNOWLEDGE

- Information, skills, and attitudes consistent with recovery.
- The client's goals, treatment plan, prognosis, and motivational level.
- Stages-of-change model.
- Assessment methods to measure progress in achieving treatment goals and objectives.

SKILLS

- Implementing motivational techniques.
- Recognizing the client's strengths.
- Assessing and providing feedback on client progress toward treatment goals.
- Assessing life and basic skills and comprehension levels of the client and all significant others involved in the treatment planning process.
- Identifying and documenting change.
- Coaching, mentoring, teaching, and validating.
- Recognizing and addressing ambivalence and resistance.

ATTITUDES

- Genuine care and concern for the client, family, and significant others.
- Appreciation for incremental progress in completing treatment goals.
- Appreciation of strengths-based principles that emphasize client autonomy and skills development.

Competency 79:

Encourage and reinforce client actions determined to be beneficial in progressing toward treatment goals.

Knowledge

- Counseling theory, treatment, and practice literature as it applies to substance use disorders.
- Relapse prevention theory, practice, and outcome literature.
- Behaviors and cognition consistent with the development, maintenance, and attainment of treatment goals.
- Counseling treatment methods that support positive client behaviors consistent with recovery.

Skills

- Using behavioral and cognitive methods and other interventions that reinforce positive client behaviors.
- Using objective observation and documentation.
- Assessing and reassessing client behaviors.

Attitudes

- Recognition of the importance of continued support, encouragement, and optimism.
- Appreciation of strengths-based principles that emphasize client autonomy and skills development.
- Appreciation for incremental progress in completing treatment goals.

Competency 80:
Work appropriately with the client to recognize and discourage all behaviors inconsistent with progress toward treatment goals.

Knowledge

- The client's history and treatment plan.
- The client's behaviors and cognition that are inconsistent with the recovery process.
- Behavioral and cognitive therapy literature relevant to substance use disorders.
- Cognitive, behavioral, and pharmacological interventions appropriate for relapse prevention.
- Strengths-based models that build on strengths of the client.

Skills

- Monitoring the client's behavior for consistency with established treatment outcomes.
- Presenting inconsistencies between the client's behaviors and goals.
- Reframing and redirecting negative behaviors.
- Teaching conflict resolution, decision-making, and problemsolving skills.
- Recognizing and addressing underlying client issues that may impede treatment progress.
- Engaging client to discover and use personal strengths and resources to achieve goals.

Attitudes

- Appreciation of strengths-based principles that emphasize client autonomy and skills development.
- Acceptance of relapse as an opportunity for positive change.
- Recognition of the value of a constructive helping relationship.

Competency 81:

Recognize how, when, and why to involve the client's significant others in enhancing or supporting the treatment plan.

Knowledge

- Theory, research, and outcome-based literature demonstrating the importance of significant others, including families and other social systems, to treatment progress.
- Social and family systems theory.
- How to apply appropriate confidentiality rules and regulations.

Skills

- Identifying the client's family and social systems.
- Recognizing the effect of the client's family and social systems on the treatment process.
- Engaging significant others in the treatment process.

Attitudes

- Appreciation for the need of significant others to be involved in the client's treatment plan, within the bounds of confidentiality rules and regulations.
- Respect for the contribution of significant others to the treatment process.

COMPETENCY 82:

Promote client knowledge, skills, and attitudes consistent with the maintenance of health and prevention of HIV/AIDS, tuberculosis, sexually transmitted diseases, hepatitis C, and other infectious diseases.

KNOWLEDGE

- The client's and system's worldviews relative to health.
- How infectious diseases are transmitted and prevented.
- The relationship among substance-abusing lifestyles, risky sexual behaviors, and the transmission of infectious diseases.
- Health enhancement concepts, research, and methods.
- Available community health care, support, and prevention resources.

SKILLS

- Using a repertoire of techniques that, based on an assessment of various client and system characteristics, promote and reinforce health-enhancing activities and safe sex practices.
- Coaching, mentoring, and teaching techniques relative to the promotion and maintenance of health.
- Demonstrating cultural and overall competence in discussing sexuality.
- Facilitating client referral to available community resources.

ATTITUDES

- Openness to discussions about health issues, lifestyle, and sexuality.
- Recognition of the counselor's potential to model a healthy lifestyle.

Competency 83:

Facilitate the development of basic and life skills associated with recovery.

Knowledge

- Basic and life skills associated with recovery.
- Theory, research, and practice literature that examines the relationship of basic and life skills to the attainment of positive treatment outcomes.
- Tools used to determine levels of basic and life skills.

Skills

- Teaching and facilitating the adoption of life skills appropriate to the client's situation and skill level.
- Applying assessment tools to determine the client's level of basic and life skills.
- Communicating how basic and life skills relate to treatment outcomes.

Attitudes

- Recognition that recovery involves a life context broader than the elimination of symptoms.
- Acceptance of relapse as an opportunity for learning and/or skills acquisition.

Competency 84:

Adapt counseling strategies to the individual characteristics of the client, including but not limited to disability, gender, sexual orientation, developmental level, culture, ethnicity, age, and health status.

Knowledge

- The effect of culture on substance use.
- Cultural factors affecting responsiveness to various counseling strategies.
- Current research concerning differences in drinking and substance use patterns based on the characteristics of the client.
- Addiction counseling strategies.
- How to apply appropriate strategies based on the client's treatment plan.
- The client's family and social systems and relationships between each.
- The client's and system's cultural norms, biases, and preferences.
- Literature relating spirituality to addiction and recovery.

Skills

- Knowing how to individualize treatment plans.
- Adapting counseling strategies to unique client characteristics and circumstances.
- Applying culturally and linguistically responsive communication styles and practices.

Attitudes

- Recognition of the need for flexibility in meeting the client's needs.
- Willingness to adjust strategies in accordance with the client's characteristics.
- A nonjudgmental, respectful acceptance of cultural, behavioral, and value differences.

PD V. Counseling

Competency 85:
Make constructive therapeutic responses when the client's behavior is inconsistent with stated recovery goals.

Knowledge

- Client behaviors that tend to be inconsistent with recovery.
- The client's social and life circumstances.
- Relapse prevention strategies.
- Therapeutic interventions.

Skills

- Monitoring the client's progress.
- Using various methods to present inconsistencies between the client's behaviors and treatment goals.
- Reframing and redirecting negative behaviors.
- Using appropriate communication and intervention strategies.

Attitudes

- Recognition of the importance of continued support, encouragement, and optimism.
- Perseverance during periods of treatment difficulty.

Competency 86:
Apply crisis prevention and management skills.

Knowledge

- Differences between crisis prevention, crisis intervention, and other kinds of therapeutic intervention.
- Characteristics of a serious crisis and typical reactions.
- Posttraumatic stress and other relevant psychiatric conditions.
- Roles played by family and significant others in the crisis development or reaction.
- Relationship of crisis to the client's stage of change.
- The client's usual coping strategies.
- Steps to aid in crisis resolution, including determination of what the client can do and what the counselor, family, or significant others in the client system should do, in accordance with the Health Insurance Portability and Accountability Act (HIPAA).

Skills

- Carrying out steps from crisis prevention to crisis resolution.
- Assessing and engaging the client's and client's system's strengths and resources.
- Assessing for immediate concerns regarding safety and potential harm to others.
- Possessing the ability to contract for safety.
- Making appropriate referrals as necessary.
- Assessing and acting on issues of confidentiality that may be part of a crisis response.
- Assisting the client in expressing emotions and normalizing feelings.

Attitudes

- Recognition of crisis as an opportunity for change.
- Confidence in the midst of crisis.
- Recognition of personal and professional limitations.
- Recognition of the need to practice crisis responses, particularly team interventions.

Competency 87:

Facilitate the client's identification, selection, and practice of strategies that help sustain the knowledge, skills, and attitudes needed for maintaining treatment progress and preventing relapse.

Knowledge

- How the client and client's family, significant others, mutual-help groups, and other systems enhance and maintain treatment progress, relapse prevention, and continuing care.
- Relapse prevention strategies.
- Skills-training methods.

Skills

- Using behavioral techniques to reinforce positive client behaviors.
- Teaching relapse prevention and life skills.
- Motivating the client toward involvement in mutual-help groups.

Attitudes

- Recognition that clients must assume responsibility for their recovery.

Addiction Counseling Competencies

Element: Group Counseling

COMPETENCY 88:
Describe, select, and appropriately use strategies from accepted and culturally appropriate models for group counseling with clients with substance use disorders.

KNOWLEDGE

- A variety of group methods appropriate to achieving client objectives in a treatment population.
- Research concerning the effectiveness of various models and strategies for group counseling with general populations.
- Research concerning the effectiveness of various models and strategies for populations with substance use disorders.
- Research and theory concerning the effectiveness of various models and strategies for group counseling with members of varying cultural groups.

SKILLS

- Designing and implementing strategies to meet the needs of specific groups.
- Recognizing and accommodating appropriate individual needs within the group.
- Leading therapeutic groups for clients with substance use disorders.
- Using humor appropriately.

ATTITUDES

- Openness and flexibility in the choice of counseling strategies that meet the needs of the group and the individuals within the group.
- Recognition of the value of the use of groups as an effective therapeutic intervention.

USES OF *THE COMPETENCIES*

In July 1999 a new mandatory Chemical Dependency Professional credentialing process was adopted in Washington State. Proficiency in specific addiction counseling competencies derived from *The Competencies* came to be required. Subsequently, college and university curricula within the State were required to be consistent with *The Competencies*.

Competency 89:

Carry out the actions necessary to form a group, including but not limited to determining group type, purpose, size, and leadership; recruiting and selecting members; establishing group goals and clarifying behavioral ground rules for participating; identifying outcomes; and determining criteria and methods for termination or graduation from the group.

Knowledge

- Specific group models and strategies relative to the client's age, gender, and cultural context.
- Selection criteria, methods, and instruments for screening and selecting group members.
- General principles for selecting group goals, outcomes, and ground rules.
- General principles for appropriately graduating group members and terminating groups.
- Principles of confidentiality rules and regulations.

Skills

- Conducting screening interviews.
- Assessing a client's appropriateness for participation in group.
- Using the group process to negotiate group goals, outcomes, and ground rules within the context of the individual needs and objectives of group members.
- Using the group process to negotiate appropriate criteria and methods for transition to the next appropriate level of care.
- Adapting group counseling skills as appropriate for the group type.
- Considering environmental factors that facilitate group interactions, such as room setup and privacy issues.

Attitudes

- Recognition of the importance of involving group members in the establishment of group goals, outcomes, ground rules, and graduation and termination criteria.
- Recognition of the fact that the nature of the specific group model depends on the needs, goals, outcomes, and cultural context of the participants.

COMPETENCY 90:
Facilitate the entry of new members and the transition of exiting members.

KNOWLEDGE

- Developmental processes affecting therapeutic groups over time.
- Issues faced by individuals and the group as a whole on entry of new members.
- Issues faced by individuals and the group as a whole on exit of members.
- Characteristics of transition stages in therapeutic groups.
- Characteristics of therapeutic group behavior.

SKILLS

- Using the group process to prepare group members for transition and to resolve transitional issues.
- Effectively addressing different types of resistant behaviors, transference issues, and countertransference issues.
- Recognizing when members are ready to exit.

ATTITUDES

- Recognition of the need to balance individual needs with group needs, goals, and outcomes.
- Appreciation for the contribution of new and continuing group members in the group process.
- Maintenance of nonjudgmental attitudes and behaviors.
- Respect for the emotional experience of the entry and exit of group members on the rest of the group.

PD V. Counseling

COMPETENCY 91:

Facilitate group growth within the established ground rules and movement toward group and individual goals by using methods consistent with group type.

KNOWLEDGE

- Leadership, facilitator, and counselor methods appropriate for each group type and therapeutic setting.
- Types and uses of power and authority in the therapeutic group process.
- Stages of group development and counseling methods appropriate to each stage.

SKILLS

- Applying group counseling methods leading to measurable progress toward group and individual goals and outcomes.
- Recognizing when and how to use appropriate power.
- Documenting measurable progress toward group and individual goals.

ATTITUDES

- Recognition of the value of the use of different group counseling methods and leadership or facilitation styles.
- Appreciation for the role and power of the group facilitator.
- Appreciation for the role and power of various group members in the group process.

COMPETENCY 92:

Understand the concepts of process and content, and shift the focus of the group when such a shift will help the group move toward its goals.

KNOWLEDGE

- Concepts of process and content.
- Difference between the group process and the content of the discussion.
- Methods and techniques of group problemsolving, decisionmaking, and addressing group conflict.
- How process variables affect the group's ability to focus on content concerns.
- How content variables affect the group's ability to focus on process concerns.

SKILLS

- Observing and documenting process and content.
- Assessing when to make appropriate process interventions.
- Using strategies congruent with enhancing both process and content to meet individual and group goals.

ATTITUDES

- Appreciation of the appropriate use of content and process interventions.

Competency 93:

Describe and summarize the client's behavior within the group to document the client's progress and identify needs and issues that may require a modification in the treatment plan.

Knowledge

- How individual treatment issues may surface in the context of group process.
- Situations in which significant differences between individual and group goals require changing either the individual's goals or the group's focus.

Skills

- Recognizing that a client's behavior can be, but is not always, reflective of the client's treatment needs.
- Documenting the client's group behavior that has implications for treatment planning.
- Recognizing the similarities and differences between individual needs and group processes.
- Redesigning individual treatment plans based on the observation of group behaviors.

Attitudes

- Recognition of the value of accurate documentation.
- Appreciation for individual differences in progress toward treatment goals and use of group intervention.

Uses of *The Competencies*

The University of California–San Diego School of Medicine Forensic Certificate is based on *The Competencies*, criminology issues, and penology. *The Competencies* also serves as the minimum standard for the California Association of Addiction Certifying Organizations, a quality assurance body for the State.

Element: Counseling Families, Couples, and Significant Others

Competency 94:
Understand the characteristics and dynamics of families, couples, and significant others affected by substance use.

Knowledge

- Dynamics associated with substance use, abuse, dependence, and recovery in families, couples, and significant others.
- The effect of interaction patterns on substance use behaviors.
- Cultural factors related to the effect of substance use disorders on families, couples, and significant others.
- Systems theory and dynamics.
- Signs and patterns of domestic violence.
- Effects of substance use behaviors on interaction patterns.

Skills

- Identifying systemic interactions that are likely to affect recovery.
- Recognizing the roles of significant others in the client's social system.
- Recognizing potential for and signs and symptoms of domestic violence.

Attitudes

- Recognition of nonconstructive family behaviors as systemic issues.
- Appreciation of the role systemic interactions play in substance use behavior.
- Appreciation for diverse cultural factors that influence characteristics and dynamics of families, couples, and significant others.

Competency 95:
Be familiar with and appropriately use models of diagnosis and intervention for families, couples, and significant others, including extended, kinship, or tribal family structures.

Knowledge

- Intervention strategies appropriate for family systems at varying stages of problem development and resolution.
- Intervention strategies appropriate for violence against persons.
- Laws and resources regarding violence against persons.
- Culturally appropriate family intervention strategies.
- Appropriate and available assessment tools for use with families, couples, and significant others.

Skills

- Applying assessment tools for use with families, couples, and significant others.
- Applying culturally appropriate intervention strategies.

Attitudes

- Recognition of the validity of viewing the system (i.e., family, significant others, and extended kinship or tribal family structures) as the client views it, while respecting the rights and needs of individuals.
- Appreciation for the diversity found in families, couples, and significant others.

Competency 96:
Facilitate the engagement of selected members of the family or significant others in the treatment and recovery process.

Knowledge

- How to apply appropriate confidentiality rules and regulations.
- Methods for engaging members of the family or significant others to focus on their concerns.

Skills

- Working within the bounds of confidentiality rules and regulations.
- Identifying goals based on both individual and systemic concerns.
- Using appropriate therapeutic interventions with system members that address established treatment goals.

Attitudes

- Recognition of the usefulness of working with those individual system members who are ready to participate in the counseling process.
- Respect for confidentiality rules and regulations.

COMPETENCY 97:
Assist families, couples, and significant others in understanding the interaction between the family system and substance use behaviors.

KNOWLEDGE

- The effect of family interaction patterns on substance use.
- The effect of substance use on family interaction patterns.
- Theory and research literature outlining systemic interventions in psychoactive substance abuse situations, including violence against persons.

SKILLS

- Describing systemic issues constructively to families, couples, and significant others.
- Assisting system members in identifying and interrupting harmful interaction patterns.
- Helping system members practice and evaluate alternative interaction patterns.

ATTITUDES

- Appreciation for the complexities of counseling families, couples, and significant others.

COMPETENCY 98:
Assist families, couples, and significant others in adopting strategies and behaviors that sustain recovery and maintain healthy relationships.

KNOWLEDGE

- Healthy behavioral patterns for families, couples, and significant others.
- Empirically based systemic counseling strategies associated with recovery.
- Stages of recovery for families, couples, and significant others.

SKILLS

- Assisting system members in identifying and practicing behaviors to resolve the crises brought about by changes in substance use behaviors.
- Assisting clients and family members with referral to appropriate support resources.
- Assisting family members in identifying and practicing behaviors associated with long-term maintenance of healthy interactions.

ATTITUDES

- Appreciation for a variety of approaches to working with families, couples, and significant others.

Bibliography

PD V. Counseling: Individual Counseling

Ackerman, S.J., & Hilsenroth, M.J. (2003). A review of therapist characteristics and techniques positively impacting the therapeutic alliance. *Clinical Psychology Review*, 23(1):1-33.

Babor, T.F. (2003). *Treatment Matching in Alcoholism*. New York: Cambridge University Press.

Bell, A., & Rollnick, S. (1996). Motivational interviewing in practice: A structured approach. In F. Rotgers, D. Keller, & J. Morgenstern (Eds.) *Treating Substance Abuse: Theory and Technique*. New York: Guilford Press, 266-285.

Bishop, F.M. (2001). *Managing Addictions: Cognitive, Emotive, and Behavioral Techniques*. Northvale, NJ: Jason Aronson.

Black, C., Paz, H., & DeBlassie, R.R. (1991). Counseling the Hispanic male adolescent. *Adolescence*, 26:223-232.

Boren, J.J., Onken, L.S., et al. (2000). *Approaches to Drug Abuse Counseling*. Rockville, MD: National Institute on Drug Abuse.

Broome, K.M., Joe, G.W., et al. (2001). Engagement models for adolescents in DATOS-A. *Journal of Adolescent Research*, 16(6):608-623.

Carroll, K.M. (1999). Behavioral and cognitive behavioral treatments. In B.S. McCrady & E.E. Epstein (Eds.) *Addictions: A Comprehensive Guidebook*. New York: Oxford University Press, 250-267.

Carroll, K.M., Libby, B., et al. (2001). Motivational interviewing to enhance treatment initiation in substance abusers: An effectiveness study. *American Journal on Addictions*, 10:335-339.

DiClemente, C.C., Carroll, K.M., et al. (2003). A look inside treatment: Therapist effects, the therapeutic alliance, and the process of intentional behavior change. In T.F. Babor (Ed.) *Treatment Matching in Alcoholism*. New York: Cambridge University Press, 166-183.

DiClemente, C.C., Schlundt, D., et al. (2004). Readiness and stages of change in addiction treatment. *American Journal on Addictions*, 13(2):103-119.

Dodes, L.M., & Khantzian, E.J. (1998). Individual psychodynamic psychotherapy. In R.J. Frances & S.I. Miller (Eds.) *Clinical Textbook of Addictive Disorders*. New York: Guilford Press, 479-495.

Donovan, D.M., Carroll, K.M., et al. (2003). Therapies for matching: Selection, development, implementation, and costs. In T.F. Babor (Ed.) *Treatment Matching in Alcoholism*. New York: Cambridge University Press, 42-61.

Donovan, D.M., & Marlatt, G.A. (1993). Behavioral treatment. In M. Galanter (Ed.) *Recent Developments in Alcoholism, Volume 11: Ten Years of Progress*. New York: Plenum Press, 397-411.

Drake, R.E., Mueser, K.T., et al. (2004). A review of treatments for people with severe mental illnesses and co-occurring substance use disorders. *Psychiatric Rehabilitation Journal*, 27(4):360-374.

Finnegan, D.G., & McNally, E.B. (2002). *Counseling Lesbian, Gay, Bisexual, and Transgender Substance Abusers: Dual Identities*. New York: Haworth Press.

Galanter, M. (Ed.) (2003). *Recent Developments in Alcoholism, Volume 16: Research on Alcoholism Treatment*. New York: Springer.

Godley, S.H., Meyers, R.J., et al. (2001). *The Adolescent Community Reinforcement Approach for Adolescent Cannabis Users*. Cannabis Youth Treatment (CYT) Series, Volume 4. DHHS Publication No. (SMA) 01-3489. Rockville, MD: Center for Substance Abuse Treatment, Substance Abuse and Mental Health Services Administration.

Godley, S.H., Risberg, R.A., et al. (2002). *Treatment Manual—Bloomington's Outpatient & Intensive Outpatient Treatment Model*. Bloomington, IL: Chestnut Health Systems.

Goldstein, E.G. (2004). Substance abusers with borderline disorders. In S.L.A. Straussner (Ed.) *Clinical Work With Substance-Abusing Clients* (2nd ed.). New York: Guilford Press, 370-391.

Gordon, K. (1993). The treatment of addictive disorders in a private clinical setting. In S.L. Straussner (Ed.) *Clinical Work With Substance Abusing Clients*. New York: Guilford Press, 88-102.

Gurnack, A.M., Atkinson, R., & Osgood N.J. (Eds.) (2002). *Treating Alcohol and Drug Abuse in the Elderly*. New York: Springer Publishing.

Heather, N., Peters, T.J., & Stockwell, T. (Eds.) (2001). *International Handbook of Alcohol Dependence and Problems*. New York: John Wiley & Sons.

Kent, C. (1997). Ending with clients: Closure in counseling. In S. Harrison & V. Carver (Eds.) *Alcohol and Drug Problems: A Practical Guide for Counselors* (2nd ed.). Toronto, Canada: Addiction Research Foundation, 203-215.

Levin, J.D. (2004). Counseling and therapy techniques in substance abuse treatment. *Issues in Psychoanalytic Psychology*, 26(2):145-162.

Marlatt, G.A., Barrett, K., & Daley, D.C. (1999). Relapse prevention. In M. Galanter & H.D. Kleber (Eds.) *Textbook of Substance Abuse Treatment* (2nd ed.). Washington, DC: American Psychiatric Association, 353-366.

Marlatt, G.A., & Donovan, D.M. (Eds.) (2005). *Relapse Prevention: Maintenance Strategies in the Treatment of Addictive Behaviors*. New York: Guilford Press.

Martino, S., Carroll, K., et al. (2002). Dual diagnosis motivational interviewing: A modification of motivational interviewing for substance-abusing patients with psychotic disorders. *Journal of Substance Abuse Treatment*, (23)4:297-308.

McCrady, B.S., & Epstein, E.E. (Eds.) (1999). *Addictions: A Comprehensive Guidebook*. New York: Oxford University Press.

Meier, P.S., Barrowclough, C., et al. (2005). The role of the therapeutic alliance in the treatment of substance misuse: A critical review of the literature. *Addiction*, 100(3):304-316.

Miller, G. (2002). *Incorporating Spirituality in Counseling and Psychotherapy: Theory and Technique*. Hoboken, NJ: John Wiley & Sons.

Miller, W.R., & Rollnick, S. (2002). *Motivational Interviewing: Preparing People To Change Addictive Behavior* (2nd ed.). New York: Guilford Press.

Monti, P.M., Kadden, R.M., et al. (2002). *Treating Alcohol Dependence: A Coping Skills Training Guide* (2nd ed.). New York: Guilford Press.

Mora, J. (1998). The treatment of alcohol dependency among Latinas: A feminist, cultural and community perspective. *Alcoholism Treatment Quarterly*, 16:163-177.

Mueser, K.T., Noordsy, D.L., et al. (2003). *Integrated Treatment of Dual Disorders: A Guide to Effective Practice*. New York: Guilford Press.

Najavits, L. (2002). *Seeking Safety: A Treatment Manual for PTSD and Substance Abuse*. New York: Guilford Press.

O'Connell, D., & Beyer, E. (Eds.) (2002). *Managing the Dually Diagnosed Patient: Current Issues and Clinical Approaches* (2nd ed.). New York: Haworth Press.

O'Leary, T.A., & Monti, P.M. (2002). Cognitive-behavioral therapy for alcohol addiction. In S.G. Hofmann & M.C. Tompson (Eds.) *Treating Chronic and Severe Mental Disorders: A Handbook of Empirically Supported Interventions*. New York: Guilford Press, 234-257.

Petry, N.M., Petrakis, I., et al. (2001). Contingency management interventions: From research to practice. *American Journal of Psychiatry*, 158(5):694-702.

Platt, J., & Husband, S. (1993). An overview of problem solving and social skills approaches in substance abuse treatment. *Psychotherapy*, 30:276-278.

Prochaska, J.O., DiClemente, C.C., & Norcross, J.C. (1997). In search of how people change: Applications to addictive behaviors. In G.A. Marlett & G.R. Vandenbos (Eds.) *Addictive Behaviors*. Washington, DC: American Psychological Association, 671-695.

Ramsay, J.R., & Newman, C.F. (2000). Substance abuse. In F.M. Dattilio & A. Freeman (Eds.) *Cognitive-Behavioral Strategies in Crisis Intervention* (2nd ed.). New York: Guilford Press, 126-149.

Rounsaville, B.J., & Carroll, K.M. (1997). Individual psychotherapy. In J.H. Lowinson, P. Ruiz, et al. (Eds.) *Substance Abuse: A Comprehensive Textbook*. Baltimore: Lippincott Williams & Wilkins, 430-439.

Sabin, C., Benally, H., et al. (n.d.). *Walking in Beauty on the Red Road: A Holistic Cultural Treatment Model for American Indian and Alaska Native Adolescents and Families*. Bloomington, IL: Chestnut Health Systems.

Senior, M., Smith, M., & Taylor, S. *EMPACT–Suicide Prevention Center Teen Substance Abuse Treatment Program Treatment Manual*. Bloomington, IL: Chestnut Health Systems.

Sheehan, M.F. (1991). Dual diagnosis. *Psychiatric Quarterly*, 62:107-134.

Siegal, H.A., Rapp, R.C., et al. (1997). The role of case management in retaining clients in substance abuse treatment: An exploratory analysis. *Journal of Drug Issues*, 27:821-832.

Springer, D.W., McNeece, C.A., et al. (2003). Individual treatment. In D.W. Springer, C.A. McNeece, & E.M. Arnold (Eds.) *Substance Abuse Treatment for Criminal Offenders: An Evidence-Based Guide for Practitioners*. Washington, DC: American Psychological Association.

Summers, R.F., & Barber, J.P. (2003). Therapeutic alliance as a measurable psychotherapy skill. *Academic Psychiatry*, 27(3):160-165.

Witkiewitz, K., & Marlatt, G.A. (2004). Relapse prevention for alcohol and drug problems: That was Zen, this is Tao. *American Psychologist*, 59(4):224-235.

Woody, G.E. (2003). Research findings on psychotherapy of addictive disorders. *American Journal on Addictions*, 12(3):S19.

Ziedonis, D., Krejci, J., et al. (2001). Integrated treatment of alcohol, tobacco, and other drug addictions. In J. Kay (Ed.) *Integrated Treatment of Psychiatric Disorders*. Washington, DC: American Psychiatric Association, 79-111.

Zweben, A., & Fleming, M.F. (1999). Brief interventions for alcohol and drug problems. In J.A. Tucker, D.M. Donovan, & G.A. Marlatt (Eds.) *Changing Addictive Behavior: Bridging Clinical and Public Health Strategies*. New York: Guilford Press, 251-282.

Zweben, J.E. (1995). Integrating psychotherapy and 12-Step approaches. In A.M. Washton (Ed.) *Psychotherapy and Substance Abuse: A Practitioner's Handbook*. New York: Guilford Press, 124-140.

PD V. Counseling: Group Counseling

Atkinson, R.M., & Misra, S. (2002). Further strategies in the treatment of aging alcoholics. In A.M. Gurnack, R. Atkinson, & N.J. Osgood (Eds.) *Treating Alcohol and Drug Abuse in the Elderly*. New York: Springer Publishing, 131-151.

Battjes, R.J., Michael, S., et al. (2004). Evaluation of a group-based substance abuse treatment program for adolescents. *Journal of Substance Abuse Treatment*, 27(2):123-134.

Brook, D.W., & Spitz, H.I. (Eds.) (2002). *The Group Therapy of Substance Abuse*. New York: Haworth Press.

Daley, D.C., & Mercer, D. (2002). *Drug Counseling for Cocaine Addiction: The Collaborative Cocaine Treatment Study Model*. Therapy Manuals for Drug Addiction, Manual 4. Rockville, MD: National Institute on Drug Abuse.

Finn, A. (2002). Group counseling for people with addictions. In D. Capuzzi & D.R. Gross (Eds.) *Introduction to Group Counseling* (3rd ed.). Denver, CO: Love Publishing Company, 351-376.

Gillaspy, J.A., Jr., Wright, A.R., et al. (2002). Group alliance and cohesion as predictors of drug and alcohol abuse treatment outcomes. *Psychotherapy Research*, 12(2):213-229.

Greif, G.L. (1996). Ten common errors beginning substance abuse workers make in group treatment. *Journal of Psychoactive Drugs*, 28:297-299.

Ingersoll, K.S., Wagner, C.C., et al. (2002). *Motivational Groups for Community Substance Abuse Programs*. Richmond, VA: Mid-Atlantic Addiction Technology Transfer Center.

Kauffman, E., Dore, M.M., & Nelson-Zlupko, L. (1995). The role of women's therapy groups in the treatment of chemical dependence. *American Journal of Orthopsychiatry*, 65:355-363.

Kent, C. (1997). Ending with clients: Closure in counseling. In S. Harrison & V. Carver (Eds.) *Alcohol and Drug Problems: A Practical Guide for Counselors* (2nd ed.). Toronto, Canada: Addiction Research Foundation, 203-215.

Khantzian, E.J., Golden, S.J., & McAuliffe, W.E. (1999). Group therapy. In M. Galanter & H.D. Kleber (Eds.) *Textbook of Substance Abuse Treatment* (2nd ed.). Washington DC: American Psychiatric Association, 367-377.

Kiresuk, T.J., Smith, A., & Cardillo, J.E. (1994). *Goal Attainment Scaling: Applications, Theory, and Measurement*. Mahwah, NJ: Lawrence Erlbaum Associates.

Lawson, G.W., Lawson, A.W., & Rivers, P.C. (1996). Group counseling in the treatment of chemical dependency. In *Essentials of Chemical Dependency Counseling*. Gaithersburg, MD: Aspen Publishers, 141-177.

Litt, M.D., Kadden, R.M., et al. (2003). Coping skills and treatment outcomes in cognitive-behavioral and interactional group therapy for alcoholism. *Journal of Consulting & Clinical Psychology*, 71(1):118-128.

Matano, R.A., & Yalom, I.D. (1991). Approaches to chemical dependency: Chemical dependency and interactive group therapy—A synthesis. *International Journal of Group Psychotherapy*, 41:269-293.

McCollum, E.E., Trepper, T.S., et al. (2004). Solution-focused group therapy for substance abuse: Extending competency-based models. *Journal of Family Psychotherapy*, 14(4):27-42.

McCrady, B.S., & Epstein, E.E. (Eds.) (1999). *Addictions: A Comprehensive Guidebook*. New York: Oxford University Press.

Nowinski, J. (1999). Self-help groups for addictions. In B.S. McCrady & E.E. Epstein (Eds.) *Addictions: A Comprehensive Guidebook*. New York: Oxford University Press, 328-346.

Nowinski, J. (2003). Self-help groups. In J.L. Sorensen, R.A. Rawson, et al. (Eds.) *Drug Abuse Treatment Through Collaboration: Practice and Research Partnerships That Work*. Washington, DC: American Psychological Association, 55-70.

Perkinson, R.R. (1997). Group therapy. In *Chemical Dependency Counseling: A Practical Guide*. Thousand Oaks, CA: Sage Publications, 69-87.

Petry, N.M., & Simcic, F., Jr. (2002). Recent advances in the dissemination of contingency management techniques: Clinical and research perspectives. *Journal of Substance Abuse Treatment*, 23(2):81-86.

Platt, J., & Husband, S. (1993). An overview of problem solving and social skills approaches in substance abuse treatment. *Psychotherapy*, 30:276-278.

Rawson, R.A., Obert, J.L., et al. (1993). Relapse prevention models for substance abuse treatment. *Psychotherapy*, 30:284-298.

Reilly, P.M., & Shopshire, M.S. (2002). *Anger Management for Substance Abuse and Mental Health Clients: A Cognitive Behavioral Therapy Manual*. Rockville, MD: Center for Substance Abuse Treatment, Substance Abuse and Mental Health Services Administration.

Rugel, R.P. (1991). Addiction treatment in groups: A review of therapeutic factors. *Small Group Research*, 22:475-491.

Sampl, S., & Kadden, R. (2001). *Motivational Enhancement Therapy and Cognitive Behavioral Therapy for Adolescent Cannabis Users: 5 Sessions*. Cannabis Youth Treatment Series, Volume 1. DHHS Publication No. (SMA) 01-3486. Rockville, MD: Center for Substance Abuse Treatment, Substance Abuse and Mental Health Services Administration.

Schwebel, R. (2004). *The Seven Challenges Manual*. Tucson, AZ: Viva Press.

Senior, M., Smith, M., & Taylor, S. *EMPACT–Suicide Prevention Center Teen Substance Abuse Treatment Program Treatment Manual*. Bloomington, IL: Chestnut Health Systems.

Shaw, S. (1999). Group therapy with adolescents. In G.W. Lawson & A.W. Lawson (Eds.) *Adolescent Substance Abuse: Etiology, Treatment, and Prevention*. Gaithersburg, MD: Aspen Publishers, 121-131.

Springer, D.W., McNeece, C.A., & Arnold, E.M. (2003). Group intervention. In D.W. Springer, C.A. McNeece, & E.M. Arnold (Eds.) *Substance Abuse Treatment for Criminal Offenders:*

An Evidence-Based Guide for Practitioners. Washington, DC: American Psychological Association.

Springer, D.W., & Orsbon, S.H. (2002). Families Helping Families: Implementing a multifamily therapy group with substance-abusing adolescents. *Health & Social Work*, 27(3):204-207.

Straussner, S.L. (1997). Group treatment with substance abusing clients. *Journal of Chemical Dependency Treatment*, 7:67-80.

Vannicelli, M. (2002). A dualistic model for group treatment of alcohol problems: Abstinence-based treatment for alcoholics, moderation training for problem drinkers. *International Journal of Group Psychotherapy*, 52(2):189-213.

Velasquez, M.M. (2001). *Group Treatment for Substance Abuse: A Stages of Change Therapy Manual*. New York: Guilford Press.

Washton, A.M. (1997). Structured outpatient group therapy. In J.H. Lowinson, P. Ruiz, et al. (Eds.) *Substance Abuse: A Comprehensive Textbook* (3rd ed.). Baltimore: Lippincott Williams & Wilkins, 440-448.

Washton, A.M. (2002). Outpatient groups at different stages of substance abuse treatment: Preparation, initial abstinence, and relapse prevention. In D.W. Brook & H.I. Spitz (Eds.) *Group Therapy of Substance Abuse*. New York: Haworth Press, 99-121.

Webb, C., Scudder, M., et al. (2002). *The Motivational Enhancement Therapy and Cognitive Behavioral Therapy Supplement: 7 Sessions of Cognitive Behavioral Therapy for Adolescent Cannabis Users*. Cannabis Youth Treatment Series, Volume 2. DHHS Publication No. (SMA) 02-3659. Rockville, MD: Center for Substance Abuse Treatment, Substance Abuse and Mental Health Services Administration.

PD V. Counseling: Counseling Families, Couples, and Significant Others

Black, C., Paz, H., & DeBlassie, R.R. (1991). Counseling the Hispanic male adolescent. *Adolescence*, 26:223-232.

Brown, A.H., Grella, C.E., & Cooper, L. (2002). Living it or learning it: Attitudes and beliefs about experience and expertise in treatment for the dually diagnosed. *Contemporary Drug Problems*, 29(4):687-710.

Brown, S. (Ed.) (1995). *Treating Alcoholism*. San Francisco: Jossey-Bass.

Brown, S., & Lewis, V. (1999). *The Alcoholic Family in Recovery: A Developmental Model*. New York: Guilford Press.

Cavacuiti, C.A. (2004). You, me, and drugs, a love triangle: Important considerations when both members of a couple are abusing substances. *Substance Use & Misuse*, 39(4):645-656.

Center for Substance Abuse Treatment. (2004). *Substance Abuse Treatment and Family Therapy*. Treatment Improvement Protocol (TIP) Series 39. DHHS Publication No. (SMA) 04-3957. Rockville, MD: Substance Abuse and Mental Health Services Administration.

Chan, J.G. (2003). An examination of family-involved approaches to alcoholism treatment. *Family Journal: Counseling & Therapy for Couples & Families*, 11(2):129-138.

Cormack, C., & Carr, A. (2000). Drug abuse. In A. Carr (Ed.) *What Works for Children and Adolescents? A Critical Review of Psychological Interventions With Children, Adolescents and Their Families*. London: Routledge, 155-177.

DeCivita, M., Dobkin, P.L., et al. (2000). A study of barriers to the engagement of significant others in adult addiction treatment. *Journal of Substance Abuse Treatment*, 19(2):135-144.

Epstein, E.E., & McCrady, B.S. (2002). Couple therapy in the treatment of alcohol problems. In A.S. Gurman & N.S. Jacobson (Eds.) *Clinical Handbook of Couple Therapy* (3rd ed.). New York: Guilford Press, 597-628.

Fenton, L.R., Cecero, J.J., et al. (2001). Perspective is everything: The predictive validity working alliance instruments. *Journal of Psychotherapy Practice & Research*, 10(4):262-268.

Freeman, E.M. (1993). Substance abuse treatment: Continuum of care in service to families. In E.M. Freeman (Ed.) *Substance Abuse Treatment: A Family Systems Perspective*. Newbury Park, CA: Sage Publications, 1-20.

Hamilton, N.L., Brantley, L.B., et al. (2001). *Family Support Network for Adolescent Cannabis Users*. Cannabis Youth Treatment Series, Volume 3. DHHS Publication No. (SMA) 01-3488. Rockville, MD: Center for Substance Abuse Treatment, Substance Abuse and Mental Health Services Administration.

Joe, G.W., Simpson, D.D., et al. (2001). Relationships between counseling rapport and drug abuse treatment outcomes. *Psychiatric Services*, 52(9):1223-1229.

Kaughman, E. (1991). The family in drug and alcohol addiction. In N.S. Miller (Ed.) *Comprehensive Handbook of Drug and Alcohol Addiction*. New York: Marcel Dekker, 851-876.

Kinney, J. (2000). Treatment techniques and approaches. In *Loosening the Grip: A Handbook of Alcohol Information* (6th ed.). New York: McGraw-Hill, 558.

Knight, D.K., & Simpson, D.D. (1999). Family assessment. In P.J. Ott, R.E. Tarter, & R.T. Ammerman (Eds.) *Sourcebook on Substance Abuse: Etiology, Assessment, and Treatment*. Boston: Allyn & Bacon, 236-247.

Latimer, W.W., Winters, K.C., et al. (2003). Integrated family and cognitive-behavioral therapy for adolescent substance abusers: A Stage I efficacy study. *Drug and Alcohol Dependence*, 71:303-317.

Lawson, A.W., & Lawson, G.W. (2005). Families and drugs. In R.H. Coombs (Ed.) *Addiction Counseling Review: Preparing for Comprehensive, Certification and Licensing Examinations*. Mahwah, NJ: Lawrence Erlbaum Associates, 175-199.

Lewis, J.A., Dana, R.Q., & Blevins, G.A. (2001). *Substance Abuse Counseling* (3rd ed.). Pacific Grove, CA: Brooks/Cole.

Lewis, V., Allen-Byrd, M., et al. (2004). Understanding successful family recovery in treating alcoholism. *Journal of Systemic Therapies*, 23:39-51.

Liddle, H.A. (2002) *Multidimensional Family Therapy for Adolescent Cannabis Users*. Cannabis Youth Treatment Series, Volume 5. DHHS Publication No. (SMA) 02-3660. Rockville, MD: Center for Substance Abuse Treatment, Substance Abuse and Mental Health Services Administration.

Liddle, H.A. (2003). *Multidimensional Family Therapy for Early Adolescent Substance Abuse Treatment Manual*. Bloomington, IL: Chestnut Health Systems.

McCollum, E.E., & Trepper, T.S. (2001). *Family Solutions for Substance Abuse: Clinical and Counseling Approaches*. New York: Haworth Press.

McCrady, B.S., & Epstein, E.E. (1996). Theoretical bases of family approaches to substance abuse treatment. In F. Rotgers, D.S. Keller, & J. Morgenstern (Eds.) *Treating Substance Abuse: Theory and Technique*. New York: Guilford Press, 117-142.

McCrady, B.S., & Epstein, E.E. (Eds.) (1999). *Addictions: A Comprehensive Guidebook*. New York: Oxford University Press.

McIntyre, J.R. (2004). Family treatment of substance abuse. In. S.L.A. Straussner (Ed.) *Clinical Work With Substance-Abusing Clients* (2nd ed.). New York: Guilford Press, 237-263.

McKay, J.R. (1996). Family therapy techniques. In F. Rotgers, D.S. Keller, & J. Morgenstern (Eds.) *Treating Substance Abuse: Theory and Technique*. New York: Guilford Press, 143-173.

Mercado, M.M. (2000). The invisible family: Counseling Asian American substance abusers and their families. *Family Journal: Counseling and Therapy for Couples and Families*, 8(3):267-272.

Meyers, R.J., Apodaca, T.R., et al. (2002). Evidence-based approaches for the treatment of substance abusers by involving family members. *Family Journal: Counseling and Therapy for Couples and Families*, 10(3):281-288.

Meyers, R.J., Smith, J.E., & Miller, E.J. (1998). Working through the concerned significant other. In W.R. Miller & N. Heather (Eds.) *Treating Addictive Behaviors* (2nd ed.). New York: Plenum Press, 149-161.

Mora, J. (1998). The treatment of alcohol dependency among Latinas: A feminist, cultural and community perspective. *Alcoholism Treatment Quarterly*, 16:163-177.

National Institute on Drug Abuse (NIDA), Szapocznik, J., et al. (2003). *Brief Strategic Family Therapy for Adolescent Drug Abuse*. Therapy Manuals for Drug Addiction, Manual 5. Rockville, MD: NIDA, 87.

O'Farrell, T.J. (Ed.) (1993). *Treating Alcohol Problems: Marital and Family Interventions*. New York: Guilford Press.

O'Farrell, T.J., Choquette, K.A., et al. (1993). Behavioral marital therapy with and without additional couples relapse prevention sessions for alcoholics and their wives. *Journal of Studies on Alcohol*, 54:652-666.

O'Farrell, T.J., & Fals-Stewart, W. (1999). Treatment models and methods: Family models. In B.S. McCrady & E.E. Epstein (Eds.) *Addictions: A Comprehensive Guidebook*. New York: Oxford University Press, 287-305.

O'Farrell, T.J., & Fals-Stewart, W. (2000). Behavioral couples therapy for alcoholism and drug abuse. *Behavior Therapist*, 23(3):49-54, 70.

O'Farrell, T.J., & Murphy, C.M. (2002). Behavioral couples therapy for alcoholism and drug abuse: Encountering the problem of domestic violence. In C. Wekerle & A.-M. Wall (Eds.) *Violence and Addiction Equation: Theoretical and Clinical Issues in Substance Abuse and Relationship Violence*. New York: Brunner-Routledge, 293-303.

Petry, N.M., & Simcic, F. (2002). Recent advances in the dissemination of contingency management techniques: Clinical and research perspectives. *Journal of Substance Abuse Treatment*, 23(2):81-86.

Platt, J., & Husband, S. (1993). An overview of problem solving and social skills approaches in substance abuse treatment. *Psychotherapy*, 30:276-278.

Rawson, R.A., Obert, J.L., et al. (1993). Relapse prevention models for substance abuse treatment. *Psychotherapy*, 30:284-298.

Robbins, M.S., Bachrach, K., et al. (2002). Bridging the research gap in adolescent substance abuse treatment: The case of brief strategic family therapy. *Journal of Substance Abuse Treatment*, 23(3):123-132.

Rotgers, F., Keller, D.S., & Morgenstern, J. (Eds.) (2003). *Treating Substance Abuse: Theory and Technique*. New York: Guilford Press, 117-142.

Rotunda, R.J., West, L., et al. (2004). Enabling behavior in a clinical sample of alcohol-dependent clients and their partners. *Journal of Substance Abuse Treatment*, 26(4):269-276.

Rowe, C., Liddle, H.A., et al. (2002). Integrative treatment development: Multidimensional family therapy for adolescent substance abuse. In F.W. Kaslow (Ed.) *Comprehensive Handbook of Psychotherapy: Integrative/Eclectic*, Volume 4. New York: John Wiley & Sons, 133-161.

Rowe, C., Parker-Sloat, E., et al. (2003). Family therapy for early adolescent substance abuse. In S.J. Stevens & A.R. Morral (Eds.) *Adolescent Substance Abuse Treatment in the United States: Exemplary Models From a National Evaluation Study*. New York: Haworth Press, 105-132.

Santisteban, D.A., & Szapocznik, J. (1994). Bridging theory, research and practice to more successfully engage substance abusing youth and their families into therapy. *Journal of Child and Adolescent Substance Abuse*, 3:9-24.

Sheehan, M.F. (1991). Dual diagnosis. *Psychiatric Quarterly*, 62:107-134.

Sholevar, G.P., & Schwoeri, L.D. (2003). Alcoholic and substance-abusing families. In G.P. Sholevar (Ed.) *Textbook of Family and Couples Therapy: Clinical Applications*. Washington, DC: American Psychiatric Association, 671-694.

Shulman, L.H., Shapira, S.R., et al. (2000). Outreach developmental services to children of patients in treatment for substance abuse. *American Journal of Public Health*, 90(12): 1930-1933.

Smith, J.E., Milford, J.C., & Meyers, R.J. (2004). CRA and CRAFT: Behavioral approaches to treating substance-abusing individuals. *Behavior Analyst Today*, 5(4):391-403.

Stanton, M. (2005). Couples and addiction. In M. Harway (Ed.) *Handbook of Couples Therapy*. New York: John Wiley & Sons, 313-336.

Stanton, M.D., & Heath, A.W. (1997). Family and marital therapy. In J.H. Lowinson, P. Ruiz, et al. (Eds.) *Substance Abuse: A Comprehensive Textbook*. Baltimore: Lippincott Williams & Wilkins, 448-454.

Stellato-Kabat, D., Stellato-Kabat, J., & Garrett, J. (1995). Treating chemical-dependent couples and families. In A.M. Washton (Ed.) *Psychotherapy and Substance Abuse: A Practitioner's Handbook*. New York: Guilford Press, 314-336.

Szapocznik, J., Hervis, O., et al. (2003). *Brief Strategic Family Therapy for Adolescent Drug Abuse*. Therapy Manuals for Drug Addiction, Manual 5. NIH Publication Number 03-4751. Rockville, MD: National Institute on Drug Abuse.

Szapocznik, J., & Williams, R.A. (2000). Brief strategic family therapy: Twenty-five years of interplay among theory, research and practice in adolescent behavior problems and drug abuse. *Clinical Child & Family Psychology Review*, 3(2):117-134.

Thomas, C., & Corcoran, J. (2001). Empirically based marital and family interventions for alcohol abuse: A review. *Research on Social Work Practice*, 11(5):549-575.

Vaughn, M.G., & Howard, M.O. (2004). Adolescent substance abuse treatment: A synthesis of controlled evaluations. *Research on Social Work Practice*, 14(5):325-335.

Vedel, E., & Emmelkamp, P.M.G. (2004). Behavioral couple therapy in the treatment of a female alcohol-dependent patient with comorbid depression, anxiety, and personality disorders. *Clinical Case Studies*, 3(3):187-205.

Velleman, R. (2001). *Counseling for Alcohol Problems* (2nd ed.). Thousand Oaks, CA: Sage Publications.

Velleman, R., & Templeton, L. (2002). Family interventions in substance misuse. In T. Petersen & A. McBride (Eds.) *Working With Substance Misusers*. New York: Routledge, 145-153.

Wakefield, P.J., Williams, R.E., et al. (1996). *Couple Therapy for Alcoholism: A Cognitive-Behavioral Treatment Manual*. New York: Guilford Press.

Waldron, H.B., & Slesnick, N. (1998). Treating the family. In W.R. Miller & N. Heather (Eds.) *Treating Addictive Behaviors* (2nd ed.). New York: Plenum Press, 271-283.

Zelvin, E. (1993). Treating the partners of substance abusers. In S.L. Straussner (Ed.) *Clinical Work With Substance-Abusing Clients*. New York: Guilford Press, 196-213.

PRACTICE DIMENSION VI

CLIENT, FAMILY, AND COMMUNITY EDUCATION

PD VI. Client, Family, and Community Education

Definition: *The process of providing clients, families, significant others, and community groups with information on risks related to psychoactive substance use, as well as available prevention, treatment, and recovery resources.*

Competency 99:
Provide culturally relevant formal and informal education programs that raise awareness and support substance abuse prevention and the recovery process.

Knowledge
- Cultural differences among ethnically and racially diverse communities.
- Cultural differences in attitudes toward consumption of psychoactive substances.
- Delivery of educational programs.
- Research and theory on prevention of substance use problems.
- Environmental strategies and prevention campaigns.
- Learning styles and teaching methods.
- Public speaking.
- Benefits of working with community coalitions.

Skills
- Delivering prevention and treatment educational programs.
- Facilitating discussion.
- Identifying, creating, and modifying relevant educational materials to meet the needs of the intended audience.
- Making public presentations.

Attitudes
- Awareness of and sensitivity to cultural differences.
- Awareness of the potential need to adapt educational materials to respond to cultural differences.
- Appreciation of the difference between educating and providing information.
- Appreciation of the historical, social, cultural, and other influences that shape the perceptions of psychoactive substance use.

COMPETENCY 100:

Describe factors that increase the likelihood for an individual, community, or group to be at risk for, or resilient to, psychoactive substance use disorders.

KNOWLEDGE

- Individual, community, and family risk and protective factors.
- The interactions of risk and protective factors and their influence on the development of substance abuse.

SKILLS

- Describing risk and protective factors as they relate to individual, community, school, and family domains.

ATTITUDES

- Sensitivity to the interaction of risk and protection in the development of substance use disorders.
- Nonjudgmental presentation of issues.

COMPETENCY 101:

Sensitize others to issues of cultural identity, ethnic background, age, and gender in prevention, treatment, and recovery.

KNOWLEDGE

- Cultural issues in planning prevention and treatment programs.
- Age and gender differences in psychoactive substance use.
- Culture, gender, and age-appropriate prevention, treatment, and recovery resources.

SKILLS

- Communicating effectively with diverse populations.
- Providing educational programs that reflect understanding of culture, ethnicity, age, and gender.

ATTITUDES

- Sensitivity to the role of culture, ethnicity, age, and gender in prevention, treatment, and recovery.
- Awareness of one's cultural biases.

PD VI. Client, Family, and Community Education

COMPETENCY 102:

Describe warning signs, symptoms, and the course of substance use disorders.

KNOWLEDGE

- The continuum of use and abuse, including the warning signs and symptoms of a developing substance use disorder.
- Current *Diagnostic and Statistical Manual of Mental Disorders* (DSM) categories or other diagnostic standards associated with psychoactive substance use.

SKILLS

- Identifying and teaching signs and symptoms of various substance use disorders.

ATTITUDES

- Recognition of the importance of research in prevention and treatment.

USES OF *THE COMPETENCIES*

The Oregon Consortium of Addiction Studies Educators (OCASE) developed a core statewide curriculum for training addiction counselors based on *The Competencies*. All colleges in the State that offer any of the nine core courses included in the curriculum have committed to a common set of competency-based learning objectives.

The Wisconsin Association on Alcohol and Other Drug Abuse (WAAODA) uses *The Competencies* as the primary framework and standard for its Minority Counselor Training Institute (MCTI) to develop highly qualified and culturally competent professionals from minority communities. WAAODA created the curriculum for MCTI by customizing and adding modules to the OCASE curriculum using *The Competencies* as a guide. Now medical schools and technical colleges in the State are considering adoption of this curriculum.

COMPETENCY 103:

Describe how substance use disorders affect families and concerned others.

KNOWLEDGE

- How psychoactive substance use by one family member affects other family members or significant others.
- The family's potential positive or negative influence on the development and continuation of a substance use disorder.
- The role of the family, couple, or significant other in treatment and recovery.

SKILLS

- Educating clients, families, and the community about the effect of substance use disorders on the family, couple, or significant others.

ATTITUDES

- Recognition of the unique response of family members and significant others to substance use disorders.

Addiction Counseling Competencies

COMPETENCY 104:
Describe the continuum of care and resources available to the family and concerned others.

KNOWLEDGE

- The continuum of care.
- Available treatment resources, including local health, allied health, and behavioral health resources.

SKILLS

- Motivating both family members and the client to seek out resources and services from the full continuum of care.
- Describing different treatment modalities and the continuum of care.
- Identifying and making referrals to local health, allied health, and behavioral health resources.

ATTITUDES

- Appreciation of strengths-based principles that emphasize client autonomy and skills development.
- Appreciation of the difficulties families and significant others may encounter in seeking help.
- Appreciation of ethnic and cultural differences.

COMPETENCY 105:
Describe principles and philosophy of prevention, treatment, and recovery.

KNOWLEDGE

- Models for prevention of, treatment of, and recovery from substance use disorders.
- Research and theory on models of prevention, treatment, and recovery.
- Influences on societal and political responses to substance use disorders.

SKILLS

- Organizing and delivering presentations that reflect basic information on prevention, treatment, and recovery.

ATTITUDES

- Appreciation of the importance of prevention and treatment.
- Recognition of the validity of a variety of prevention and treatment strategies.

COMPETENCY 106:

Understand and describe the health and behavior problems related to substance use, including transmission and prevention of HIV/AIDS, tuberculosis, sexually transmitted diseases, hepatitis C, and other infectious diseases.

KNOWLEDGE

- Health risks associated with substance use.
- High-risk behaviors related to substance use.
- Prevention and transmission of infectious diseases.
- Factors that may be associated with the prevention or transmission of infectious diseases.
- Community health and allied health resources.

SKILLS

- Teaching clients and community members about disease transmission and prevention.
- Facilitating small- and large-group discussions.

ATTITUDES

- Awareness of one's biases when presenting information.

COMPETENCY 107:

Teach life skills, including but not limited to stress management, relaxation, communication, assertiveness, and refusal skills.

KNOWLEDGE

- The importance of life skills to the prevention and treatment of substance use disorders.
- How these skills are typically taught to individuals and groups.
- Resources available to teach these skills.

SKILLS

- Delivering educational sessions.
- Identifying and accessing other instructional resources for training.
- Facilitating the practice and acquisition of life skills.

ATTITUDES

- Recognition of the importance of life skills training to the process of recovery.

USES OF *THE COMPETENCIES*

In Iowa *The Competencies* is being used in a number of ways. The master's program in Substance Abuse Counseling at the University of Iowa is based on *The Competencies*. *The Competencies* also is the basis for a "toolbox" training, through a subcontractor of the Prairielands ATTC, designed to educate entry-level substance abuse counselors about the skills needed for quality treatment and passing the State's certification exam.

In addition, a graduate assistant at the Center of Excellence for Substance Abuse and Dually Diagnosed Persons at the University of Iowa is using the practice dimensions as a framework for his dissertation. He is assessing substance abuse counselors and their perceptions of the content areas in which they need and desire more supervision.

Bibliography

PD VI. Client, Family, and Community Education

Amodeo, M., & Robb, N. (1997). Modifying methods and content to teach about alcohol and drug abuse cross-culturally. *Substance Abuse*, 18(1):1-12.

Bahr, S.J., & Hawks, R.D. (1993). Family and religious influences on adolescent substance abuse. *Youth & Society*, 24(4):443-465.

Brook, J.S., & Brook, D.W. (1996). Risk and protective factors for drug use. In C.B. McCoy, L.R. Metsch, & J.A. Inciardi (Eds.) *Intervening With Drug-Involved Youth*. Thousand Oaks, CA: Sage Publications, 23-44.

Brown, E.D., Maisto, S.A., & Boies-Hickman, K. Education. (1997). In E.D. Brown, T.J. O'Farrell, et al. (Eds.) *Substance Abuse Program Accreditation Guide*. Thousand Oaks, CA: Sage Publications, 71-76.

Center for Substance Abuse Prevention (1997). *Technical Assistance Bulletin: Communicating Appropriately With Asian and Pacific Islander Audiences*. Rockville, MD: Substance Abuse and Mental Health Services Administration.

Center for Substance Abuse Prevention (1997). *Technical Assistance Bulletin: Developing Effective Messages and Materials for Hispanic/Latino Audiences*. Rockville, MD: Substance Abuse and Mental Health Services Administration.

Center for Substance Abuse Prevention (1998). *Technical Assistance Bulletin: Communicating With 9- to 14-Year-Old Girls*. Rockville, MD: Substance Abuse and Mental Health Services Administration.

Center for Substance Abuse Prevention (1999). *Understanding Substance Abuse Prevention— Toward the 21st Century: A Primer on Effective Programs*. DHHS Publication No. (SMA) 99-3301. Rockville, MD: Substance Abuse and Mental Health Services Administration.

Coggans, N., & Watson, J. (1995). Drug education: Approaches, effectiveness and delivery. *Drugs: Education, Prevention and Policy*, 2(3):211-224.

Connor, K.R., & Gunther, M.W. (1996). Educational lectures and films in the clinical treatment of alcoholism: A critique. *Substance Use & Misuse*, 31(9):1117-1129.

Delgado, M. (1997). Strengths-based practice with Puerto Rican adolescents: Lessons from a substance abuse prevention project. *Social Work in Education*, 19(2):101-112.

Dubas, J.S., Lynch, K.B., et al. (1998). Preliminary evaluation of a resiliency-based preschool substance abuse and violence prevention project. *Journal of Drug Education*, 28(3):235-255.

Dusenbury, L., & Botvin, G.J. (1992). Substance abuse prevention: Competence enhancement and the development of positive life options. *Journal of Addictive Diseases*, 11(3):29-45.

Finn, P. (1994). Addressing the needs of cultural minorities in drug treatment. *Journal of Substance Abuse Treatment*, 11(4):325-337.

Gloria, A.M., & Peregoy, J.J. (1996). Counseling Latino alcohol and other substance users/ abusers. *Journal of Substance Abuse Treatment*, 13(2):119-126.

Goldberg, M.E. (1995). Substance-abusing women: False stereotypes and real needs. *Social Work*, 40(6):789-798.

Harrington, N.G., & Donohew, L. (1997). Jump Start: A targeted substance abuse prevention program. *Health Education & Behavior*, 24(5):568-586.

Herring, R.D. (1994). Substance use among Native American Indian youth: A selected review of causality. *Journal of Counseling & Development*, 72(6):578-584.

Herrmann, D.S., & McWhirter, J.J. (1997). Refusal and resistance skills for children and adolescents: A selected review. *Journal of Counseling & Development*, 75(3):177-187.

Hogan, J. A., Gabrielson, K.R., et al. (2003). *Substance Abuse Prevention: The Intersection of Science and Practice*. Boston: Allyn & Bacon.

Joanning, H., Thomas, F., et al. (1992). Treating adolescent drug abuse: A comparison of family systems therapy, group therapy, and family drug education. *Journal of Marital & Family Therapy*, 18(4):345-356.

Kaskutas, L.A., Marsh, D., & Kohn, A. (1998). Didactic and experiential education in substance abuse programs. *Journal of Substance Abuse Treatment*, 15(1):43-53.

Leal, A. (1990). Hispanics and substance abuse: Implications for rehabilitation counselors. *Journal of Applied Rehabilitation Counseling*, 21(3):52-54.

Mirabeau, F. (1997). Evaluation outcome study of family education in the treatment of alcoholic patients. *Journal of Addictions Nursing*, 9(2):77-80.

Negreiros, J. (1994). Theoretical orientations in drug abuse prevention research. *Drugs: Education, Prevention and Policy*, 1(2):135-142.

Niemann, S.H. (2001). Guidance/psychoeducational groups. In D. Capuzzi & D.R. Gross (Eds.) *Introduction to Group Counseling* (3rd ed.). Denver, CO: Love Publishing Company, 265-290.

O'Hara, P., Parris, D., et al. (1998). Influence of alcohol and drug use on AIDS risk behavior among youth in dropout prevention. *Journal of Drug Education*, 28(2):159-168.

O'Leary, T.A., Brown, S., et al. (2002). Treating adolescents together or individually? Issues in adolescent substance abuse interventions. *Alcoholism: Clinical and Experimental Research*, 26(6):890-899.

Orenstein, A., & Ullman, A. (1996). Characteristics of alcoholic families and adolescent substance use. *Journal of Alcohol and Drug Education*, 41(3):86-101.

Pilgrim, C., Abbey, A., et al. (1998). Implementation and impact of a family-based substance abuse prevention program in rural communities. *Journal of Primary Prevention*, 18(3):341-361.

Sheridan, M.J., & Green, R.G. (1993). Family dynamics and individual characteristics of adult children of alcoholics: An empirical analysis. *Journal of Social Service Research*, 17(1-2):73-97.

Slaght, E., Lyman, S., et al. (2004). Promoting healthy lifestyles as a biopsychosocial approach to addictions counseling. *Journal of Alcohol and Drug Education*, 48(2):5-16.

Snow, D.L., Tebes, J.K., & Ayers, T.S. (1997). Impact of two social-cognitive interventions to prevent adolescent substance use: Test of an amenability to treatment model. *Journal of Drug Education*, 27(1):1-17.

Zweben, J.E. (2001). Hepatitis C: Education and counseling issues. *Journal of Addictive Diseases*, 20(1):33-42.

Practice Dimension VII

DOCUMENTATION

PD VII. Documentation

Definition: *The recording of the screening and intake process, assessment, treatment plan, clinical reports, clinical progress notes, discharge summaries, and other client-related data.*

Competency 108:
Demonstrate knowledge of accepted principles of client record management.

Knowledge
- Regulations pertaining to client records.
- The essential components of client records, including release forms, assessments, treatment plans, progress notes, and discharge summaries and plans.

Skills
- Composing timely, clear, complete, and concise records that comply with regulations.
- Documenting information in an objective manner.
- Writing legibly.
- Using new technologies in the production of client records.

Attitudes
- Appreciation of the importance of accurate documentation.

Uses of *The Competencies*

During a 1999 survey of inpatient and outpatient programs at Georgia's largest State psychiatric facility, Georgia Regional Hospital in Atlanta, ***The Competencies*** was used to develop standards for determining the competency of counselors, psychologists, and clinical supervisors working in substance abuse treatment services. ***The Competencies*** also was used to develop a policy procedure and test instrument for the facility by the Joint Commission on Accreditation of Healthcare Organizations.

Competency 109:

Protect client rights to privacy and confidentiality in the preparation and handling of records, especially in relation to the communication of client information with third parties.

Knowledge

- Federal, State, and program confidentiality rules and regulations.
- The application of confidentiality rules and regulations.
- Confidentiality rules and regulations regarding infectious diseases.
- The legal nature of records.

Skills

- Applying Federal, State, and agency regulations regarding client confidentiality.
- Requesting, preparing, and completing release of information when appropriate.
- Protecting and communicating clients' rights.
- Explaining regulations to clients and third parties.
- Applying infectious disease regulations as they relate to addictions treatment.
- Providing security for clinical records.

Attitudes

- Willingness to seek and accept supervision regarding confidentiality rules and regulations.
- Respect for clients' rights to privacy and confidentiality.
- Commitment to professionalism.
- Recognition of the absolute necessity of safeguarding records.

Competency 110:

Prepare accurate and concise screening, intake, and assessment reports.

Knowledge

- Essential elements of screening, intake, and assessment reports, including but not limited to:
  - psychoactive substance use and abuse history
  - physical health
  - psychological information
  - social information
  - history of criminality
  - spiritual information
  - recreational information
  - nutritional information
  - educational or vocational information
  - sexual information
  - legal information.

Skills

- Analyzing, synthesizing, and summarizing information.
- Keeping a concise and relevant record of information.
- Organizing information in a presentable format for ease of access and review.
- Documenting referral information.
- Documenting source of referral information.

Attitudes

- Willingness to develop accurate reports.
- Recognition of the importance of accurate records.

Competency 111:

Record treatment and continuing care plans that are consistent with agency standards and comply with applicable administrative rules.

Knowledge

- Current Federal, State, local, and program regulations.
- Regulations regarding informed consent.

Skills

- Keeping timely, clear, complete, and concise records that comply with regulations.

Attitudes

- Recognition of the importance of recording treatment and continuing care plans.
- Willingness to incorporate professional assessment in records.

COMPETENCY 112:
Record progress of client in relation to treatment goals and objectives.

KNOWLEDGE

- Appropriate clinical terminology used to describe client's response to intervention and progress made toward completing treatment goals and objectives.
- How to review and update records.

SKILLS

- Preparing clear and legible documents.
- Documenting changes in the treatment plan, client status, client response to and outcome of interventions, level of care provided, and discharge status.
- Using appropriate clinical terminology and standardized abbreviations.
- Noting client's strengths and limitations in achieving treatment goals.
- Recording client's response to and outcome of interventions.
- Recording changes in client's status, behavior, and level of functioning.
- Noting limitations of treatment provided to client.

ATTITUDES

- Recognition of the value of objectively recording progress.
- Recognition that timely recording is critical to accurate documentation.

PD VII. Documentation

COMPETENCY 113:
Prepare accurate and concise discharge summaries.

KNOWLEDGE

- The components of a discharge summary, including but not limited to:
  - client profile and demographics
  - presenting symptoms
  - diagnoses
  - selected interventions
  - critical incidents
  - progress toward treatment goals
  - outcome
  - continuing care plan
  - prognosis
  - recommendations.

SKILLS

- Summarizing information.
- Preparing concise discharge summaries.
- Completing records in a timely manner.
- Reporting measurable results.

ATTITUDES

- Recognition that treatment is not a static, singular event.
- Recognition that recovery is ongoing.
- Recognition that timely recording is critical to accurate documentation.

COMPETENCY 114:
Document treatment outcome, using accepted methods and instruments.

KNOWLEDGE

- Accepted measures of treatment outcome.
- Current research related to defining treatment outcomes.
- Methods of gathering outcome data.
- Principles of using outcome data for program evaluation.
- Distinctions between process and outcome evaluation.

SKILLS

- Gathering and recording outcome data.
- Incorporating outcome measures during the treatment process.

ATTITUDES

- Recognition that treatment and evaluation should occur simultaneously.
- Appreciation of the importance of using data to improve clinical practice.

Bibliography

PD VII. Documentation

Anderson, D. (1992). Case standards for counseling practice. *Journal of Counseling & Development*, 71(September/October):22-26.

Badding, N.C. (1989). Client involvement in case recording: Social casework. *Journal of Contemporary Social Work*, (November):539-548.

Brown, E.D., O'Farrell, T.J., et al. (1997). *Substance Abuse Program Accreditation Guide*. Thousand Oaks, CA: Sage Publications.

Clemens, N.A. (2001). Documenting psychotherapy: Getting help on HIPAA. *Journal of Psychiatric Practice*, 7(2):138-140.

Clemens, N.A. (2004). Documentation: The doctor's dilemma. *Journal of Psychiatric Practice*, 10(1):64-67.

Committee on Professional Practice and Standards (1993). Recordkeeping guidelines. *American Psychologist*, 48(September):984-986.

Eggland, E.T. (1995). Charting smarter: Using new mechanisms to organize your paperwork. *Nursing*, 25(September):34-42.

Finley, J.R., & Lenz, B.S. (Eds.) (2005). *The Addiction Counselor's Documentation Sourcebook: The Complete Paperwork Resource for Treating Clients With Addictions* (2nd ed.). Hoboken, NJ: John Wiley & Sons.

Fulero, S.M., & Wilbert, J.R. (1988). Recordkeeping practices of clinical and counseling psychologists: A survey of practitioners. *Professional Psychology Research and Practice*, 19:658-660.

Gwodz, D.T., & Del Togno, V. (1992). Streamlining patient care documentation. *Journal of Nursing Administration*, 22(May):35-39.

Johnson, S.L. (2004). *Therapist's Guide to Clinical Intervention* (2nd ed.). San Diego, CA: Elsevier, Inc.

Joint Commission on Accreditation of Healthcare Organizations (JCAHO) (2002). *A Practical Guide to Documentation in Behavioral Health Care* (2nd ed.). Oakbrook Terrace, IL: JCAHO.

Joint Commission on Accreditation of Healthcare Organizations (JCAHO) (2005). *2006-2007 Comprehensive Accreditation Manual for Behavioral Health Care*. Oakbrook Terrace, IL: JCAHO.

Joint Commission on Accreditation of Healthcare Organizations (JCAHO) (2005). *2006-2007 Standards for Behavioral Health Care*. Oakbrook Terrace, IL: JCAHO.

Kaczmarek, P., Barclay, D., & Smith, M. (1996). Systematic training in client documentation: Strategies for counselor educators. *Counselor Education and Supervision*, 36(September):77-84.

Kerr, S.D. (1992). A comparison of four nursing documentation systems. *Journal of Nursing Staff Development*, 8(January/February):276-331.

Kozier, B., Erb, G., & Oliveri, R. (1991). *Fundamentals of Nursing: Concepts, Process and Practice* (4th ed.). Redwood City, CA: Addison-Wesley.

Loganbill, C., & Stoltenberg, C. (1983). The case conceptualization format: A training device for practicum. *Counselor Education and Supervision*, 22: 235-241.

Lopez, F. (1994). *Confidentiality of Patient Records for Alcohol and Other Drug Treatment*. Technical Assistance Publication (TAP) Series 13. DHHS Publication No. (SMA) 95-3018. Rockville, MD: Center for Substance Abuse Treatment, Substance Abuse and Mental Health Services Administration.

Makover, R.B. (2004). *Treatment Planning for Psychotherapists: A Practical Guide to Better Outcomes*. Arlington, VA: American Psychiatric Publishing, Inc.

Marrelli, T.M. (2000). *Nursing Documentation Handbook* (3rd ed.). St. Louis, MO: Mosby.

Mitchell, R. (2001). *Documentation in Counseling Records* (2nd ed.). Alexandria, VA: American Counseling Association.

Moline, M.E., Williams, G.T., & Austin, K.M. (1997). *Documenting Psychotherapy: Essentials for Mental Health Practitioners*. Thousand Oaks, CA: Sage Publications.

Montemuro, M. (1988). CORE: Documentation: A complete system for documenting nursing care. *Nursing Management*, 19(August):28-32.

Presser, N.R., & Pfost, K.S. (1985). A format for individual psychotherapy session notes. *Professional Psychology Research and Practice*, 16:11-16.

Rehabilitation Accreditation Commission (RAC) (1998). *Introduction to Outcomes Management in Behavioral Health*. Tucson, AZ: RAC.

Rehabilitation Accreditation Commission (RAC) (1999). *Opioid Treatment Program Accreditation Standards*. Tucson, AZ: RAC.

Rehabilitation Accreditation Commission (RAC) (1999). *2000 Behavioral Health Standards Manual*. Tucson, AZ: RAC.

Scharf, L. (1997). Revising nursing documentation to meet patient outcomes. *Nursing Management*, 28(April):38-39.

Scoates, G.H., Fishman, M., & McAdam, B. (1997). Health Care Focus Documentation—More Efficient Charting. *Nursing Management*, 27(April):30-32.

Springhouse Corporation (1994). *Nursing Fundamentals*. Springhouse, PA: Springhouse Corporation.

Springhouse Corporation (2002). *Illustrated Manual of Nursing Practice* (3rd ed.). Philadelphia: Lippincott Williams & Wilkins.

Sullivan, G. (1996). Is your documentation all it should be? *RN*, 59(October):59-61.

Weed, L.L. (1968). Medical records that guide and teach. *New England Journal of Medicine*, 278:593-600.

Wiger, D.E. (2005). *The Clinical Documentation Sourcebook: The Complete Paperwork Resource for Your Mental Health Practice* (3rd ed.). New York: John Wiley & Sons.

Wiger, D.E. (2005). *The Psychotherapy Documentation Primer*. New York: John Wiley & Sons.

Wiger, D.E., & Solberg, K.B. (2001). *Tracking Mental Health Outcomes: A Therapist's Guide to Measuring Client Progress, Analyzing Data, and Improving Your Practice*. New York: John Wiley & Sons.

Zuckerman, E.L. (2003). *The Paper Office: Forms, Guidelines, and Resources To Make Your Practice Work Ethically, Legally, and Profitably* (3rd ed.). New York: Guilford Press.

Practice Dimension VIII

Professional and Ethical Responsibilities

PD VIII. Professional and Ethical Responsibilities

Definition: *The obligations of an addiction counselor to adhere to accepted ethical and behavioral standards of conduct and continuing professional development.*

Competency 115:
Adhere to established professional codes of ethics that define the professional context within which the counselor works to maintain professional standards and safeguard the client.

Knowledge

- Federal, State, agency, and professional codes of ethics.
- Clients' rights and responsibilities.
- Professional standards and scope of practice.
- Boundary issues between client and counselor.
- Difference between the role of the professional counselor and that of a peer counselor or sponsor.
- Consequences of violating codes of ethics.
- Means for addressing alleged ethical violations.
- Nondiscriminatory practices.
- Mandatory reporting requirements.

Skills

- Demonstrating ethical and professional behavior.

Attitudes

- Openness to changing personal behaviors and attitudes that may conflict with ethical guidelines.
- Willingness to participate in self, peer, and supervisory assessment of clinical skills and practice.
- Respect for professional standards.

Addiction Counseling Competencies

COMPETENCY 116:
Adhere to Federal and State laws and agency regulations regarding the treatment of substance use disorders.

KNOWLEDGE

- Federal, State, and agency regulations that apply to addiction counseling.
- Confidentiality rules and regulations.
- Clients' rights and responsibilities.
- Legal ramifications of noncompliance with confidentiality rules and regulations.
- Legal ramifications of violating clients' rights.
- Grievance processes.

SKILLS

- Interpreting and applying appropriate Federal, State, and agency regulations regarding addiction counseling.
- Making ethical decisions that reflect unique needs and situations.
- Providing treatment services that conform to Federal, State, and local regulations.

ATTITUDES

- Appreciation of the importance of complying with Federal, State, and agency regulations.
- Willingness to learn the appropriate application of Federal, State, and agency guidelines.

COMPETENCY 117:
Interpret and apply information from current counseling and psychoactive substance use research literature to improve client care and enhance professional growth.

KNOWLEDGE

- Professional literature on substance use disorders.
- Information on current trends in addiction and related fields.
- Professional associations.
- Resources to promote professional growth and competency.

SKILLS

- Reading and interpreting current professional and research-based literature.
- Applying professional knowledge to client-specific situations.
- Applying research findings to clinical practice.
- Applying new skills in clinically appropriate ways.

ATTITUDES

- Commitment to life-long learning and professional growth and development.
- Willingness to adjust clinical practice to reflect advances in the field.

PD VIII. Professional and Ethical Responsibilities

COMPETENCY 118:

Recognize the importance of individual differences that influence client behavior, and apply this understanding to clinical practice.

KNOWLEDGE

- Differences found in diverse populations.
- How individual differences affect assessment and response to treatment.
- Personality, culture, lifestyle, and other factors influencing client behavior.
- Culturally sensitive counseling methods.
- Dynamics of family systems in diverse cultures and lifestyles.
- Client advocacy needs specific to diverse cultures and lifestyles.
- Signs, symptoms, and patterns of violence against persons.
- Risk factors that relate to potential harm to self or others.
- Hierarchy of needs and motivation.

SKILLS

- Assessing and interpreting culturally specific client behaviors and lifestyles.
- Conveying respect for cultural and lifestyle diversity in the therapeutic process.
- Adapting therapeutic strategies to client needs.

ATTITUDES

- Willingness to appreciate the life experiences of individuals.
- Appreciation for diverse populations and lifestyles.
- Recognition of one's biases toward other cultures and lifestyles.

USES OF *THE COMPETENCIES*

In 2000, the Northwest Frontier (NF) ATTC solicited a substance abuse treatment workforce survey in its region. Evaluators surveyed substance abuse treatment professionals (both front line and management) in Alaska, Idaho, Oregon, and Washington. Of 469 respondents, 63 percent were familiar with *The Competencies*. When asked how they used *The Competencies*, respondents indicated they used it for the following:

- 49 percent to improve their job performance
- 46 percent to guide their professional development
- 35 percent to improve treatment outcomes
- 32 percent for self-assessment
- 27 percent to assess job performance
- 22 percent to guide supervisory decisions.

A 2002 update of this survey in Alaska, Hawaii, Idaho, Oregon, and Washington showed that, of 609 respondents, the majority of agency directors (79%) and treatment staff (61%) were familiar with *The Competencies* and, of those who reported familiarity, 80 percent actively used it in their work, showing a pattern of increasing use over time. A 2005 survey update, currently underway, will provide data on the most current uses of *The Competencies*. NFATTC has convened a regional workgroup, with participants from Alaska, Hawaii, Idaho, Oregon, and Washington, to develop teaching strategies specific to *The Competencies*. An educators' "toolkit" of student exercises to use with *The Competencies* will be available on an educator's Web page and in printed form and will be presented at educators' workshops.

Competency 119:

Use a range of supervisory options to process personal feelings and concerns about clients.

Knowledge

- The role of supervision.
- Models of supervision.
- Potential barriers in the counselor–client relationship.
- Transference and countertransference.
- Resources for exploration of professional concerns.
- Problemsolving methods.
- Conflict resolution.
- The process and effect of client reassignment.
- The process and effect of termination of the counseling relationship.
- Phases of treatment and client responses.

Skills

- Recognizing situations in which supervision is appropriate.
- Developing a plan for resolution or improvement of feelings and concerns that may interfere with the counselor–client relationship.
- Seeking supervisory feedback.
- Resolving conflicts.
- Identifying overt and covert feelings and their effect on the counseling relationship.
- Communicating feelings and concerns openly and respectfully.

Attitudes

- Willingness to accept feedback.
- Acceptance of responsibility for personal and professional growth.
- Awareness that one's personal recovery issues have an effect on job performance and interactions with clients.

PD VIII. Professional and Ethical Responsibilities

COMPETENCY 120:
Conduct self-evaluations of professional performance applying ethical, legal, and professional standards to enhance self-awareness and performance.

KNOWLEDGE

- Personal and professional strengths and limitations.
- Legal, ethical, and professional standards affecting addiction counseling.
- Consequences of failure to comply with professional standards.
- Self-evaluation methods.
- Regulatory guidelines and restrictions.

SKILLS

- Developing professional goals and objectives.
- Interpreting and applying ethical, legal, and professional standards.
- Using self-assessment tools for personal and professional growth.
- Eliciting and applying feedback from colleagues and supervisors.

ATTITUDES

- Appreciation of the importance of self-evaluation.
- Recognition of personal strengths, weaknesses, and limitations.
- Willingness to change behaviors as necessary.

COMPETENCY 121:
Obtain appropriate continuing professional education.

KNOWLEDGE

- Education and training methods that promote professional growth.
- Recredentialing requirements.

SKILLS

- Assessing personal training needs.
- Selecting and participating in appropriate training programs.
- Using consultation and supervision as enhancements to professional growth.

ATTITUDES

- Recognition that professional growth continues throughout one's professional career.
- Willingness to expose oneself to information that may conflict with personal or professional beliefs.
- Recognition that professional development is an individual responsibility.

Addiction Counseling Competencies

Competency 122:
Participate in ongoing supervision and consultation.

Knowledge

- The rationale for regular assessment of professional skills and development.
- Models of clinical and administrative supervision.
- The rationale for using consultation.
- Agency policy and protocols.
- Case presentation methods.
- How to identify needs for clinical or technical assistance.
- Interpersonal dynamics in a supervisory relationship.

Skills

- Identifying professional progress and limitations.
- Communicating the need for assistance.
- Preparing and making case presentations.
- Eliciting feedback from others.

Attitudes

- Willingness to accept both constructive criticism and positive feedback.
- Respect for the value of clinical and administrative supervision.

Competency 123:
Develop and use strategies to maintain one's physical and mental health.

Knowledge

- Rationale for periodic self-assessment regarding physical health, mental health, and recovery from substance use disorders.
- Available resources for maintaining physical health, mental health, and recovery from substance use disorders.
- Consequences of failing to maintain physical health, mental health, and recovery from substance use disorders.
- Relationship between physical health and mental health.
- Health promotion strategies.

Skills

- Carrying out regular self-assessment with regard to physical health, mental health, and recovery from substance use disorders.
- Using prevention measures to guard against burnout.
- Employing stress-reduction strategies.
- Locating and accessing resources to achieve physical health, mental health, and recovery from substance use disorders.
- Modeling self-care as an effective treatment tool.

Attitudes

- Recognition that counselors serve as role models.
- Appreciation that maintaining a healthy lifestyle enhances the counselor's effectiveness.

Bibliography

PD VIII. Professional and Ethical Responsibilities

American Counseling Association (ACA) (2005). *ACA Code of Ethics*. Alexandria, VA: ACA.

American Methadone Treatment Association (AMTA) (1997). AMTA ethical canon for programs and individuals providing methadone treatment. *Journal of Maintenance in the Addictions*, 1(1):133.

American Psychological Association (APA) (2002). *Ethical Principles of Psychologists and Code of Conduct*. Washington, DC: APA.

Bernard, J.M., & Goodyear, R.K. (2003). *Fundamentals of Clinical Supervision* (3rd ed.). Boston: Allyn & Bacon.

Bissell, L., & Royce, J.E. (1994). *Ethics for Addiction Professionals* (2nd ed.). Center City, MN: Hazelden.

Brooks, M.K. (1997). Ethical and legal aspects of confidentiality. In J.H. Lowinson, P. Ruiz, et al. (Eds.) *Substance Abuse: A Comprehensive Textbook* (3rd ed.). Baltimore: Lippincott Williams & Wilkins, 884-899.

Brown, E.D., Maisto, S.A., & Boies-Hickman, K. (1997). Patient rights and responsibilities and organizational ethics. In E.D. Brown, T.J. O'Farrell, et al. (Eds.) *Substance Abuse Program Accreditation Guide*. Thousand Oaks, CA: Sage Publications, 3-11.

Cheng, Z. (2002). Issues to consider when counseling gay people with alcohol dependency. *Journal of Applied Rehabilitation Counseling*, 33(3):10-17.

Corey, G., Corey, M.S., & Callahan, P. (2000). *Issues and Ethics in the Helping Professions* (5th ed.). Pacific Grove, CA: Brooks/Cole.

Dove, W.R. (1995). Ethics training for the alcohol/drug abuse professional. *Alcoholism Treatment Quarterly*, 12(4):19-30.

Doyle, K. (1997). Substance abuse counselors in recovery: Implications for the ethical issue of dual relationships. *Journal of Counseling & Development*, 75(6):428-432.

Garcia, S. (1997). Ethical and legal issues associated with substance abuse by pregnant and parenting women. *Journal of Psychoactive Drugs*, 29(1):101-111.

Glaser, F.B., & Warren, D.G. (1999). Legal and ethical issues. In B.S. McCrady & E.E. Epstein (Eds.) *Addictions: A Comprehensive Guidebook*. New York: Oxford University Press, 399-413.

Legal Action Center (2003). *Confidentiality and Communication: A Guide to the Federal Drug and Alcohol Confidentiality Law and HIPAA*. New York: Legal Action Center.

Lopez, F. (1994). *Confidentiality of Patient Records for Alcohol and Other Drug Treatment*. Technical Assistance Publication (TAP) Series 13. DHHS Publication No. (SMA) 95-3018. Rockville, MD: Center for Substance Abuse Treatment, Substance Abuse and Mental Health Services Administration.

Manhal-Baugus, M. (1996). Confidentiality: The legal and ethical issues for chemical dependency counselors. *Journal of Addictions and Offender Counseling*, 17(1):3-11.

Manhal-Baugus, M. (1996). Reducing the risk of malpractice in chemical dependency counseling. *Journal of Addictions and Offender Counseling*, 17(1):35-42.

NAADAC–The Association for Addiction Professionals (2004). *NAADAC Code of Ethics*. Alexandria, VA: NAADAC.

Najavits, L.M., Crits-Christoph, P., et al. (2000). Clinicians' impact on the quality of substance use disorder treatment. *Substance Use & Misuse*, 35(12-14):2161-2190.

National Association of Social Workers (NASW) (1999). *Code of Ethics*. Washington, DC: NASW.

Petrila, J. (1998). *Ethical Issues for Behavioral Health Care Practitioners and Organizations in a Managed Care Environment. Managed Care Technical Assistance Series 5*. Rockville, MD: Substance Abuse and Mental Health Services Administration.

Powell, D.J., & Brodsky, A. (2004). *Clinical Supervision in Alcohol and Drug Abuse Counseling: Principles, Models, Methods* (Revised ed.). San Francisco: Jossey-Bass.

Scott, C.G. (2000). Ethical issues in addiction counseling. *Rehabilitation Counseling Bulletin*, 43(4):209-214.

Substance Abuse and Mental Health Services Administration (SAMHSA) (2004). *The Confidentiality of Alcohol and Drug Abuse Patient Records Regulation and the HIPAA Privacy Rule: Implications for Alcohol and Substance Abuse Programs*. Rockville, MD: SAMHSA.

Ward, K. (2002). Confidentiality in substance abuse counseling. *Journal of Social Work Practice in the Addictions*, 2(2):39-52.

White, W.L., & Popovitz, R.E. (2001). *Critical Incidents: Ethical Issues in the Prevention and Treatment of Addictions* (2nd ed.). Bloomington, IL: Chestnut Health Systems.

Whittinghill, D. (2002). Ethical considerations for the use of family therapy in substance abuse treatment. *Family Journal: Counseling and Therapy for Couples and Families*, 10(1):75-78.

Section 3:

ADDITIONAL RESOURCES

- **CULTURAL COMPETENCY**
- **INTERNET RESOURCES**
- **ATTITUDES BIBLIOGRAPHY**
- **RECOVERY BIBLIOGRAPHY**

Cultural Competency

Clients' experiences of culture predate and influence their interaction with substance abuse treatment professionals. The majority of substance abuse treatment counselors are White, whereas nearly half of people who seek treatment are not White.[1] Regarding mental health services, clients who are not White express, at much higher rates than do White clients, the belief that they would have received better treatment if they were of another race.[2]

In addition to the references found in the bibliography for Transdisciplinary Foundation IV: Professional Readiness on pages 32 to 34, three Treatment Improvement Protocols (TIPs) provide information about cultural competency and substance abuse treatment. The forthcoming TIP *Improving Cultural Competence in Substance Abuse Treatment* is wholly devoted to the subject of culturally competent care. Information about the administrative challenges of preparing a program to provide culturally competent treatment can be found in chapter 4 of TIP 46, *Substance Abuse: Administrative Issues in Outpatient Treatment*, which includes an appendix listing resources for program assessment and cultural competency training. Chapter 10 of TIP 47, *Substance Abuse: Clinical Issues in Intensive Outpatient Treatment*, addresses the clinical implications of culturally competent treatment and includes the following:

- An introduction to current research supporting the need for individualized treatment that is sensitive to culture
- Principles in the delivery of culturally competent treatment services
- Topics of special concern, including foreign-born clients, women from other cultures, and religious considerations
- Clinical implications of culturally competent treatment
- Sketches of diverse client populations, including Hispanics/Latinos; African Americans; Native Americans; Asian Americans and Pacific Islanders; persons with HIV/AIDS; lesbian, gay, and bisexual populations; persons with physical and cognitive disabilities; rural populations; homeless populations; and older adults
- An appendix that lists resources on culturally competent treatment for various populations.

---

[1] Mulvey, K.P., Hubbard, S., & Hayashi, S. (2003). A national study of the substance abuse treatment workforce. *Journal of Substance Abuse Treatment*, 24:51-57.

[2] La Veist, T.A., Diala, C., & Jarrett, N.C. (2000). Social status and perceived discrimination: Who experiences discrimination in the health care system, how, and why? In C.J.R. Hogue, M.A. Hargraves, & K.S. Collins (Eds.) *Minority Health in America*. Baltimore: Johns Hopkins University Press, 194-208.

Additional Resources

INTERNET RESOURCES

The list below includes Web sites that address knowledge dissemination. These sites provide good starting points for those wishing to follow up on the competencies, knowledge, skills, and attitudes discussed in this Technical Assistance Publication.

- Substance Abuse and Mental Health Services Administration (SAMHSA) (http://www.samhsa.gov)
- SAMHSA's Fetal Alcohol Spectrum Disorders Center for Excellence (http://fasdcenter.samhsa.gov)
- SAMHSA's Addiction Technology Transfer Centers (ATTCs): Click on http://attcnetwork.org/regional-centers/search.aspx to find a regional center. (http://www.attcnetwork.org)
  - Central East ATTC (http://www.attcnetwork.org/regional-centers/?rc=centraleast)
  - Central Rockies ATTC (http://www.attcnetwork.org/regional-centers/?rc=centralrockies)
  - Great Lakes ATTC (http://www.attcnetwork.org/regional-centers/?rc=greatlakes)
  - Mid-America ATTC (http://www.attcnetwork.org/regional-centers/?rc=midamerica)
  - New England ATTC (http://www.attcnetwork.org/regional-centers/?rc=newengland)
  - Northeast & Caribbean ATTC (http://www.attcnetwork.org/regional-centers/?rc=northeastcaribbean)
  - Northwest ATTC (http://www.attcnetwork.org/regional-centers/?rc=northwest)
  - Pacific Southwest ATTC (http://www.attcnetwork.org/regional-centers/?rc=pacificsouthwest)
  - Southeast ATTC (http://www.attcnetwork.org/regional-centers/?rc=southeast)
  - South Southwest ATTC (http://www.attcnetwork.org/regional-centers/?rc=southsouthwest)
- Health Resources and Services Administration (http://www.hrsa.gov/index.html)
- National Institute on Alcohol Abuse and Alcoholism (http://www.niaaa.nih.gov)
- National Institute on Drug Abuse (http://www.drugabuse.gov)
- Office of National Drug Control Policy (http://www.whitehouse.gov/ondcp)

ATTITUDES BIBLIOGRAPHY

Counselors' attitudes toward clients and the treatment process are important because they shape the therapeutic relationship that is at the core of treatment for substance use disorders. Negative counselor attitudes need to be considered within the framework of stigma and its consequences for the counselor, the client, and the field. Attitudes of treatment professionals toward the multiple systems of bureaucracy with which they interact—agency priorities, clinic hierarchies, the criminal justice system, departments of social services, community organizations—may also affect their ability to deliver effective treatment.

Albery, I.P., Heuston, J., et al. (2003). Measuring therapeutic attitude among drug workers. *Addictive Behaviors*, 28(5):995-1005.

Ball, S., Bachrach, K., et al. (2002). Characteristics, beliefs, and practices of community clinicians trained to provide manual-guided therapy for substance abusers. *Journal of Substance Abuse Treatment*, 23(4):309-318.

Beauvais, F., Jumper-Thurman, P., et al. (2002). A survey of attitudes among drug user treatment providers toward the treatment of inhalant users. *Substance Use & Misuse*, 37(11): 1391-1410.

Campbell, T.C., Catlin, L.A., & Melchert, T.P. (2003). Alcohol and other drug abuse counselors' attitudes and resources for integrating research and practice. *Journal of Drug Education*, 33(3):307-323.

Caplehorn, J.R., Lumley, T.S., & Irwig, L. (1998). Staff attitudes and retention of patients in methadone maintenance programs. *Drug and Alcohol Dependence*, 52(1):57-61.

Carone, S.S., & LaFleur, N.K. (2000). The effect of adolescent sex offender abuse history on counselor attitudes. *Journal of Addictions and Offender Counseling*, 20(2):56-63.

Culbreth, J.R., & Borders, L.D. (1998). Perceptions of the supervisory relationship: A preliminary qualitative study of recovering and nonrecovering substance abuse counselors. *Journal of Substance Abuse Treatment*, 15(4):345-352.

Culbreth, J.R., & Borders, L.D. (1999). Perceptions of the supervisory relationship: Recovering and nonrecovering substance abuse counselors. *Journal of Counseling & Development*, 77(3):330-338.

Davis, T.D. (2005). Beliefs about confrontation among substance abuse counselors: Are they consistent with the evidence? In C. Hilarski (Ed.) *Addiction, Assessment, and Treatment With Adolescents, Adults, and Families*. Binghamton, NY: Haworth Social Work Practice Press, 1-17.

Eliason, M.J., & Hughes, T. (2004). Treatment counselor's attitudes about lesbian, gay, bisexual, and transgendered clients: Urban vs. rural settings. *Substance Use & Misuse*, 39(4):625-644.

Forman, R.F., Bovasso, G., & Woody, G. (2001). Staff beliefs about addiction treatment. *Journal of Substance Abuse Treatment*, 21(1):1-9.

Additional Resources

Forman, R.F., Bovasso, G., et al. (2002). Staff beliefs about drug abuse clinical trials. *Journal of Substance Abuse Treatment*, 23(1):55-60.

Goddard, P. (2003). Changing attitudes towards harm reduction among treatment professionals: A report from the American Midwest. *International Journal of Drug Policy*, 14(3):257-260.

Grosenick, J.K., & Hatmaker, C.M. (2000). Perceptions of staff attributes in substance abuse treatment. *Journal of Substance Abuse Treatment*, 19(3):273-284.

Jacka, D., Clode, D., et al. (1999). Attitudes and practices of general practitioners training to work with drug-using patients. *Drug and Alcohol Review*, 18(3):287-291.

Janikowski, T.P., & Glover-Graf, N.M. (2003). Qualifications, training, and perceptions of substance abuse counselors who work with victims of incest. *Addictive Behaviors*, 28(6):1193-1201.

Kasarabada, N.D., Hser, Y.I., et al. (2002). Do patients' perceptions of their counselors influence outcomes of drug treatment? *Journal of Substance Abuse Treatment*, 23(4):327-334.

Laudet, A.B. (2003). Attitudes and beliefs about 12-step groups among addiction treatment clients and clinicians: Toward identifying obstacles to participation. *Substance Use & Misuse*, 38(14):2017-2047.

Lawson, K.A., Wilcox, R.E., et al. (2004). Educating treatment professionals about addiction science research: Demographics of knowledge and belief changes. *Substance Use & Misuse*, 39(8):1235-1258.

Mark, T.L., Kranzler, H.R., et al. (2003). Physicians' opinions about medications to treat alcoholism. *Addiction*, 98(5):617-626.

Ogborne, A.C., Wild, T.C., et al. (1998). Measuring treatment process beliefs among staff of specialized addiction treatment services. *Journal of Substance Abuse Treatment*, 15(4):301-312.

Palm, J. (2004). The nature of and responsibility for alcohol and drug problems: Views among treatment staff. *Addiction Research & Theory*, 12(5):413-431.

Project MATCH Research Group (1998). Therapist effects in three treatments for alcohol problems. *Psychotherapy Research*, 8(4):455-474.

Rassool, G.H., & Lind, J.E. (2000). Perception of addiction nurses toward clinical supervision: An exploratory study. *Journal of Addictions Nursing*, 12(1):23-29.

Shoptaw, S., Stein, J.A., & Rawson, R.A. (2000). Burnout in substance abuse counselors: Impact of environment, attitudes, and clients with HIV. *Journal of Substance Abuse Treatment*, 19(2):117-126.

Tuchman, E., Gregory, C., et al. (2005). Office-based opioid treatment (OBOT): Practitioner's knowledge, attitudes, and expectations in New Mexico. *Addictive Disorders and Their Treatment*, 4(1):11-19.

Walton, M.A., Blow, F.C., & Booth, B.M. (2000). A comparison of substance abuse patients' and counselors' perceptions of relapse risk: Relationship to actual relapse. *Journal of Substance Abuse Treatment*, 19(2):161-169.

Wild, T.C., Newton-Taylor, B., et al. (2001). Attitudes toward compulsory substance abuse treatment: A comparison of the public, counselors, probationers and judges' views. *Drugs: Education, Prevention & Policy*, 8(1):33-45.

RECOVERY BIBLIOGRAPHY

In substance use disorders treatment, much attention is paid to what happens during acute episodes of treatment. There is often significant emphasis on treatment issues, such as treatment approach, therapeutic alliance, client retention, family involvement, cultural competency, and pharmacological intervention. The importance of the ongoing recovery process is sometimes not given sufficient attention. It is crucial to identify and address clients' needs for case management, continuing care, housing, employment, transportation, education, life skills, social support—all the things that help clients reintegrate into the community, build a meaningful life, and sustain their recovery.

Blume, S. (1977). Role of the recovered alcoholic in the treatment of alcoholism. In B. Kissin & H. Begliester (Eds.) *The Biology of Alcoholism, Volume 5: Treatment and Rehabilitation of the Chronic Alcoholic*. New York: Plenum Press, 545-565.

Bond, J., Kaskutas, L., & Weisner, C. (2003). The persistent influence of social networks and Alcoholics Anonymous on abstinence. *Journal of Studies on Alcohol*, 64(4):579-588.

Borkman, T. (1998). Is recovery planning any different from treatment planning? *Journal of Substance Abuse Treatment*, 15(1):37-42.

Boyle, M.G., White, W.L., et al. *Behavioral Health Recovery Management: A Statement of Principles*. Behavioral Health Recovery Management Project. Peoria, IL: Fayette Companies; Bloomington, IL: Chestnut Health Systems.

Broome, M., Simpson, D.D., & Joe, G.W. (2002). The role of social support following short-term inpatient treatment. *Journal on Addictions*, 11(1):57-65.

Cloud, W., & Granfield, R. (2001). Natural recovery from substance dependency: Lessons for treatment providers. *Journal of Social Work Practice in the Addictions*, 1(1):83-104.

Coyhis, D., & White, W. (2002). Addiction and recovery in Native America: Lost history, enduring lessons. *Counselor*, 3(5):16-20.

Dennis, M., Scott, C.K., & Funk, R. (2003). An experimental evaluation of recovery management checkups (RMC) for people with chronic substance use disorders. *Evaluation and Program Planning*, 26(3):339-352.

Dodd, M.H. (1997). Social model of recovery: Origin, early features, changes, and future. *Journal of Psychoactive Drugs*, 29(2):133-139.

Frese, F.J., Stanley, J., et al. (2001). Integrating evidence-based practices and the recovery model. *Psychiatric Services*, 52(11):1462-1468.

Galanter, M. (2002). Healing through social and spiritual affiliation. *Psychiatric Services*, 53(9):1072-1074.

Gordon, A.J., & Zrull, M. (1991). Social networks and recovery: One year after inpatient treatment. *Journal of Substance Abuse Treatment*, 8(3):146-152.

Gorski, T.T., & Kelley, J.M. (1996). *Counselor's Manual for Relapse Prevention With Chemically Dependent Criminal Offenders*. Technical Assistance Publication (TAP) Series No. 19. DHHS Publication No. (SMA) 96-3115. Rockville, MD: Center for Substance Abuse Treatment, Substance Abuse and Mental Health Services Administration.

Granfield, R., & Cloud, W. (2001). Social capital and natural recovery: The role of social resources and relationships in overcoming addiction without treatment. *Substance Use & Misuse*, 36(11):1543-1549.

Gregoire, T.K., & Snively, C.A. (2001). The relationship of social support and economic self-sufficiency to substance abuse outcomes in a long-term recovery program for women. *Journal of Drug Education*, 31(3):221-237.

Humphreys, K. (2004). *Circles of Recovery: Self-Help Organizations for Addictions*. New York: Cambridge University Press.

Kirby, M.W. (2004). Self-help organizations for alcohol and drug problems: Toward evidence-based practice and policy. *Journal of Substance Abuse Treatment*, 26(3):161-162.

Laudet, A.B. (April 2005). Exploring the recovery process: Patterns, supports, challenges and future directions. Presented at the Seminar Series of the Division of Epidemiology, Services and Prevention Research, conducted at the National Institute on Drug Abuse, Center for the Study of Addiction and Recovery.

Laudet, A.B., Magura, S., et al. (2000). Recovery challenges among dually diagnosed individuals. *Journal of Substance Abuse Treatment*, 18(4):321-329.

Lemieux, C.M. (2002). Social support among offenders with substance abuse problems: Overlooked and underused? *Journal of Addictions & Offender Counseling*, 23:41-57.

Longabaugh, R. (2003). Involvement of support networks in treatment. *Recent Developments in Alcoholism*, 16:133-147.

McIntosh, J., & McKeganey, N. (2000). The recovery from dependent drug use: Addicts' strategies for reducing the risk of relapse. *Drugs: Education, Prevention & Policy*, 7(2): 179-192.

McLellan, A., McKay, J., et al. (2005). Reconsidering the evaluation of addiction treatment: From retrospective follow-up to concurrent recovery monitoring. *Addiction*, 100(4): 447-458.

Moxley, D.P., & Washington, O.G. (2001). Strengths-based recovery practice in chemical dependency: A transpersonal perspective. *Families in Society: the Journal of Contemporary Human Services*, 82(3):251-262.

Nebelkopf, E., & Phillips, M. (2003). Morning star rising: Healing in Native American communities. *Journal of Psychoactive Drugs*, 35(1):1-5.

Snow, M.G., Prochaska, J.O., & Rossi, J.S. (1994). Processes of change in Alcoholics Anonymous: Maintenance factors in long term sobriety. *Journal of Studies on Alcohol*, 55(3):362-371.

Sullivan, E., Mino, M., et al. (2002). *Families as a Resource in Recovery From Drug Abuse: An Evaluation of la Bodega de la Familia*. New York, NY: Vera Institute of Justice.

Tims, F.M., Leukefeld, C.G., & Platt, J.J. (Eds.) (2001). *Relapse and Recovery in Addictions*. New Haven, CT: Yale University Press.

White, W. (1996). *Pathways From the Culture of Addiction to the Culture of Recovery: A Travel Guide for Addiction Professionals*. Center City, MN: Hazelden.

White, W. (2002). *An Addiction Recovery Glossary: The Languages of American Communities of Recovery*. Behavioral Health Recovery Management Project. Peoria, IL: Fayette Companies; Bloomington, IL: Chestnut Health Systems.

White, W. (2004). Recovery: The new frontier. *Counselor*, 5(1):18-21.

White, W. (2004). *Recovery Rising: Radical Recovery in America*. Behavioral Health Recovery Management Project. Peoria, IL: Fayette Companies; Bloomington, IL: Chestnut Health Systems.

White, W., Boyle, M., & Loveland, D. (2003). A model to transcend the limitations of addiction treatment. *Behavioral Health Management*, 23(3):38-44.

White, W., Boyle, M., et al. (2004). *What Is Behavioral Health Recovery Management? A Brief Primer*. Behavioral Health Recovery Management Project. Peoria, IL: Fayette Companies; Bloomington, IL: Chestnut Health Systems.

White, W., & Sanders, M. (2004). *Recovery Management and People of Color: Redesigning Addiction Treatment for Historically Disempowered Communities*. Behavioral Health Recovery Management Project. Peoria, IL: Fayette Companies; Bloomington, IL: Chestnut Health Systems.

White Bison, Inc. (2002). *The Red Road to Wellbriety: In the Native American Way*. Colorado Springs, CO: White Bison, Inc.

Section 4:

APPENDICES

- **APPENDIX A – GLOSSARY**
- **APPENDIX B – THE COMPETENCIES**
- **APPENDIX C – NATIONAL VALIDATION STUDY**
- **APPENDIX D – COMPLETE BIBLIOGRAPHY**
- **APPENDIX E – OTHER CONTRIBUTORS**

Appendix A – Glossary

This glossary contains descriptions of key words used in this Technical Assistance Publication. The descriptions of the terms reflect the usage of the terms in this document. The descriptions are not intended as universal or complete definitions of the terms.

Active listening – a counseling skill that enhances rapport and demonstrates interest and understanding through the use of verbal and nonverbal acknowledgment of client statements.

Addiction – a chronic, relapsing disease of the brain with social and behavioral manifestations marked by continued alcohol or drug use despite negative consequences.

Addiction counseling – professional and ethical application of specific competencies that constitute eight practice dimensions, including clinical evaluation; treatment planning; referral; service coordination; individual, group, and family counseling; client, family, and community education; and documentation.

Advocacy – (1) a social or political movement working for changes in legislation, policy, and funding to reflect clients' concerns and protect their rights (i.e., advocacy for clients); (2) a philosophy of substance abuse treatment practice maintaining that clients should be involved actively in their own treatment and have rights in its planning and implementation (i.e., advocacy by clients). Much of advocacy is about shifting the system from the directive model to one in which the client is an empowered, involved participant in treatment decisions.

Biomedical – pertaining to the biological and physiological aspects of clinical medicine.

Biopsychosocial – the biological, psychosocial, and social influences in human development and behavior.

Case management – see "Service coordination."

Client – individual, significant other, or community agent who presents for alcohol and drug abuse education, prevention, intervention, treatment, and consultation services.

Collateral sources – persons or organizations providing pertinent information about a client (can include family members and legal, educational, and medical personnel).

Competency – specific counselor functions comprising requisite knowledge, skills, and attitudes.

Confidentiality – a client's right to privacy as defined by applicable Federal and State statutes.

Confidentiality rules and regulations – rules established by Federal and State agencies to limit disclosure of information about a client's substance use disorder and treatment (described in 42 CFR, Part 2B 16). Programs must notify clients of their rights to confidentiality, provide a written summary of these rights, and establish written procedures regulating access to and use of client records.

Confrontation – a form of interpersonal exchange in which individuals present to one another their observations of, and reactions to, behaviors and attitudes that are matters of concern. Feedback is provided on behavior, and an appeal is made to the client for personal honesty, truthfulness in dealing with others, and responsible behavior.

Content – the subjects discussed in the context of counseling.

Continuing care – care that supports a client's progress, monitors his or her condition, and responds to a return to substance use or a return of mental disorder symptoms. It is both a process of posttreatment monitoring and a form of treatment itself; sometimes referred to as aftercare.

Continuum of care – the array of services that differ in terms of unique needs of clients throughout the course of treatment and recovery.

Contracting – the process by which the client and the counselor enter into an agreement to address specific problems, issues, or behaviors.

Co-occurring disorder/coexisting disorder – the presence of concurrent psychiatric or medical disorders in combination with a substance use disorder.

Counseling – a therapeutic process aimed at meeting specific identified needs of the client.

Countertransference – a counselor's unresolved feelings for significant others that may be transferred to the client.

Craving – an urgent, seemingly overpowering desire to use a substance, which often is associated with tension, anxiety, or other dysphoric, depressive, or negative affective states.

Cultural competency – the capacity of a service provider or organization to understand and work effectively in accord with the beliefs and practices of persons from a given ethnic/racial/religious/social group or sexual orientation. It includes the holding of knowledge, skills, and attitudes that allow the treatment provider and program to understand the full context of a client's current and past socioenvironmental situation.

Cultural diversity – the vast array of different cultural groups based on varying behaviors, attitudes, values, languages, celebrations, rituals, and histories.

Culture – the vast structure of behaviors, ideas, attitudes, values, habits, beliefs, customs, language, rituals, ceremonies, histories, and practices distinctive to a particular group of people.

Diagnosis – classification of the nature and severity of the substance use, medical, mental health, or other problems present. DSM-IV-TR and ICD-10 commonly are used to classify substance use and mental disorders.

Disorder – an affliction that affects the functions of the mind and/or body, disturbing physical and/or mental health.

Duty to warn – the legal obligation of a counselor (healthcare provider) to notify the appropriate authorities as defined by statute and/or the potential victim when there is serious danger of a client's inflicting injury on an identified individual.

Efficacy – the power to produce a desired effect.

Elements – specific, definable areas found in three of the practice dimensions (clinical evaluation, service coordination, and counseling).

Empirical – relying on observation or experience rather than theoretical principles or theory.

Engagement – a client's commitment to and maintenance of treatment in all of its forms. A successful engagement program helps clients view the treatment facility as an important resource.

Appendix A – Glossary

Epidemiology – the study of the incidence, distribution, and consequences of a particular problem in one or more populations.

Etiology – the study of origins (what causes a disorder).

Extrinsic motivator – a rationale for changing substance use that comes from outside the client. Examples include threat of losing a job, legal charges, or a spouse/significant other ending a relationship.

Harmful use – patterns of alcohol or drug use for nonmedical reasons that result in negative health consequences and some degree of impairment in social, psychological, and occupational functioning for the user.

Helping strategy – an activity employed by the counselor to help the client accomplish his or her therapeutic goals.

Hepatitis C – a viral disease of the liver that is a major cause of liver damage and cirrhosis.

Incidence – the number of new cases of a disorder that occur in a population during a specific period.

Indicated preventive interventions – strategies designed for persons who are identified as having minimal but detectable signs or symptoms or precursors of some illness or condition, but whose condition is below the threshold of a formal diagnosis of the condition.

Individualized treatment plan – a strategy that addresses the identified substance use disorder(s), as well as issues related to treatment progress, including relationships with family and significant others, employment, education, spirituality, health concerns, and legal needs. Plans are developed in collaboration with the client and significant others and tailored to fit the client's unique biopsychosocial strengths and needs.

Infectious – a contagious illness or disease transmitted by direct or indirect contact.

Initiation – the individual's introduction to and onset of alcohol or drug use.

Intervention – the specific treatment strategies, therapies, or techniques that are used to treat one or more disorders.

Intoxication – an altered physical and mental state resulting from the overuse of alcohol or drugs.

Intrinsic motivator – an individual's internal reason for changing substance use behaviors, such as poor health or low self-esteem, resulting from his or her substance use.

Life skills training – activities that include development of job, vocational, life (budgeting, leisure, etc.), anger management, general coping, communication, and social skills; literacy classes and GED preparation; parenting classes; and relationship building.

Managed care – an approach to delivery of health and mental health services that seeks to reduce the cost of care by monitoring the access to and use of medical services and supplies, as well as outcomes of that care.

Modality/treatment modality – any specific treatment method or procedure used to relieve symptoms or motivate behaviors that lead to recovery.

Model – a collection of beliefs or unifying theory about what is needed to bring about change with a particular client in a particular treatment context.

Motivational interviewing – a direct, client-centered counseling style implemented to elicit behavior change by helping clients resolve their ambivalence to change.

Multiaxial diagnostic criteria – the system used by the DSM-IV-TR that evaluates the acute, longstanding medical conditions as well as stressors and level of functioning (current and past).

Multidisciplinary approach – a planned and coordinated program of care involving two or more health professions for the purpose of improving health care as a result of their joint contributions.

Multidisciplinary assessment approach – an organized process by which professionals of different specialties collaborate to assess the needs of the client.

Mutual help – a process present in many self-help groups by which the members of such groups rely on and receive support from other members who share the same condition.

Outcome monitoring – collection and analysis of data during and following alcohol and drug treatment to determine the effects of treatment, especially in relation to improvements in client functioning.

Outcome statement – an agreement between the client and the counselor that identifies the desired results of treatment.

Outreach strategies – approaches that actively seek out persons in a community who have substance use disorders and engage them in substance abuse treatment.

Patient – see "Client."

Peer counselor – individuals in recovery from substance use disorders who have been trained to work in substance abuse treatment settings.

Practice dimensions – the eight essential areas of practice that addiction counselors must master to effectively provide treatment activities identified in *The Competencies*.

Prevalence – the percentage of people in the population that has a specific disorder.

Prevention – the theory and means for reducing the harmful effects of drug use in specific populations. Prevention objectives are to protect individuals before they manifest signs or symptoms of substance use problems, identify persons in the early stages of substance abuse and intervene, and end compulsive use of psychoactive substances through treatment.

Problem statement – a statement that describes a client's current condition in behavioral terms.

Process – the way in which a client, counselor, or group engages or interacts.

Professionalism – a demonstration of knowledge, skills, and attitudes consistently applied when working with people who use substances and abiding by a code of ethics most commonly held by addiction professionals.

Projective identification – the process by which a person places internal negative feelings or concepts about oneself onto others.

Protective factors – conditions that promote bonding to prosocial values and institutions and can serve to buffer the negative effects of risks.

Psychoactive substance – a pharmacological agent that can change mood, behavior, and cognition process.

Rapport – the degree to which trust and openness are present in the relationship between counselor and client; an essential element of the therapeutic relationship.

Appendix A – Glossary

Recovery – achieving and sustaining a state of health in which the individual no longer engages in problem behavior or psychoactive substance use and is able to establish a lifestyle that embraces health and positive goals.

Regression – a mechanism whereby an individual retreats to the use of early-life or less mature responses in attempting to cope with stress, fears, pain, or memories.

Relapse – the return to a pattern of substance abuse or the process during which indicators appear before the client's resumption of substance use.

Relapse prevention – a variety of interventions designed to teach people with substance use disorders to cope more effectively and to overcome the stressors/triggers in their environments that may lead them back into drug use and dependence. The interventions can be placed in five categories: assessment procedures, insight/awareness raising techniques, coping skills training, cognitive strategies, and lifestyle modification.

Reliability – the degree to which a measure is consistent.

Resilience – the ability of an individual to cope with or overcome the negative effects of risk factors or to "bounce back" from a problem. This capability develops and changes over time, is enhanced by protective factors, and contributes to the maintenance or enhancement of health.

Risk factors – conditions for a group, individual, or identified geographic area that increase the likelihood of a substance use problem or substance abuse.

Screening – gathering and sorting of information used to determine whether an individual has a problem with substance use and, if so, whether a detailed clinical assessment is appropriate.

Selective preventive interventions – activities targeted to individuals or a subgroup of the population whose risk of developing a disorder is significantly higher than average.

Self-determination – the extent to which individuals control their lives.

Self-help group – a supportive, educational, usually change-oriented mutual-help group that addresses a single life problem or condition shared by all members.

Service coordination – the process of prioritizing, managing, and implementing activities in an individual's treatment plan.

Significant others – family member, sexual partner, and others on whom an individual is dependent for meeting all or part of his or her needs.

Sobriety – the quality or condition of abstinence from psychoactive substance abuse supported by personal responsibility in recovery.

Special populations – diverse groups of individuals sharing a particular characteristic, circumstance, or problem.

Spirituality – a belief system that acknowledges and appreciates the influence in one's life of a higher power or state of being.

Stage of change – transtheoretical description of one of several stages through which a person passes in moving from active use to treatment and abstinence.

Stage of readiness – the individual's awareness of need to change. Can be influenced by external pressure (family, legal system, or employer) or internal pressure (physical health concerns).

Substance abuse – a maladaptive pattern of substance use leading to clinically significant impairment or distress such as failure to fulfill major role responsibilities or use in spite of physical hazards, legal problems, or interpersonal and social problems. (See also DSM-IV-TR for specific criteria.)

Substance dependence – the need for alcohol or a drugs that results from the use of that substance. This need includes both mental and physical changes that make it difficult for individuals to control when they use the substance and how much they use. Psychological dependence occurs when individuals need the substance to feel good or normal or to function. Physical dependence occurs when the body adapts to the substance and needs increasing amounts to achieve the same effect or to function. (See also DSM-IV-TR for specific criteria.)

Substance use – consumption of low and/or infrequent doses of alcohol or drugs, sometimes called "experimental," "casual," "recreational," or "social" use, such that consequences may be rare or minor.

Systems theory – view of behavior as an interactive part of a larger social structure.

Theory – a framework to organize and integrate knowledge to facilitate answering the question, "why?"

Transdisciplinary – knowledge and attitudes that both transcend and are needed by all disciplines working with persons with substance use disorders.

Transference – the process in which a client's strong feelings for significant others may be transferred to the counselor.

Treatment barriers – anything that hinders treatment. Examples include financial problems, language difficulties, ethnic and social attitudes, logistics (e.g., child care, transportation), and unhelpful patient behaviors (e.g., tardiness, missed appointments).

Treatment goals – objectives based on resolving problems identified during assessment and reasonably achievable in the active treatment phase.

Treatment interventions – strategies the counselor and other professionals use to assist the client in achieving treatment goals.

Treatment objectives – incremental steps a client takes in achieving treatment goals.

Universal prevention – prevention designed for everyone in the eligible population, both the general public and all members of specific eligible groups. Also, activities targeted to the general public or a whole population group that has not been identified on the basis of individual risk.

Validity – the degree to which an instrument or process measures what it is designed to measure.

Appendix B – The Competencies: A Complete List

This is a complete list of the competencies without the knowledge, skills, and attitudes.

Transdisciplinary Foundation I: Understanding Addiction

Competency 1:
Understand a variety of models and theories of addiction and other problems related to substance use.

Competency 2:
Recognize the social, political, economic, and cultural context within which addiction and substance abuse exist, including risk and resiliency factors that characterize individuals and groups and their living environments.

Competency 3:
Describe the behavioral, psychological, physical health, and social effects of psychoactive substances on the person using and significant others.

Competency 4:
Recognize the potential for substance use disorders to mimic a variety of medical and mental health conditions and the potential for medical and mental health conditions to coexist with addiction and substance abuse.

Transdisciplinary Foundation II: Treatment Knowledge

Competency 5:
Describe the philosophies, practices, policies, and outcomes of the most generally accepted and scientifically supported models of treatment, recovery, relapse prevention, and continuing care for addiction and other substance-related problems.

Competency 6:
Recognize the importance of family, social networks, and community systems in the treatment and recovery process.

Competency 7:
Understand the importance of research and outcome data and their application in clinical practice.

Competency 8:
Understand the value of an interdisciplinary approach to addiction treatment.

TRANSDISCIPLINARY FOUNDATION III: APPLICATION TO PRACTICE

COMPETENCY 9:
Understand the established diagnostic criteria for substance use disorders, and describe treatment modalities and placement criteria within the continuum of care.

COMPETENCY 10:
Describe a variety of helping strategies for reducing the negative effects of substance use, abuse, and dependence.

COMPETENCY 11:
Tailor helping strategies and treatment modalities to the client's stage of dependence, change, or recovery.

COMPETENCY 12:
Provide treatment services appropriate to the personal and cultural identity and language of the client.

COMPETENCY 13:
Adapt practice to the range of treatment settings and modalities.

COMPETENCY 14:
Be familiar with medical and pharmacological resources in the treatment of substance use disorders.

COMPETENCY 15:
Understand the variety of insurance and health maintenance options available and the importance of helping clients access those benefits.

COMPETENCY 16:
Recognize that crisis may indicate an underlying substance use disorder and may be a window of opportunity for change.

COMPETENCY 17:
Understand the need for and use of methods for measuring treatment outcome.

TRANSDISCIPLINARY FOUNDATION IV: PROFESSIONAL READINESS

COMPETENCY 18:
Understand diverse cultures, and incorporate the relevant needs of culturally diverse groups, as well as people with disabilities, into clinical practice.

COMPETENCY 19:
Understand the importance of self-awareness in one's personal, professional, and cultural life.

COMPETENCY 20:
Understand the addiction professional's obligations to adhere to ethical and behavioral standards of conduct in the helping relationship.

COMPETENCY 21:
Understand the importance of ongoing supervision and continuing education in the delivery of client services.

COMPETENCY 22:
Understand the obligation of the addiction professional to participate in prevention and treatment activities.

COMPETENCY 23:
Understand and apply setting-specific policies and procedures for handling crisis or dangerous situations, including safety measures for clients and staff.

PRACTICE DIMENSION I: CLINICAL EVALUATION
Element: Screening

COMPETENCY 24:
Establish rapport, including management of a crisis situation and determination of need for additional professional assistance.

COMPETENCY 25:
Gather data systematically from the client and other available collateral sources, using screening instruments and other methods that are sensitive to age, developmental level, culture, and gender. At a minimum, data should include current and historic substance use; health, mental health, and substance-related treatment histories; mental and functional statuses; and current social, environmental, and/or economic constraints.

COMPETENCY 26:
Screen for psychoactive substance toxicity, intoxication, and withdrawal symptoms; aggression or danger to others; potential for self-inflicted harm or suicide; and co-occurring mental disorders.

COMPETENCY 27:
Assist the client in identifying the effect of substance use on his or her current life problems and the effects of continued harmful use or abuse.

COMPETENCY 28:
Determine the client's readiness for treatment and change as well as the needs of others involved in the current situation.

COMPETENCY 29:
Review the treatment options that are appropriate for the client's needs, characteristics, goals, and financial resources.

COMPETENCY 30:
Apply accepted criteria for diagnosis of substance use disorders in making treatment recommendations.

COMPETENCY 31:
Construct with the client and appropriate others an initial action plan based on client needs, client preferences, and resources available.

COMPETENCY 32:
Based on the initial action plan, take specific steps to initiate an admission or referral and ensure followthrough.

PRACTICE DIMENSION I: CLINICAL EVALUATION
Element: Assessment

COMPETENCY 33:
Select and use a comprehensive assessment process that is sensitive to age, gender, racial and ethnic culture, and disabilities that includes but is not limited to:

- History of alcohol and drug use
- Physical health, mental health, and addiction treatment histories
- Family issues
- Work history and career issues
- History of criminality
- Psychological, emotional, and worldview concerns
- Current status of physical health, mental health, and substance use
- Spiritual concerns of the client
- Education and basic life skills
- Socioeconomic characteristics, lifestyle, and current legal status
- Use of community resources
- Treatment readiness
- Level of cognitive and behavioral functioning.

COMPETENCY 34:
Analyze and interpret the data to determine treatment recommendations.

COMPETENCY 35:
Seek appropriate supervision and consultation.

COMPETENCY 36:
Document assessment findings and treatment recommendations.

PRACTICE DIMENSION II: TREATMENT PLANNING

COMPETENCY 37:
Use relevant assessment information to guide the treatment planning process.

Appendix B – The Competencies

COMPETENCY 38:
Explain assessment findings to the client and significant others.

COMPETENCY 39:
Provide the client and significant others with clarification and additional information as needed.

COMPETENCY 40:
Examine treatment options in collaboration with the client and significant others.

COMPETENCY 41:
Consider the readiness of the client and significant others to participate in treatment.

COMPETENCY 42:
Prioritize the client's needs in the order they will be addressed in treatment.

COMPETENCY 43:
Formulate mutually agreed-on and measurable treatment goals and objectives.

COMPETENCY 44:
Identify appropriate strategies for each treatment goal.

COMPETENCY 45:
Coordinate treatment activities and community resources in a manner consistent with the client's diagnosis and existing placement criteria.

COMPETENCY 46:
Develop with the client a mutually acceptable treatment plan and method for monitoring and evaluating progress.

COMPETENCY 47:
Inform the client of confidentiality rights, program procedures that safeguard them, and the exceptions imposed by regulations.

COMPETENCY 48:
Reassess the treatment plan at regular intervals or when indicated by changing circumstances.

PRACTICE DIMENSION III: REFERRAL

COMPETENCY 49:
Establish and maintain relationships with civic groups, agencies, other professionals, governmental entities, and the community at large to ensure appropriate referrals, identify service gaps, expand community resources, and help address unmet needs.

COMPETENCY 50:
Continuously assess and evaluate referral resources to determine their appropriateness.

COMPETENCY 51:
Differentiate between situations in which it is most appropriate for the client to self-refer to a resource and situations requiring counselor referral.

Addiction Counseling Competencies

COMPETENCY 52:
Arrange referrals to other professionals, agencies, community programs, or appropriate resources to meet the client's needs.

COMPETENCY 53:
Explain in clear and specific language the necessity for and process of referral to increase the likelihood of client understanding and followthrough.

COMPETENCY 54:
Exchange relevant information with the agency or professional to whom the referral is being made in a manner consistent with confidentiality rules and regulations and generally accepted professional standards of care.

COMPETENCY 55:
Evaluate the outcome of the referral.

PRACTICE DIMENSION IV: SERVICE COORDINATION
Element: Implementing the Treatment Plan

COMPETENCY 56:
Initiate collaboration with the referral source.

COMPETENCY 57:
Obtain, review, and interpret all relevant screening, assessment, and initial treatment planning information.

COMPETENCY 58:
Confirm the client's eligibility for admission and continued readiness for treatment and change.

COMPETENCY 59:
Complete necessary administrative procedures for admission to treatment.

COMPETENCY 60:
Establish accurate treatment and recovery expectations with the client and involved significant others, including but not limited to:

- The nature of services
- Program goals
- Program procedures
- Rules regarding client conduct
- The schedule of treatment activities
- Costs of treatment
- Factors affecting duration of care
- Clients' rights and responsibilities
- The effect of treatment and recovery on significant others.

Competency 61:
Coordinate all treatment activities with services provided to the client by other resources.

Practice Dimension IV: Service Coordination
Element: Consulting

Competency 62:
Summarize the client's personal and cultural background, treatment plan, recovery progress, and problems inhibiting progress to ensure quality of care, gain feedback, and plan changes in the course of treatment.

Competency 63:
Understand the terminology, procedures, and roles of other disciplines related to the treatment of substance use disorders.

Competency 64:
Contribute as part of a multidisciplinary treatment team.

Competency 65:
Apply confidentiality rules and regulations appropriately.

Competency 66:
Demonstrate respect and nonjudgmental attitudes toward clients in all contacts with community professionals and agencies.

Practice Dimension IV: Service Coordination
Element: Continuing Assessment and Treatment Planning

Competency 67:
Maintain ongoing contact with the client and involved significant others to ensure adherence to the treatment plan.

Competency 68:
Understand and recognize stages of change and other signs of treatment progress.

Competency 69:
Assess treatment and recovery progress, and, in consultation with the client and significant others, make appropriate changes to the treatment plan to ensure progress toward treatment goals.

Competency 70:
Describe and document the treatment process, progress, and outcome.

Competency 71:
Use accepted treatment outcome measures.

Addiction Counseling Competencies

COMPETENCY 72:
Conduct continuing care, relapse prevention, and discharge planning with the client and involved significant others.

COMPETENCY 73:
Document service coordination activities throughout the continuum of care.

COMPETENCY 74:
Apply placement, continued stay, and discharge criteria for each modality on the continuum of care.

Practice Dimension V: Counseling
Element: Individual Counseling

COMPETENCY 75:
Establish a helping relationship with the client characterized by warmth, respect, genuineness, concreteness, and empathy.

COMPETENCY 76:
Facilitate the client's engagement in the treatment and recovery process.

COMPETENCY 77:
Work with the client to establish realistic, achievable goals consistent with achieving and maintaining recovery.

COMPETENCY 78:
Promote client knowledge, skills, and attitudes that contribute to a positive change in substance use behaviors.

COMPETENCY 79:
Encourage and reinforce client actions determined to be beneficial in progressing toward treatment goals.

COMPETENCY 80:
Work appropriately with the client to recognize and discourage all behaviors inconsistent with progress toward treatment goals.

COMPETENCY 81:
Recognize how, when, and why to involve the client's significant others in enhancing or supporting the treatment plan.

COMPETENCY 82:
Promote client knowledge, skills, and attitudes consistent with the maintenance of health and prevention of HIV/AIDS, tuberculosis, sexually transmitted diseases, hepatitis C, and other infectious diseases.

COMPETENCY 83:
Facilitate the development of basic and life skills associated with recovery.

Competency 84:
Adapt counseling strategies to the individual characteristics of the client, including but not limited to disability, gender, sexual orientation, developmental level, culture, ethnicity, age, and health status.

Competency 85:
Make constructive therapeutic responses when the client's behavior is inconsistent with stated recovery goals.

Competency 86:
Apply crisis prevention and management skills.

Competency 87:
Facilitate the client's identification, selection, and practice of strategies that help sustain the knowledge, skills, and attitudes needed for maintaining treatment progress and preventing relapse.

Practice Dimension V: Counseling
Element: Group Counseling

Competency 88:
Describe, select, and appropriately use strategies from accepted and culturally appropriate models for group counseling with clients with substance use disorders.

Competency 89:
Carry out the actions necessary to form a group, including but not limited to determining group type, purpose, size, and leadership; recruiting and selecting members; establishing group goals and clarifying behavioral ground rules for participating; identifying outcomes; and determining criteria and methods for termination or graduation from the group.

Competency 90:
Facilitate the entry of new members and the transition of exiting members.

Competency 91:
Facilitate group growth within the established ground rules and movement toward group and individual goals by using methods consistent with group type.

Competency 92:
Understand the concepts of process and content, and shift the focus of the group when such a shift will help the group move toward its goals.

Competency 93:
Describe and summarize the client's behavior within the group to document the client's progress and identify needs and issues that may require a modification in the treatment plan.

Practice Dimension V: Counseling
Element: Counseling Families, Couples, and Significant Others

Competency 94:
Understand the characteristics and dynamics of families, couples, and significant others affected by substance use.

Competency 95:
Be familiar with and appropriately use models of diagnosis and intervention for families, couples, and significant others, including extended, kinship, or tribal family structures.

Competency 96:
Facilitate the engagement of selected members of the family or significant others in the treatment and recovery process.

Competency 97:
Assist families, couples, and significant others in understanding the interaction between the family system and substance use behaviors.

Competency 98:
Assist families, couples, and significant others in adopting strategies and behaviors that sustain recovery and maintain healthy relationships.

Practice Dimension VI: Client, Family, and Community Education

Competency 99:
Provide culturally relevant formal and informal education programs that raise awareness and support substance abuse prevention and the recovery process.

Competency 100:
Describe factors that increase the likelihood for an individual, community, or group to be at risk for, or resilient to, psychoactive substance use disorders.

Competency 101:
Sensitize others to issues of cultural identity, ethnic background, age, and gender in prevention, treatment, and recovery.

Competency 102:
Describe warning signs, symptoms, and the course of substance use disorders.

Competency 103:
Describe how substance use disorders affect families and concerned others.

Competency 104:
Describe the continuum of care and resources available to the family and concerned others.

Competency 105:
Describe principles and philosophy of prevention, treatment, and recovery.

Competency 106:
Understand and describe the health and behavior problems related to substance use, including transmission and prevention of HIV/AIDS, tuberculosis, sexually transmitted diseases, hepatitis C, and other infectious diseases.

Competency 107:
Teach life skills, including but not limited to stress management, relaxation, communication, assertiveness, and refusal skills.

Practice Dimension VII: Documentation

Competency 108:
Demonstrate knowledge of accepted principles of client record management.

Competency 109:
Protect client rights to privacy and confidentiality in the preparation and handling of records, especially in relation to the communication of client information with third parties.

Competency 110:
Prepare accurate and concise screening, intake, and assessment reports.

Competency 111:
Record treatment and continuing care plans that are consistent with agency standards and comply with applicable administrative rules.

Competency 112:
Record progress of client in relation to treatment goals and objectives.

Competency 113:
Prepare accurate and concise discharge summaries.

Competency 114:
Document treatment outcome, using accepted methods and instruments.

Practice Dimension VIII: Professional and Ethical Responsibilities

Competency 115:
Adhere to established professional codes of ethics that define the professional context within which the counselor works to maintain professional standards and safeguard the client.

Competency 116:
Adhere to Federal and State laws and agency regulations regarding the treatment of substance use disorders.

Competency 117:
Interpret and apply information from current counseling and psychoactive substance use research literature to improve client care and enhance professional growth.

Competency 118:
Recognize the importance of individual differences that influence client behavior, and apply this understanding to clinical practice.

Competency 119:
Use a range of supervisory options to process personal feelings and concerns about clients.

Competency 120:
Conduct self-evaluations of professional performance applying ethical, legal, and professional standards to enhance self-awareness and performance.

Competency 121:
Obtain appropriate continuing professional education.

Competency 122:
Participate in ongoing supervision and consultation.

Competency 123:
Develop and use strategies to maintain one's physical and mental health.

APPENDIX C — NATIONAL VALIDATION STUDY: DEFINING AND MEASURING THE COMPETENCE OF ADDICTION COUNSELORS

Paula K. Horvatich, Ph.D., and Jon F. Wergin, Ph.D.
Virginia Commonwealth University[1]

INTRODUCTION

The education of addiction counselors, once based on tradition, myth, and politics, is becoming increasingly professionalized, based on competencies, research, and best practice (Fisher 1997). Treatment for psychoactive substance abuse and dependence has traditionally been provided by addiction counselors. Although many counselors have academic degrees, many others have become counselors following personal experiences with treatment and recovery (Deitch & Carleton 1997). Formal education for addiction counselors has traditionally consisted of specialty training provided by treatment agencies, professional or certification organizations, or human service programs of community colleges that confer associate's degrees. Certification of addiction counselors varies from State to State but usually requires a high school diploma and a specified number of years of experience in the field. A bachelor's degree is required in only some States. In others, addiction counselors require no certification as long as they work in a State-approved facility.

Because of a variety of policy and economic factors, training requirements for certification in addiction counseling have become more rigorous. These factors include, among others, the pervasiveness and effect of substance abuse on society, expanded treatment research efforts, and managed behavioral health care. If substance use problems were not so widespread and costly to society, there would be less interest in the credentials of addiction counselors and the outcomes of the treatment they provide.

Although treatment research has grown rapidly and has provided useful insights, new information will be useless unless it is implemented by frontline practitioners. Addiction counselors must be able to understand and apply new knowledge, but traditionally these connections have not been made (Fisher 1997).

Efforts to make treatment more efficient have resulted in the integration of substance abuse treatment with mental health services, thereby increasing the role of mental health and other healthcare professionals in substance abuse treatment. Addiction specialties have emerged in medicine, nursing, social work, psychology, and counseling, including rehabilitation counseling. Managed care has made it increasingly likely that master's-level addiction

---

[1] An earlier version of this paper was presented at the American Educational Research Association Annual Meeting, April 13–17, 1998, in San Diego, California. This study was funded by the Substance Abuse and Mental Health Services Administration's Center for Substance Abuse Treatment Grant Number 5U98 TI 00837. The original version is archived on the Education Resources Information Center (ERIC) Web site under ERIC document number ED422545.

counselors will be reimbursed for services provided. Addiction counselors who are currently certified with only a high school diploma may have difficulty making the leap to a master's degree. Many addiction counselors may not be able to obtain the advanced education needed fast enough to survive in the market.

In 1993 the Center for Substance Abuse Treatment (CSAT) created the Addiction Technology Transfer Center (ATTC) Program to foster improvements in the preparation of addiction treatment professionals (Rohrer et al. 1996). As part of the ATTC Program, a National Curriculum Committee (the Committee) was established to evaluate existing curricula and to set priorities for current academic programs. At its first meeting, the Committee realized that the field had not defined the knowledge, skills, and attitudes that should be shared by all addiction counselors. Identifying and delineating these competencies became the Committee's first task to professionalize the field.

Representing a range of specialties within the substance abuse treatment field, members of the Committee provided practice-related information through a brainstorming process. Once the general responsibilities of the field were identified, the Committee developed task statements for each. Committee members ordered the responsibilities and task statements in a learning sequence, based on the order in which responsibilities are generally performed on the job. The process of identifying responsibilities was considered complete when the Committee reached consensus regarding the accuracy and sequence of the task statements produced. The Committee identified four transdisciplinary foundations and eight practice dimensions encompassing 121 competencies. These results are consistent with the DACUM (Develop a Curriculum) process (Norton 1985), which typically results in 8 to 12 responsibilities and 50 to 200 tasks. The four transdisciplinary foundation categories were understanding addiction, treatment knowledge, application to practice, and professional readiness. The eight practice dimension categories were clinical evaluation; treatment planning; referral; case management; counseling; client, family, and community education; documentation; and professional and ethical responsibilities. Each category had between 3 and 20 competencies in it. This effort resulted in the publication of *Addiction Counselor Competencies* (Addiction Technology Transfer Centers 1995).

Although the Committee incorporated existing literature related to the work of addiction counselors, particularly the practice analysis conducted by Birch and Davis Corporation (1986) and the International Certification and Reciprocity Consortium Role Delineation Study (International Certification and Reciprocity Commission/Alcohol and Other Drug Abuse 1991) when developing the competencies that made up *Addiction Counselor Competencies*, it also relied on its own contributions. The Committee felt that job-related data provided a snapshot of what is, not what could be. And in the addiction counseling field, *what is* has been questioned. Because of its peer counselor and personal experience history, treatment provided by some addiction counselors has been described as narrow and inflexible, impeding the adoption of new treatment methods that may better meet the needs of clients. Moreover, lacking traditional academic preparation, some counselors have difficulty understanding literature and incorporating new research results. Consequently, the Committee's work emphasized moving the field forward. To gauge the potential value of the competencies, the Committee conducted a study to determine which of 121 competencies were perceived as necessary for practice by addiction counselors in the field.

Method

The purposes of this study were the following:

- Validate a set of 121 competencies for the profession of addiction counseling
- Determine gaps between actual and needed competencies displayed by entry-level counselors
- Determine congruence among the perceptions of three practitioner groups.

The study was conducted in partnership with the ATTCs, CSAT, and the Northwest Regional Educational Laboratory (Adams & Gallon 1997).

A survey was conducted in 16 States and Puerto Rico from November 1996 to January 1997. The survey instrument was distributed through the ATTCs to State-approved substance abuse treatment agencies. State authorities worked with ATTCs to select qualified treatment sites, distribute the surveys with appropriate cover letters from the State authority, and implement followup strategies to ensure an adequate return rate.

A random sample of 60 State-approved treatment facilities was selected in each participating State. For States with fewer than 60 qualifying facilities, all State-approved treatment facilities were included in the study, if the facilities were large enough to have a separate clinical supervisor who was not also an administrator in the facility.

Each treatment agency director was sent a cover letter and instructions, three copies of the 16-page survey listing 121 competencies, and corresponding postage-paid return envelopes. Directors were asked to distribute the surveys to a *clinical supervisor, a least experienced counselor,* and a *most proficient counselor.* "Least experienced" was defined as nonsupervisory, direct-care counselors having no more than 3 years of paid experience as an addiction treatment professional. Each respondent rated the level of proficiency "typically demonstrated" by entry-level counselors at the time of hire, as well as the level of competency "needed" at the time of hire. Each respondent was instructed to provide a rating for each item on a five-point scale, ranging from 1 ("very little to no knowledge/skill/attitude") to 5 ("excellent knowledge/skill/attitude"). Beginning 1 week following the due date of the responses, telephone calls were placed with nonresponding agencies, encouraging them to submit finished surveys. Final response rates varied by State, ranging from 25 percent in North Carolina to 82 percent in Maryland; the response rate nationally was 46 percent. The total number of respondents was 1,238.

Results

Demographics. (See exhibits 1–6.) Respondents included 369 least experienced counselors, 412 most proficient counselors, and 457 clinical supervisors (N=1,238). Females outnumbered males in all respondent groups. The sample was mostly middle-aged, and age increased with level of experience. Seventy-five percent of the respondents were Caucasian, 14 percent African American, 7 percent Hispanic, and 4 percent filled other minority categories or were undeclared.

The respondents were well educated with 74 percent reporting bachelor's or master's degrees. As expected, clinical supervisors reported the greatest number of graduate degrees. Clinical supervisors and most experienced counselors reported the longest employment in the field (i.e., more than 5 years). Although "least experienced" was defined as no more than 3 years' paid

Exhibit 1. Gender*

Gender	Supervisor	Most Proficient	Least Experienced	Total
Male	198	153	130	481
Female	259	259	239	757
TOTAL	457	412	369	1,238

Exhibit 2. Age*

Age	Supervisor	Most Proficient	Least Experienced	Total
<21	0	0	1	1
21–29	19	30	72	121
30–39	104	112	106	322
40–49	194	169	118	481
50–59	115	79	53	247
60+	17	18	15	50
TOTAL	449	408	365	1,222

Exhibit 3. Race/Ethnicity*

Race/Ethnicity	Supervisor	Most Proficient	Least Experienced	Total
African American	60	56	57	173
Hispanic	28	32	31	91
White	345	305	262	912
Native American	5	8	5	18
Asian/Pacific Islander	3	1	2	6
Other	7	1	1	9
Undeclared	5	5	4	14
TOTAL	453	408	362	1,223

Exhibit 4. Education*

Education	Supervisor	Most Proficient	Least Experienced	Total
GRE/high school diploma	9	6	13	28
Some college or technical/trade school	50	65	70	185
Associate's degree	23	49	37	109
Bachelor's degree	112	130	135	377
Graduate degree (master's level and above)	257	161	110	528
TOTAL	451	411	365	1,227

Exhibit 5. Period of Employment in the Addictions Profession*

Employment History	Supervisor	Most Proficient	Least Experienced	Total
Less than 6 months	4	10	30	44
6 months to 18 months	13	17	78	108
19 months to 3 years	20	31	68	119
3 to 5 years	49	67	69	185
5 to 10 years	113	159	80	352
More than 10 years	251	126	40	417
TOTAL	450	410	365	1,225

Exhibit 6. Addictions Certification*

Certificate Status	Supervisor	Most Proficient	Least Experienced	Total
Certified	308	264	156	728
Not certified	144	141	209	494
TOTAL	452	405	365	1,222

*Adams and Gallon 1997.

experience, many "least experienced" counselors reported more than 3 years of employment in the addiction profession. This may be the result of a mistaken inclusion of other experiences in the field such as volunteer service, internships, or personal treatment and recovery. The least experienced counselors had the smallest proportion certified, whereas clinical supervisors had the highest proportion certified.

Data reduction procedures. Given the huge number of possible cross-tabulations with a survey this size, results have been summarized in three different ways. First, because the purpose of the study was to identify "essential" competencies, survey responses were collapsed into percentages of respondents rating each item "4" or "5" ("good" or "excellent"). Excluding the "moderate" ratings provides a more stringent standard for judging the content validity of the competencies. Second, results were provided for the national sample only. Third, responses were summarized across individual competencies within the 12 competency categories.

Validation of the 121 competencies. Internal consistency of the survey was high: Cronbach's Alpha for the 12 sections of the survey ranged from 0.91 to 0.98. Among the clinical supervisors, 40 percent of respondents indicated that entering practitioners needed to be "good" or "excellent" in *all* 121 competencies; 60 percent gave these ratings for 118 of the 121 competencies; and 70 percent gave these ratings for 107 of the 121 competencies. Clearly, the surveyed competencies had high content validity for these experienced practitioners.

Gaps between actual and needed competencies. Large differences were found between perceived *needed* and *actual* proficiency, across all three respondent groups. As exhibit 7 indicates, the gap was most pronounced among clinical supervisors. For all but 1 of the 121 items, less than half the supervisors rated actual proficiencies as "good" or "excellent." Exhibit 8 displays the percentage gaps for each of the 12 categories, as reported by clinical supervisors only. Gaps between actual and needed proficiencies are evident across categories, ranging from a 44-percent gap for the "Referral" category to a 54-percent gap for the "Counseling" category. Just as the perceived need for counselor competencies was consistently high, the perceived level of *actual* competencies was consistently low.

Congruence among perceptions of counselor groups. As exhibit 7 indicates, although the three counselor groups are consistent with one another in their ratings of need, they differ consistently in their ratings of actual proficiency. In each category the lowest ratings were given by supervisors, followed by "most proficient" and then "least experienced" counselors. Differences between supervisors and least experienced counselors were lowest in the "Treatment Planning" category and greatest—not surprisingly—in the "Professional Readiness" category.

Competency subsets. Ratings of some subsets of the competencies indicate a need for further study. For example, supervisors and counselors seemed to undervalue competencies related to research and treatment outcome assessment. The Committee included these competencies because it felt that the counselors' abilities to assess and monitor outcomes and apply research findings to their own practices were important and would contribute to the professionalization of the field.

In sum, this survey revealed large and consistent gaps between actual and needed competencies across all categories, with clinical supervisors perceiving the largest differences.

Addiction Counseling Competencies

EXHIBIT 7. RATINGS OF ACTUAL VS. NEEDED PROFICIENCY*

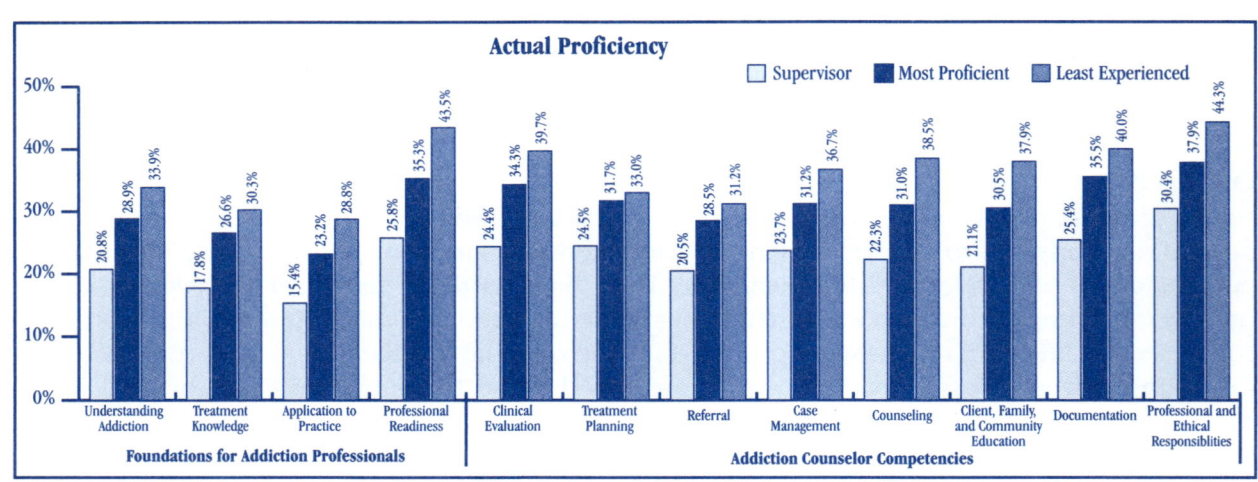

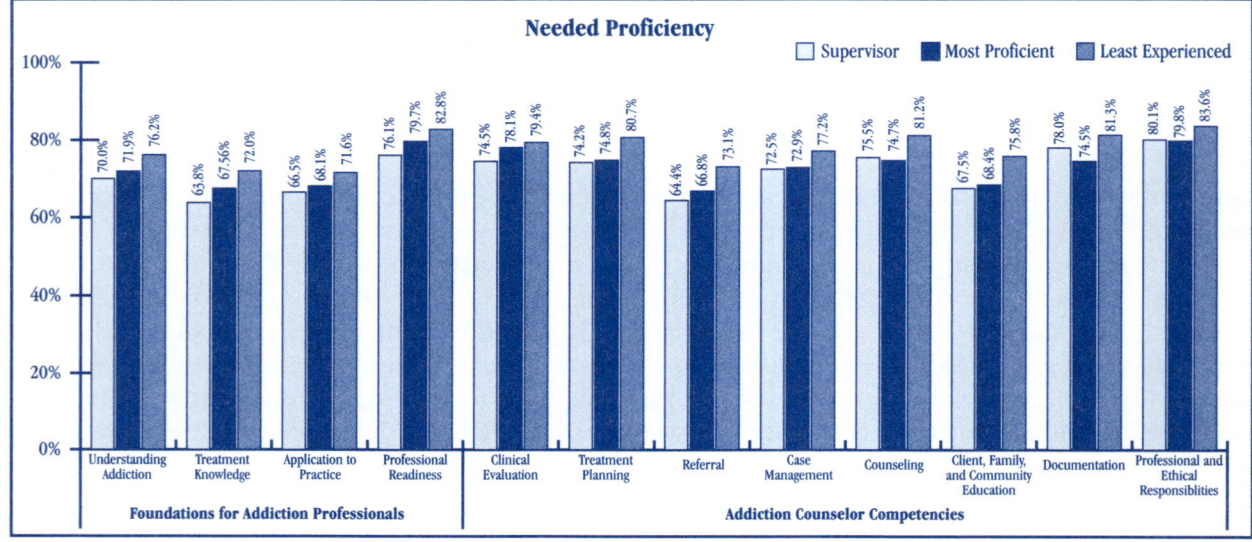

*Adams and Gallon 1997.

EXHIBIT 8. PERCENTAGE GAP BETWEEN ACTUAL AND NEEDED LEVEL AS PERCEIVED BY SUPERVISORS*

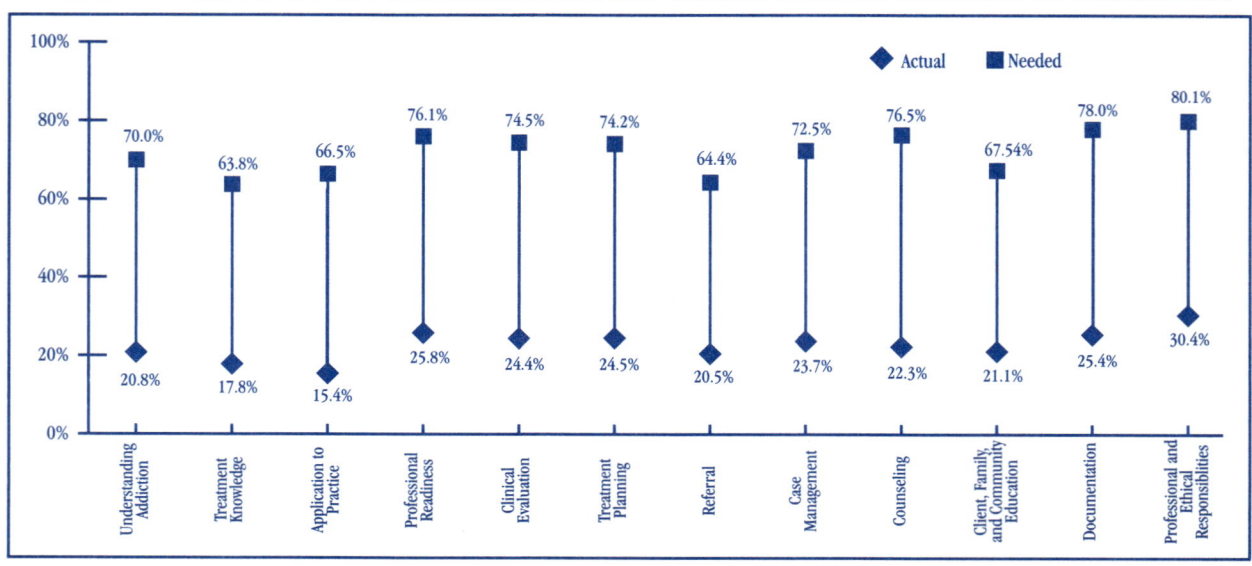

*Adams and Gallon 1997.

Discussion

Clinical supervisors, entry-level counselors, and most proficient counselors endorsed almost all 121 competencies as important. However, the responses of each professional group also show relatively little discrimination among items and categories, which may account for the high Alpha coefficients. Given the large number of items in the survey, this level of consistency could indicate a substantial halo effect: that is, respondents could have been answering individual items on the basis of an overall impression and not making fine discriminations among the individual competencies.

The results also indicate large gaps between what is needed and observed in proficiency for entry-level counselors, even among entry-level counselors themselves. Supervisors noted the greatest gaps, followed by the most proficient and entry-level counselors. Although the least experienced counselors reported the smallest gaps, the gaps were still substantial, indicating that what counselors know they *need* to do the job and what they *can do* are two different things.

What accounts for supervisors' ratings of entry-level proficiency being more critical than the other respondent groups? One possibility is a contrast effect. That is, supervisors may be using their own level of expertise as the standard for comparison resulting in unrealistically high expectations for entry-level counselors. In this instance, counselors with average proficiency would receive lower ratings against the supervisors' higher standard representing significantly more experience.

As a content validation strategy, the survey has limited value. Respondents were given 121 statements to respond to, and little discrimination among the items was observed. However, all the competencies were perceived to be important, and the preparation for each was always reported as inadequate. Respondents appeared to address the list as a whole, rather than the individual competencies. Those who would embark on curricular change should do the same. That is, formal preparation for addiction counselors cannot just be bolstered here and there; it needs to be comprehensively redesigned.

The main benefit of the survey results may be as a catalyst for curricular change. This has already proven to be the case. While the survey was being conducted, the Committee was already working on an expanded document that listed the knowledge, skills, and attitudes for each of the 121 competencies. Feedback from the field was obtained on the draft document. Then the International Certification and Reciprocity Consortium (ICRC) convened a national leadership group to assess the need for model addiction counselor training. After careful deliberation, the group concluded that much of the work to define such a curriculum standard had already been accomplished by the Committee and the ICRC in the Committee's *Addiction Counselor Competencies* and the ICRC's 1996 *Role Delineation Study*, respectively.

Soon after, CSAT agreed to fund a collaborative effort to finalize a document that could be used as a national standard. CSAT convened a panel—The National Steering Committee for Addiction Counseling Standards (NSC)—that comprised representatives from five national educational, certification, and professional associations. The NSC was successful in achieving unanimous endorsement of the *Addiction Counselor Competencies*—a milestone in the addiction counseling field. In 1998 CSAT published the results of this groundbreaking work as TAP 21: *Addiction Counseling Competencies: The Knowledge, Skills, and Attitudes of Professional Practice*.

The significance of TAP 21 for addiction counseling was that it provided a single frame of reference for curriculum development, student advising, professional development, and clinical supervision. The current updated edition of TAP 21 continues the work of furthering the professionalization of the addiction counseling field.

Conclusions

Although this is a study of perceptions and professional judgment and further inquiry is needed into the reasons for the discrepancies, these results suggest that clinical supervisors are getting far less than they need in entry-level counselors. More systematic discussions between clinical practitioners and faculty of training programs in addiction counseling should produce a redefinition of curricular goals based on the competencies described in this document.

Addiction counseling is a profession in the making. Rather than maintaining its professional culture by relying on tradition, addiction counseling is building its identity from the ground up, by first identifying competencies all addiction counselors are expected to possess. Such an approach addresses directly the "education–practice discontinuity" cited by Cavanaugh (1993) as one of the most critical problems in professional education.

References

Adams, R.J., & Gallon, S.L. (1997). *Entry Level Addiction Counselor Competency Survey: National Results*. Portland, OR: Northwest Regional Educational Laboratory.

Addiction Technology Transfer Centers, National Curriculum Committee (1995). *Addiction Counselor Competencies*. Rockville, MD: Center for Substance Abuse Treatment.

Birch and Davis Corporation (1986). *Development of Model Professional Standards for Counselor Credentialing*. Dubuque, IA: Kendall/Hunt Publishing.

Cavanaugh, S.H. (1993). Connecting education and practice. In L. Curry & J.F. Wergin (Eds.) *Educating Professionals*. San Francisco: Jossey-Bass.

Deitch, D.A., & Carleton, S.A. (1997). Education and training of clinical personnel. In J.H. Lowinson, P. Ruiz, et al. (Eds.) *Substance Abuse: A Comprehensive Textbook*. Baltimore, MD: William & Wilkins.

Fisher, G. (September 1997). Training Issues for Addiction Counselors and Other Helping Professions. Paper presented at the meeting of the Mid-Atlantic Addiction Educator's Conference, Williamsburg, VA.

International Certification and Reciprocity Consortium/Alcohol and Other Drug Abuse (1991). *Role Delineation Study for Alcohol and Other Drug Abuse Counselors*. Raleigh, NC: National Certification Reciprocity Consortium/Alcohol and Other Drug Abuse.

Norton, R.E. (1985). *DACUM Handbook*. Columbus, OH: Ohio State University National Center for Research in Vocational Education.

Rohrer, S.R., Diesenhaus, D.I., et al. (1996). Addiction Technology Transfer Centers (ATTCs). *Substance Abuse*, 4:193-199.

Appendix D – Complete Bibliography

Purposes

This updated version of *The Competencies* includes bibliographies for each of the four transdisciplinary foundations and the eight practice dimensions. Bibliographies appear at the end of each section and are combined into a complete, alphabetized list here.

The Competencies bibliographies serve a number of purposes including the following:

- Serving as a guide to educators in teaching and curriculum development
- Offering assistance to counselors preparing for certification or licensure exams
- Contributing to practitioners' understanding and knowledge of research- and consensus-based practices
- Furnishing clinical supervisors with current reading suggestions for supervisees
- Providing counselors and other practitioners with a study resource
- Supplying administrators with current citations regarding the practice of addiction counseling for use in grant preparation.

Literature Search Methodology

This updated version of *The Competencies* represents the work of two Committees. In 2000, a Committee began revising the 1998 version of *The Competencies*. In 2005, a second Committee was convened to review *The Competencies* and update the 2000 bibliography.

The bibliographies in *The Competencies* do not represent a complete reference list of meaningful addiction counseling-related citations. However, they are the result of a thoughtful and extensive literature review, and they represent the intent and spirit of *The Competencies.*

Both literature searches pointed up gaps in literature for several practice dimensions. A scarcity of citations was especially notable in the documentation; service coordination; client, family, and community education; and referral practice dimensions. Addiction counseling professionals might explore these subjects if they are looking for research and writing agendas.

2000 Methodology

The literature search for the 2000 update was conducted by members of the National Addiction Technology Transfer Center Curriculum Committee for each transdisciplinary foundation and practice dimension. Library facilities at Brown University, the State University of New York at Albany, the University of Iowa, the University of Missouri, and the University of Nevada–Reno were used. Criteria for the searches specified that resources be the following:

- Timely—no citation published before 1989 unless it was deemed seminal
- Empirically sound
- Relevant to a particular practice dimension and its associated knowledge, skills, and attitudes.

The results of the searches were mixed. Some practice dimensions yielded many citations, whereas few relevant citations were found for others. The research methods used also differed from institution to institution. The lack of uniformity in search methodology concerned the Committee. Thus, a professional library association specializing in substance abuse—the Substance Abuse Librarians and Information Specialists (SALIS), which uses specially trained librarians to manage, organize, collect, and distribute substance abuse-related information—was hired.

SALIS was asked to search materials relevant to the eight practice dimensions using the following online databases:

- Medline
- Psych Info
- ETOH
- ERIC (U.S. Department of Education)
- SALIS's library catalog databases (ADAI Library in Seattle, Washington; Wisconsin Clearinghouse Library in Madison, Wisconsin; and Alcohol Research Group in Berkeley, California).

Keywords were used to find other relevant terms and articles. Review articles were gleaned for items not found with online databases, such as chapters from edited works and government documents.

Because large numbers of citations were retrieved for a majority of the practice dimensions, SALIS conducted an initial screening of articles based on topic, major researchers, descriptions in abstracts, and source documents. Because entire books are rarely found through online database literature searches, tables of contents for appropriate books were included from citations found on SALIS catalog databases.

When SALIS completed the search, it provided the Committee with a list of citations and articles for each practice dimension. Committee members then reviewed the results of the SALIS literature search. Each article received an independent review by two Committee members based on whether it met the following criteria:

- Relevance to the practice dimension being reviewed
- Relevance to another practice dimension or transdisciplinary foundation
- Empirically or evidence based
- Based on clinical practice
- Contribution to further understanding of the practice dimension or transdisciplinary foundation
- Published between 1989 and 2000, unless considered exemplary or a "classic."

After critiquing both the SALIS-generated articles and articles from the Committee's initial search, the Committee cross-referenced the results of each article's evaluation. An article was selected for inclusion only if two Committee members agreed that it correctly represented the intent of a given practice dimension. When consensus was not reached between the primary reviewers, a third Committee member reviewed the article. Articles were considered for inclusion only if a third review was positive. Articles found to be irrelevant to the practice dimensions or those that did not meet the established criteria were excluded from the bibliography.

Appendix D – Complete Bibliography

2005 Methodology

The literature search for the 2005 update was conducted by the Center for Substance Abuse Research (CESAR). The literature search was for each of the four transdisciplinary foundations and each of the eight practice dimensions. It covered literature from 2000 to 2005. The literature search used the same methodology as the search conducted in 2000.

When CESAR completed the search, it provided the Committee with a list of citations and articles for each practice dimension. Committee members also recommended articles that were pertinent to a particular practice dimension. Each article received an independent review by two Committee members based on the following criteria:

- Relevance to the practice dimension being reviewed
- Relevance to another practice dimension or transdisciplinary foundation
- Contribution to further understanding of the practice dimension or transdisciplinary foundation.

The 2005 Committee followed the same methodology as the 2000 Committee in deciding whether to include or exclude articles from the practice dimension bibliographies. Group consensus focusing on creating a balanced representation of the available literature was used to determine whether to include or exclude books for the transdisciplinary foundation bibliographies. Articles and books selected by the 2005 update Committee were added to the bibliographies created by the 2000 update Committee.

Bibliography

Ackerman, S.J., & Hilsenroth, M.J. (2003). A review of therapist characteristics and techniques positively impacting the therapeutic alliance. *Clinical Psychology Review*, 23(1):1-33.

Adams, N., & Grieder, D.M. (2005). *Treatment Planning for Person-Centered Care: The Road to Mental Health and Addiction Recovery*. Burlington, MA: Elsevier Academic Press.

Adesso, V.J., Cisler, R.A., et al. (2004). Substance abuse. In M. Hersen (Ed.) *Psychological Assessment in Clinical Practice: A Pragmatic Guide*. New York: Brunner-Routledge, 147-173.

Akers, R.L. (1992). *Drugs, Alcohol, and Society: Social Structure, Process, and Policy*. Monterey, CA: Brooks/Cole.

Albanese, M., & Khantzian, E. (2001). The difficult-to-treat patient with substance abuse. In M.J. Dewan & R.W. Pies (Eds.) *The Difficult-to-Treat Psychiatric Patient*. Arlington, VA: American Psychiatric Publishing, Inc., 273-298.

Albery, I.P., Heuston, J., et al. (2003). Measuring therapeutic attitude among drug workers. *Addictive Behaviors*, 28(5):995-1005.

Allen, J.P., & Litten, R.Z. (1998). Screening instruments and biochemical screening tests. In A.W. Graham, T.K. Schultz, & B.B. Wilford (Eds.) *Principles of Addiction Medicine* (2nd ed.). Chevy Chase, MD: American Society of Addiction Medicine, 263-271.

Allen, J.P., & Mattson, M.E. (1993). Psychometric instruments to assist in alcoholism treatment planning. *Journal of Substance Abuse Treatment*, 10(3):289-296.

American Counseling Association (ACA) (2005). *ACA Code of Ethics*. Alexandria, VA: ACA.

American Methadone Treatment Association (AMTA) (1997). AMTA ethical canon for programs and individuals providing methadone treatment. *Journal of Maintenance in the Addictions*, 1(1):133.

American Psychiatric Association (1994). *Diagnostic and Statistical Manual of Mental Disorders* (4th ed.). Washington, DC: American Psychiatric Press.

American Psychological Association (APA) (2002). *Ethical Principles of Psychologists and Code of Conduct*. Washington, DC: APA.

Amodeo, M., & Robb, N. (1997). Modifying methods and content to teach about alcohol and drug abuse cross-culturally. *Substance Abuse*, 18(1):1-12.

Anderson, A.J. (1999). Comparative impact evaluation of two therapeutic programs for mentally ill chemical abusers. *International Journal of Psychosocial Rehabilitation*, 4:11-26.

Anderson, D. (1992). Case standards for counseling practice. *Journal of Counseling and Development*, 71(September/October):22-26.

Annis, H.M., Sobell, L.C., et al. (1996). Drinking-related assessment instruments: Cross-cultural studies. *Substance Use & Misuse*, 31(11&12):1525-1546.

Anton, R.F., Litten, R.Z., & Allen, J.P. (1995). Biological assessment of alcohol consumption. In J.P. Allen & M. Columbus (Eds.) *Assessing Alcohol Problems: A Guide for Clinicians and Researchers*. NIAAA Treatment Handbook Series, No. 4. Bethesda, MD: National Institute on Alcohol Abuse and Alcoholism, 31-39.

Appelbaum, P.S., & Gutheil, T.G. (1982). Clinical aspects of treatment refusal. *Comprehensive Psychiatry*, 23(6):560-566.

Argeriou, M., & Daley, M. (1998). An examination of racial and ethnic differences within a sample of Hispanic, White (non-Hispanic), and African American Medicaid-eligible pregnant substance abusers: The MOTHERS Project. *Journal of Substance Abuse Treatment*, 14(5):489-498.

Armstrong, T.D., & Costello, E.J. (2002). Community studies on adolescent substance use, abuse or dependence and psychiatric comorbidity. *Journal of Consulting and Clinical Psychology*, 70(6):1224-1239.

Atkinson, D.R., Morten, G., & Sue, D.W. (1997). *Counseling American Minorities*. New York: McGraw-Hill.

Atkinson, R.M., & Misra, S. (2002). Further strategies in the treatment of aging alcoholics. In A.M. Gurnack, R. Atkinson, & N.J. Osgood (Eds.) *Treating Alcohol and Drug Abuse in the Elderly*. New York: Springer Publishing, 131-151.

Babor, T.F. (2003). *Treatment Matching in Alcoholism*. New York: Cambridge University Press.

Badding, N.C. (1989). Client involvement in case recording: Social casework. *Journal of Contemporary Social Work*, (November):539-548.

Baer, J.S., Marlatt, G.A., & McMahon, R.J. (Eds.) (1993). *Addictive Behaviors Across the Life Span*. Newbury Park, CA: Sage Publications.

Bahr, S.J., & Hawks, R.D. (1993). Family and religious influences on adolescent substance abuse. *Youth & Society*, 24(4):443-465.

Ball, S., Bachrach, K., et al. (2002). Characteristics, beliefs, and practices of community clinicians trained to provide manual-guided therapy for substance abusers. *Journal of Substance Abuse Treatment*, 23(4):309-318.

Ball, S.A., & Kosten, T.A. (1998). Diagnostic classification systems. In A.W. Graham, T.K. Schultz, & B.B. Wilford (Eds.) *Principles of Addiction Medicine* (2nd ed.). Chevy Chase, MD: American Society of Addiction Medicine, 279-290.

Barber, J.P., Luborsky, L., et al. (1999). Therapeutic alliance as a predictor of outcome in treatment of cocaine dependence. *Psychotherapy Research*, 9(1):54-73.

Barber, J.P., Luborsky, L., et al. (2001). Therapeutic alliance as a predictor of outcome in retention in the National Institute on Drug Abuse collaborative cocaine treatment study. *Journal of Consulting and Clinical Psychology*, 69(1):119-124.

Barker, S.B., Kerns, L.L., & Schnoll, S.H. (1996). Assessment of medical history, health status, intoxication, and withdrawal. In B.J. Rounsaville, F.M. Tims, et al. (Eds.) *Diagnostic Source Book on Drug Abuse Research and Treatment*. Rockville, MD: National Institute on Drug Abuse, 35-48.

Appendix D – Complete Bibliography

Battjes, R.J., Michael, S., et al. (2004). Evaluation of a group-based substance abuse treatment program for adolescents. *Journal of Substance Abuse Treatment*, 27(2):123-134.

Beauvais, F., Jumper-Thurman, P., et al. (2002). A survey of attitudes among drug user treatment providers toward the treatment of inhalant users. *Substance Use & Misuse*, 37(11):1391-1410.

Bell, A., & Rollnick, S. (1996). Motivational interviewing in practice: A structured approach. In F. Rotgers, D. Keller, & J. Morgenstern (Eds.) *Treating Substance Abuse: Theory and Technique*. New York: Guilford Press, 266-285.

Bell, P. (2002). *Chemical Dependency and the African American: Counseling and Prevention Strategies* (2nd ed.). Center City, MN: Hazelden.

Bennett, L.A., Reiss, D., et al. (1987). *The Alcoholic Family*. New York: Basic Books.

Benshoff, J.J., & Janikowski, T.P. (2000). *The Rehabilitation Model of Substance Abuse Counseling*. Pacific Grove, CA: Brooks/Cole.

Bepko, C. (Ed.) (1992). *Feminism and Addiction*. New York: Haworth Press.

Berg, I.K., & Miller, S.D. (1992). *Working With the Problem Drinker: A Solution-Focused Approach*. New York: W.W. Norton.

Bernard, J.M., & Goodyear, R.K. (2003). *Fundamentals of Clinical Supervision* (3rd ed.). Boston: Allyn & Bacon.

Bishop, F.M. (2001). *Managing Addictions: Cognitive, Emotive, and Behavioral Techniques*. Northvale, NJ: Jason Aronson.

Bissell, L., & Royce, J.E. (1994). *Ethics for Addiction Professionals* (2nd ed.). Center City, MN: Hazelden.

Black, C., Paz, H., & DeBlassie, R.R. (1991). Counseling the Hispanic male adolescent. *Adolescence*, 26:223-232.

Blevins, G.A., Dana, R.Q., & Lewis, J.A. (1994). *Substance Abuse Counseling: An Individual Approach* (2nd ed.). Pacific Grove, CA: Brooks/Cole.

Blume, S. (1977). Role of the recovered alcoholic in the treatment of alcoholism. In B. Kissin & H. Begliester (Eds.) *The Biology of Alcoholism, Volume 5: Treatment and Rehabilitation of the Chronic Alcoholic*. New York: Plenum Press, 545-565.

Bois, C., & Graham, K. (1997). Case management. In S. Harrison & V. Carver (Eds.) *Alcohol and Drug Problems: A Practical Guide for Counselors* (2nd ed.). Toronto, Canada: Addiction Research Foundation, 61-76.

Bokos, P.J., Mejta, C.L., et al. (1993). A case management model for intravenous drug users. In J.A. Inciardi, R.M. Tims, & B.W. Fletcher (Eds.) *Innovative Approaches in the Treatment of Drug Abuse—Program Models and Strategies*. Westport, CT: Greenwood Press, 87-96.

Bond, J., Kaskutas, L., & Weisner, C. (2003). The persistent influence of social networks and Alcoholics Anonymous on abstinence. *Journal of Studies on Alcohol*, 64(4):579-88.

Boren, J.J., Onken, L.S., et al. (2000). *Approaches to Drug Abuse Counseling*. Rockville, MD: National Institute on Drug Abuse.

Borkman, T.J. (1998). Is recovery planning any different from treatment planning? *Journal of Substance Abuse Treatment*, 15(1):37-42.

Boyle, M.G., White, W.L., et al. *Behavioral Health Recovery Management: A Statement of Principles*. Behavioral Health Recovery Management Project. Peoria, IL: Fayette Companies; Bloomington, IL: Chestnut Health Systems.

Bradley, K.A., Boyd-Wickizer, B.A., et al. (1998). Alcohol screening questionnaires in women: A critical review. *JAMA*, 280(2):166-171.

Brindis, C., Pfeffer, R., & Wolfe, A. (1995). A case management program for chemically dependent clients with multiple needs. *Journal of Case Management*, 4:22-28.

Brindis, C.D., & Theidon, K.S. (1997). The role of case management in substance abuse treatment services for women and their children. *Journal of Psychoactive Drugs*, 29:79-88.

Brook, D.W., & Spitz, H.I. (Eds.) (2002). *The Group Therapy of Substance Abuse*. New York: Haworth Press.

Brook, J.S., & Brook, D.W. (1996). Risk and protective factors for drug use. In C.B. McCoy, L.R. Metsch, & J.A. Inciardi (Eds.) *Intervening With Drug-Involved Youth*. Thousand Oaks, CA: Sage Publications, 23-44.

Brooks, M.K. (1997). Ethical and legal aspects of confidentiality. In J.H. Lowinson, P. Ruiz, et al. (Eds.) *Substance Abuse: A Comprehensive Textbook* (3rd ed.). Baltimore: Lippincott Williams & Wilkins, 884-899.

Broome, K.M., Joe, G.W., et al. (2001). Engagement models for adolescents in DATOS-A. *Journal of Adolescent Research*, 16(6):608-623.

Broome, M., Simpson, D.D., & Joe, G.W. (2002). The role of social support following short-term inpatient treatment. *Journal on Addictions*, 11(1):57-65.

Brown, A.H., Grella, C.E., & Cooper, L. (2002). Living it or learning it: Attitudes and beliefs about experience and expertise in treatment for the dually diagnosed. *Contemporary Drug Problems*, 29(4):687-710.

Brown, E.D., Maisto, S.A., & Boies-Hickman, K. (1997). Education. In E.D. Brown, T.J. O'Farrell, et al. (Eds.) *Substance Abuse Program Accreditation Guide*. Thousand Oaks, CA: Sage Publications, 71-76.

Brown, E.D., Maisto, S.A., & Boies-Hickman, K. (1997). Patient rights and responsibilities and organizational ethics. In E.D. Brown, T.J. O'Farrell, et al. (Eds.) *Substance Abuse Program Accreditation Guide*. Thousand Oaks, CA: Sage Publications, 3-11.

Brown, E.D., O'Farrell, T.J., et al. (1997). *Substance Abuse Program Accreditation Guide*. Thousand Oaks, CA: Sage Publications.

Brown, S. (Ed.) (1995). *Treating Alcoholism*. San Francisco: Jossey-Bass.

Brown, S., & Lewis, V. (1999). *The Alcoholic Family in Recovery: A Developmental Model*. New York: Guilford Press.

Brown, T.G., Seraganian, P., et al. (2002). Matching substance abuse aftercare treatment to client characteristics. *Addictive Behavior*, 27(4):585-604.

Cacciola, J.S., Koppenhaver, J.M., et al. (1999). Test-retest reliability of the lifetime items on the Addiction Severity Index. *Psychological Assessment*, 11(1):86-93.

Campbell, T.C., Catlin, L.A., & Melchert, T.P. (2003). Alcohol and other drug abuse counselors' attitudes and resources for integrating research and practice. *Journal of Drug Education*, 33(3):307-323.

Caplehorn, J.R., Lumley, T.S., & Irwig, L. (1998). Staff attitudes and retention of patients in methadone maintenance programs. *Drug and Alcohol Dependence*, 52(1):57-61.

Carey, K.B. (2002). Clinically useful assessments: Substance use and comorbid psychiatric disorders. *Behaviour Research & Therapy*, 40:1345.

Carey, K.B., & Correia, C.J. (1998). Severe mental illness and addictions: Assessment considerations. *Addictive Behaviors*, 23(6):735-748.

Carise, D., Gurel, O., et al. (2005). Getting patients the services they need using a computer-assisted system for patient assessment and referral—CASPAR. *Drug and Alcohol Dependence*, 80(2):177-189.

Carone, S.S., & LaFleur, N.K. (2000). The effect of adolescent sex offender abuse history on counselor attitudes. *Journal of Addictions and Offender Counseling*, 20(2):56-63.

Carroll, K.M. (1999). Behavioral and cognitive behavioral treatments. In B.S. McCrady & E.E. Epstein (Eds.) *Addictions: A Comprehensive Guidebook*. New York: Oxford University Press, 250-267.

Carroll, K.M., Libby, B., et al. (2001). Motivational interviewing to enhance treatment initiation in substance abusers: An effectiveness study. *American Journal on Addictions*, 10:335-339.

Carroll, K.M., & Rounsaville, B.J. (2002). On beyond urine: Clinically useful assessment instruments in the treatment of drug dependence. *Behaviour Research & Therapy*, 40:1329.

Cavacuiti, C.A. (2004). You, me, and drugs, a love triangle: Important considerations when both members of a couple are abusing substances. *Substance Use & Misuse*, 39(4):645-656.

Appendix D – Complete Bibliography

Cavanaugh, E.R., Ginzburg, H.M., et al. (1989). *Drug Abuse Treatment: A National Study of Effectiveness*. Chapel Hill, NC: University of North Carolina Press.

Center for Substance Abuse Prevention (1993). *Maternal Substance Use Assessment Methods Reference Manual: A Review of Screening and Clinical Assessment Instruments for Examining Maternal Use of Alcohol, Tobacco and Other Drugs*. CSAP Special Report 13. Rockville, MD: Substance Abuse and Mental Health Services Administration.

Center for Substance Abuse Prevention (1997). *Technical Assistance Bulletin: Communicating Appropriately With Asian and Pacific Islander Audiences*. Rockville, MD: Substance Abuse and Mental Health Services Administration.

Center for Substance Abuse Prevention (1997). *Technical Assistance Bulletin: Developing Effective Messages and Materials for Hispanic/Latino Audiences*. Rockville, MD: Substance Abuse and Mental Health Services Administration.

Center for Substance Abuse Prevention (1998). *Technical Assistance Bulletin: Communicating With 9- to 14-Year-Old Girls*. Rockville, MD: Substance Abuse and Mental Health Services Administration.

Center for Substance Abuse Prevention (1999). *Understanding Substance Abuse Prevention— Toward the 21st Century: A Primer on Effective Programs*. DHHS Publication No. (SMA) 99-3301. Rockville, MD: Substance Abuse and Mental Health Services Administration.

Center for Substance Abuse Treatment (1998). *Comprehensive Case Management for Substance Abuse Treatment*. Treatment Improvement Protocol (TIP) Series 27. DHHS Publication No. (SMA) 98-3222. Rockville, MD: Substance Abuse and Mental Health Services Administration.

Center for Substance Abuse Treatment (2004). *Substance Abuse Treatment and Family Therapy*. Treatment Improvement Protocol (TIP) Series 39. DHHS Publication No. (SMA) 04-3957. Rockville, MD: Substance Abuse and Mental Health Services Administration.

Center for Substance Abuse Treatment (2006). *Substance Abuse: Administrative Issues in Outpatient Treatment*. Treatment Improvement Protocol (TIP) Series 46. DHHS Publication No. (SMA) 06-4151. Rockville, MD: Substance Abuse and Mental Health Services Administration.

Center for Substance Abuse Treatment (2006). *Substance Abuse: Clinical Issues in Intensive Outpatient Treatment*. Treatment Improvement Protocol (TIP) Series 47. DHHS Publication No. (SMA) 06-4182. Rockville, MD: Substance Abuse and Mental Health Services Administration.

Center for Substance Abuse Treatment (2007). *Competencies for Substance Abuse Treatment Clinical Supervisors*. Technical Assistance Publication (TAP) Series 21-A. Rockville, MD: Substance Abuse and Mental Health Services Administration.

Center for Substance Abuse Treatment (forthcoming). *Improving Cultural Competence in Substance Abuse Treatment*. Treatment Improvement Protocol (TIP) Series. Rockville, MD: Substance Abuse and Mental Health Services Administration.

Chan, J.G. (2003). An examination of family-involved approaches to alcoholism treatment. *Family Journal: Counseling & Therapy for Couples & Families*, 11(2):129-138.

Cheng, Z. (2002). Issues to consider when counseling gay people with alcohol dependency. *Journal of Applied Rehabilitation Counseling*, 33(3):10-17.

Cherpital, C.J. (1998). Differences in performance of screening instruments for problem drinking among Blacks, Whites, and Hispanics in an emergency room population. *Journal of Studies on Alcohol*, July:420-426.

Chiauzzi, E.J. (1991). *Preventing Relapse in the Addictions: A Biopsychosocial Approach*. New York: Pergamon.

Clemens, N.A. (2001). Documenting psychotherapy: Getting help on HIPAA. *Journal of Psychiatric Practice*, 7(2):138-140.

Clemens, N.A. (2004). Documentation: The doctor's dilemma. *Journal of Psychiatric Practice*, 10(1):64-67.

Cloud, W., & Granfield, R. (2001). Natural recovery from substance dependency: Lessons for treatment providers. *Journal of Social Work Practice in the Addictions*, 1(1):83-104.

Coggans, N., & Watson, J. (1995). Drug education: Approaches, effectiveness and delivery. *Drugs: Education, Prevention and Policy*, 2(3):211-224.

Cohen, W.E., Holstein, M.E., & Inaba, D.S. (1997). *Uppers, Downers, All Arounders: Physical and Mental Effects of Psychoactive Drugs* (3rd ed.). Ashland, OR: CNS Publications.

Collins, R.L., Leonard, K.E., & Searles, J.S. (Eds.) (1990). *Alcohol and the Family: Research and Clinical Perspectives*. New York: Guilford Press.

Committee on Professional Practice and Standards (1993). Recordkeeping guidelines. *American Psychologist*, 48(September):984-986.

Connor, K.R., & Gunther, M.W. (1996). Educational lectures and films in the clinical treatment of alcoholism: A critique. *Substance Use & Misuse*, 31(9):1117-1129.

Connors, G.J. (1995). Screening for alcohol problems. In J.P. Allen & M. Columbus (Eds.) *Assessing Alcohol Problems: A Guide for Clinicians and Researchers*. NIAAA Treatment Handbook Series, No. 4. Bethesda, MD: National Institute on Alcohol Abuse and Alcoholism, 17-29.

Cooney, N.L., Zweben, A., & Fleming, M.F. (2002). Screening for alcohol problems and at-risk drinking in health-care settings. In R.K. Hester & W.R. Miller (Eds.) *Handbook of Alcoholism Treatment Approaches* (3rd ed.). Boston: Allyn & Bacon, 45-60.

Corey, G., Corey, M.S., & Callahan, P. (2000). *Issues and Ethics in the Helping Professions* (5th ed.). Pacific Grove, CA: Brooks/Cole.

Cormack, C., & Carr, A. (2000). Drug abuse. In A. Carr (Ed.) *What Works for Children and Adolescents? A Critical Review of Psychological Interventions With Children, Adolescents and Their Families*. London: Routledge, 155-177.

Coyhis, D., & White, W. (2002). Addiction and recovery in Native America: Lost history, enduring lessons. *Counselor*, 3(5):16-20.

Crevecoeur, D., Finnerty, B., & Rawson, R. (2004). Los Angeles County Evaluation System (LACES): Bringing accountability to alcohol and drug abuse treatment through a collaboration between providers, payers, and researchers. *Journal of Drug Issues*, 32(1): 881-892.

Culbreth, J.R., & Borders, L.D. (1998). Perceptions of the supervisory relationship: A preliminary qualitative study of recovering and nonrecovering substance abuse counselors. *Journal of Substance Abuse Treatment*, 15(4):345-352.

Culbreth, J.R., & Borders, L.D. (1999). Perceptions of the supervisory relationship: Recovering and nonrecovering substance abuse counselors. *Journal of Counseling & Development*, 77(3):330-338.

Curtis, O. (1998). *Chemical Dependency: A Family Affair*. Pacific Grove, CA: Brooks/Cole.

Cushner, K., & Brislin, R.W. (1997). *Improving Intercultural Interactions—Modules for Cross-Cultural Training Programs*. Thousand Oaks, CA: Sage Publications.

Daley, D.C., & Mercer, D. (2002). *Drug Counseling for Cocaine Addiction: The Collaborative Cocaine Treatment Study Model*. Therapy Manuals for Drug Addiction, Manual 4. Rockville, MD: National Institute on Drug Abuse.

Davis, T.D. (2005). Beliefs about confrontation among substance abuse counselors: Are they consistent with the evidence? In C. Hilarski (Ed.) *Addiction, Assessment, and Treatment With Adolescents, Adults, and Families*. Binghamton, NY: Haworth Social Work Practice Press, 1-17.

DeCivita, M., Dobkin, P.L., et al. (2000). A study of barriers to the engagement of significant others in adult addiction treatment. *Journal of Substance Abuse Treatment*, 19(2):135-144.

Deitch, D., & Solit, R. (1993). Training of drug abuse treatment personnel in therapeutic community methodology. *Psychotherapy*, 30(2):305-316.

Delgado, M. (1997). Strengths-based practice with Puerto Rican adolescents: Lessons from a substance abuse prevention project. *Social Work in Education*, 19(2):101-112.

Delgado, M. (Ed.) (1998). *Alcohol Use/Abuse Among Latinos: Issues and Examples of Culturally Competent Services*. New York: Haworth Press.

Delgado, M., Segal, B., & Lopex, R. (Eds.) (1999). *Conducting Drug Abuse Research With Minority Populations: Advances and Issues*. New York: Haworth Press.

Dennis, M., Scott, C.K., & Funk, R. (2003). An experimental evaluation of recovery management checkups (RMC) for people with chronic substance use disorders. *Evaluation and Program Planning*, 26(3):339-352.

Dennis, M.L., Dawud-Noursi, S., et al. (2003). The need for developing and evaluating adolescent treatment models. In S.J. Stevens & H.R. Morral (Eds.) *Adolescent Substance Abuse Treatment in the United States*. New York: Haworth Press, 3-35.

Dennis, M.L., & Stevens, S.J. (2003). Maltreatment issues and outcomes of adolescents enrolled in substance abuse treatment. *Child Maltreatment*, 8(1):3-6.

DiClemente, C.C., Carroll, K.M., et al. (2003). A look inside treatment: Therapist effects, the therapeutic alliance, and the process of intentional behavior change. In T.F. Babor (Ed.) *Treatment Matching in Alcoholism*. New York: Cambridge University Press, 166-183.

DiClemente, C.C., Schlundt, D., et al. (2004). Readiness and stages of change in addiction treatment. *American Journal on Addictions*, 13(2):103-119.

DiClemente, C.C., & Scott, C.W. (1997). Stages of change: Interactions with treatment compliance and involvement. In L.S. Onken, J.D. Blaine, & J.J. Boren (Eds.) *Beyond the Therapeutic Alliance: Keeping the Drug-Dependent Individual in Treatment*. NIDA Research Monograph No. 165. Rockville, MD: National Institute on Drug Abuse, 131-156.

DiNitto, D.M., & Crisp, C. (2002). Addictions and women with major psychiatric disorders. In S.L.A. Straussner & S. Brown (Eds.) *The Handbook of Treatment for Women*. San Francisco: Jossey-Bass, 423-450.

Dodd, M.H. (1997). Social model of recovery: Origin, early features, changes, and future. *Journal of Psychoactive Drugs*, 29(2):133-139.

Dodes, L.M., & Khantzian, E.J. (1998). Individual psychodynamic psychotherapy. In R.J. Frances & S.I. Miller (Eds.) *Clinical Textbook of Addictive Disorders*. New York: Guilford Press, 479-495.

Donigian, J., & Malnati, R. (1996). *Systemic Group Therapy: A Triadic Model*. Pacific Grove, CA: Brooks/Cole.

Donovan, D.M. (1995). Assessments to aid in the treatment planning process. In J.P. Allen & M. Columbus (Eds.) *Assessing Alcohol Problems: A Guide for Clinicians and Researchers*. NIAAA Treatment Handbook Series 4. Bethesda, MD: National Institute on Alcohol Abuse and Alcoholism, 75-122.

Donovan, D.M. (1999). Assessment strategies and measures in addictive behaviors. In B.S. McCrady & E.E. Epstein (Eds.) *Addictions: A Comprehensive Guidebook*. New York: Oxford University Press, 187-215.

Donovan, D.M., Carroll, K.M., et al. (2003). Therapies for matching: Selection, development, implementation, and costs. In T.F. Babor (Ed.) *Treatment Matching in Alcoholism*. New York: Cambridge University Press, 42-61.

Donovan, D.M., & Marlatt, G.A. (1993). Behavioral treatment. In M. Galanter (Ed.) *Recent Developments in Alcoholism, Volume 11: Ten Years of Progress*. New York: Plenum Press, 397-411.

Donovan, D.M., & Marlatt, G.A. (Eds.) (2005). *Assessment of Addictive Behaviors* (2nd ed.). New York: Guilford Press.

Dove, W.R. (1995). Ethics training for the alcohol/drug abuse professional. *Alcoholism Treatment Quarterly*, 12(4):19-30.

Doyle, K. (1997). Substance abuse counselors in recovery: Implications for the ethical issue of dual relationships. *Journal of Counseling & Development*, 75(6):428-432.

Drake, R.E., & Mueser, K.T. (2000). Psychosocial approaches to dual diagnosis. *Schizophrenia Bulletin*, 26(1):105-118.

Drake, R.E., Mueser, K.T., et al. (2004). A review of treatments for people with severe mental illnesses and co-occurring disorders. *Psychiatric Rehabilitation Journal*, 27(4):360-374.

Drake, R.E., & Noordsy, D.L. (1994). Case management for people with coexisting severe mental disorder and substance use disorder. *Psychiatric Annals*, 24:427-431.

Dubas, J.S., Lynch, K.B., et al. (1998). Preliminary evaluation of a resiliency-based preschool substance abuse and violence prevention project. *Journal of Drug Education*, 28(3): 235-255.

Dusenbury, L., & Botvin, G.J. (1992). Substance abuse prevention: Competence enhancement and the development of positive life options. *Journal of Addictive Diseases*, 11(3):29-45.

Eggland, E.T. (1995). Charting smarter: Using new mechanisms to organize your paperwork. *Nursing*, 25(September):34-42.

Eliason, M.J., & Hughes, T. (2004). Treatment counselor's attitudes about lesbian, gay, bisexual, and transgendered clients: Urban vs. rural settings. *Substance Use & Misuse*, 39(4):625-644.

Epstein, E.E., & McCrady, B.S. (Eds.) (1999). *Addictions: A Comprehensive Guidebook*. New York: Oxford University Press.

Epstein, E.E., & McCrady, B.S. (2002). Couple therapy in the treatment of alcohol problems. In A.S. Gurman & N.S. Jacobson (Eds.) *Clinical Handbook of Couple Therapy* (3rd ed.). New York: Guilford Press, 597-628.

Erickson, J.R., Chong, J., et al. (1995). Service linkages: Understanding what fosters and what deters from service coordination for homeless adult drug users. *Contemporary Drug Problems*, 22:343-362.

Ettore, E. (1992). *Women and Substance Use*. New Brunswick, NJ: Rutgers University Press.

Evans, K., & Sullivan, J.M. (2001). *Dual Diagnosis: Counseling the Mentally Ill Substance Abuser* (2nd ed.). New York: Guilford Press.

Feld, B.C. (1999). *Bad Kids: Race and the Transformation of the Juvenile Court*. New York: Oxford University Press.

Fenton, L.R., Cecero, J.J., et al. (2001). Perspective is everything: The predictive validity working alliance instruments. *Journal of Psychotherapy Practice & Research*, 10(4):262-268.

Finley, J.R., & Lenz, B.S. (Eds.) (2005). *The Addiction Counselor's Documentation Sourcebook: The Complete Paperwork Resource for Treating Clients With Addictions* (2nd ed.). Hoboken, NJ: John Wiley & Sons.

Finn, A. (2002). Group counseling for people with addictions. In D. Capuzzi & D.R. Gross (Eds.) *Introduction to Group Counseling* (3rd ed.). Denver, CO: Love Publishing Company, 351-376.

Finn, P. (1994). Addressing the needs of cultural minorities in drug treatment. *Journal of Substance Abuse Treatment*, 11(4):325-337.

Finnegan, D.G., & McNally, E.B. (2002). *Counseling Lesbian, Gay, Bisexual, and Transgender Substance Abusers: Dual Identities*. New York: Haworth Press.

Fisher, G.L., & Harrison, T.C. (2004). *Substance Abuse: Information for School Counselors, Social Workers, Therapists, and Counselors*. Boston: Allyn & Bacon.

Fleming, M.F. (2002). Identification and treatment of alcohol use disorders in older adults. In A.M. Gurnack, R. Atkinson, & N. Osgood (Eds.) *Treating Alcohol and Drug Abuse in the Elderly*. New York: Springer Publishing, 85-108.

Flores, P.J. (1997). *Group Psychotherapy With Addicted Populations: An Integration of Twelve-Step and Psychodynamic Theory* (2nd ed.). New York: Haworth Press.

Forman, R.F., Bovasso, G., & Woody, G. (2001). Staff beliefs about addiction treatment. *Journal of Substance Abuse Treatment*, 21(1):1-9.

Forman, R.F., Bovasso, G., et al. (2002). Staff beliefs about drug abuse clinical trials. *Journal of Substance Abuse Treatment*, 23(1):55-60.

Freeman, E.M. (1993). Substance abuse treatment: Continuum of care in service to families. In E.M. Freeman (Ed.) *Substance Abuse Treatment: A Family Systems Perspective*. Newbury Park, CA: Sage Publications, 1-20.

Frese, F.J., Stanley, J., et al. (2001). Integrating evidence-based practices and the recovery model. *Psychiatric Services*, 52(11):1462-1468.

Fulero, S.M., & Wilbert, J.R. (1988). Recordkeeping practices of clinical and counseling psychologists: A survey of practitioners. *Professional Psychology Research and Practice*, 19:658-660.

Galanter, M. (1993). *Network Therapy for Alcohol and Drug Abuse*. New York: Guilford Press.

Galanter, M. (2002). Healing through social and spiritual affiliation. *Psychiatric Services*, 53(9):1072-1074.

Galanter, M. (Ed.) (2003). *Recent Developments in Alcoholism, Volume 16: Research on Alcoholism Treatment*. New York: Springer.

Garcia, S. (1997). Ethical and legal issues associated with substance abuse by pregnant and parenting women. *Journal of Psychoactive Drugs*, 29(1):101-111.

Gardenswartz, L., & Rowe, A. (1994). *The Managing Diversity Survival Guide: A Complete Collection of Checklists, Activities, and Tips* (book and disk). Chicago: Irwin Professional Publishing.

Garito, P.J. (2002). Assessing and treating psychiatric comorbidity in chemically dependent analysis. In D. O'Connell, E. Beyer, et al. (Eds.) *Managing the Dually Diagnosed Patient: Current Issues and Clinical Approaches* (2nd ed.). New York: Haworth Press, 153-185.

Gavetti, M.F., & Constantine, M.G. (2001). Assessment and treatment of alcoholism in older adults: Considerations for mental health clinicians. *Journal of Psychiatry in Independent Practice*, 2(3):61-71.

Gillaspy, J.A., Jr., Wright, A.R., et al. (2002). Group alliance and cohesion as predictors of drug and alcohol abuse treatment outcomes. *Psychotherapy Research*, 12(2):213-229.

Glaser, F.B., & Warren, D.G. (1999). Legal and ethical issues. In B.S. McCrady & E.E. Epstein (Eds.) *Addictions: A Comprehensive Guidebook*. New York: Oxford University Press, 399-413.

Gloria, A.M., & Peregoy, J.J. (1996). Counseling Latino alcohol and other substance users/abusers. *Journal of Substance Abuse Treatment*, 13(2):119-126.

Goddard, P. (2003). Changing attitudes towards harm reduction among treatment professionals: A report from the American Midwest. *International Journal of Drug Policy*, 14(3):257-260.

Godley, S.H., Godley, M.D., et al. (1994). Case management services for adolescent substance abusers: A program description. *Journal of Substance Abuse Treatment*, 11:309-317.

Godley, S.H., Meyers, R.J., et al. (2001). *The Adolescent Community Reinforcement Approach for Adolescent Cannabis Users*. Cannabis Youth Treatment (CYT) Series, Volume 4. DHHS Publication No. (SMA) 01-3489. Rockville, MD: Center for Substance Abuse Treatment, Substance Abuse and Mental Health Services Administration.

Godley, S.H., Risberg, R.A., et al. (2002). *Treatment Manual—Bloomington's Outpatient & Intensive Outpatient Treatment Model*. Bloomington, IL: Chestnut Health Systems.

Goldberg, M.E. (1995). Substance-abusing women: False stereotypes and real needs. *Social Work*, 40(6):789-798.

Goldstein, E.G. (2004). Substance abusers with borderline disorders. In S.L.A. Straussner (Ed.) *Clinical Work With Substance-Abusing Clients* (2nd ed.). New York: Guilford Press, 370-391.

Gomberg, E.S.L., & Nirenberg, T.D. (Eds.) (1993). *Women and Substance Abuse*. Norwood, NJ: Ablex Publishing.

Gordon, A.J., & Zrull, M. (1991). Social networks and recovery: One year after inpatient treatment. *Journal of Substance Abuse Treatment*, 8(3):146-152.

Gordon, J.U. (Ed.) (1994). *Managing Multiculturalism in Substance Abuse Services*. Thousand Oaks, CA: Sage Publications.

Gordon, K. (1993). The treatment of addictive disorders in a private clinical setting. In S.L. Straussner (Ed.) *Clinical Work With Substance Abusing Clients*. New York: Guilford Press, 88-102.

Gorski, T.T., & Kelley, J.M. (1996). *Counselor's Manual for Relapse Prevention With Chemically Dependent Criminal Offenders*. Technical Assistance Publication (TAP) Series 19. DHHS Publication No. (SMA) 96-3115. Rockville, MD: Center for Substance Abuse Treatment, Substance Abuse and Mental Health Services Administration.

Graham, K., Brett, P.J., & Bois, C. (1995). Treatment entry and engagement: A study of the process at assessment/referral centers. *Journal of Contemporary Drug Problems*, 22(1): 61-104.

Graham, K., Timney, C.B., et al. (1995). Continuity of care in addictions treatment: The role of advocacy and coordination in case management. *American Journal of Drug and Alcohol Abuse*, 21:433-451.

Granfield, R., & Cloud, W. (2001). Social capital and natural recovery: The role of social resources and relationships in overcoming addiction without treatment. *Substance Use & Misuse*, 36(11):1543-1549.

Grant, R.M., Ernst, C.C., et al. (1996). When case management isn't enough: A model of paraprofessional advocacy for drug- and alcohol-abusing mothers. *Journal of Case Management*, 5:3-11.

Greenlick, M., Lamb, S., & McCarty, D. (Eds.) (1998). *Bridging the Gap Between Practice and Research: Forging Partnerships With Community-Based Drug and Alcohol Treatment*. Washington, DC: National Academy Press.

Gregoire, T.K., & Snively, C.A. (2001). The relationship of social support and economic self-sufficiency to substance abuse outcomes in a long-term recovery program for women. *Journal of Drug Education*, 31(3):221-237.

Greif, G.L. (1996). Ten common errors beginning substance abuse workers make in group treatment. *Journal of Psychoactive Drugs*, 28:297-299.

Grella, C.E., & Gilmore, J. (2002). Improving service delivery to the dually diagnosed in Los Angeles County. *Journal of Substance Abuse Treatment*, 23(2):115-122.

Grosenick, J.K., & Hatmaker, C.M. (2000). Perceptions of staff attributes in substance abuse treatment. *Journal of Substance Abuse Treatment*, 19(3):273-284.

Gruber, K.J., & Fleetwood, T.W. (2004). In-home continuing care services for substance use affected families. *Substance Use & Misuse*, 39(9):1379-1403.

Gullotta, T.P., Adams, G.R., & Montemayor, R. (Eds.) (1994). *Substance Misuse in Adolescence*. Thousand Oaks, CA: Sage Publications.

Gurnack, A.M., Atkinson, R., & Osgood, N.J. (Eds.) (2002). *Treating Alcohol and Drug Abuse in the Elderly*. New York: Springer Publishing.

Guthmann, D., & Sandberg, K. (1998). Assessing substance abuse problems in deaf and hard of hearing individuals. *American Annals of the Deaf*, 143(1):14-19.

Gwodz, D.T., & Del Togno, V. (1992). Streamlining patient care documentation. *Journal of Nursing Administration*, 22(May):35-39.

Hamilton, N.L., Brantley, L.B., et al. (2001). *Family Support Network for Adolescent Cannabis Users*. Cannabis Youth Treatment Series, Volume 3. DHHS Publication No. (SMA) 01-3488. Rockville, MD: Center for Substance Abuse Treatment, Substance Abuse and Mental Health Services Administration.

Harkness, A.R., & Lilienfeld, S.O. (1997). Individual differences science for treatment planning: Personality traits. *Psychological Assessment*, 9(4):349-360.

Harrington, N.G., & Donohew, L. (1997). Jump Start: A targeted substance abuse prevention program. *Health Education & Behavior*, 24(5):568-586.

Hawkins, J.D., & Catalano, R.F. (1992). *Communities That Care: Action for Drug Abuse Prevention*. San Francisco: Jossey-Bass.

Heather, N., & Miller, W.R. (Eds.) (1998). *Treating Addictive Behaviors* (2nd ed.). New York: Plenum Press.

Heather, N., Peters, T.J., & Stockwell, T. (Eds.) (2001). *International Handbook of Alcohol Dependence and Problems*. New York: John Wiley & Sons.

Heinemann, A. (Ed.) (1993). *Substance Abuse and Physical Disability*. New York: Haworth Press.

Herring, R.D. (1994). Substance use among Native American Indian youth: A selected review of causality. *Journal of Counseling & Development*, 72(6):578-584.

Herring, R.D. (1999). *Counseling Native American Indians and Alaska Natives: Strategies for Helping Professionals*. Thousand Oaks, CA: Sage Publications.

Herrmann, D.S., & McWhirter, J.J. (1997). Refusal and resistance skills for children and adolescents: A selected review. *Journal of Counseling & Development*, 75(3):177-187.

Hogan, J.A., Gabrielson, K.R., et al. (2003). *Substance Abuse Prevention: The Intersection of Science and Practice*. Boston: Allyn & Bacon.

Hser, Y. (1995). A referral system that matches drug users to treatment programs: Existing research and relevant issues. *Journal of Drug Issues*, 25(1):209-224.

Hser, Y.-I., & Anglin, M.D. (2005). Drug treatment and aftercare programs. In R.H. Coombs (Ed.) *Addiction Counseling Review*. Mahwah, NJ: Lawrence Erlbaum Associates.

Hser, Y.-I., Polinsky, M.L., et al. (1999). Matching client's needs with drug treatment services. *Journal of Substance Abuse Treatment*, 16(4):299-305.

Huitt, W.G. (2004). Maslow's hierarchy of needs. *Educational Psychology Interactive*. Valdosta, GA: Valdosta State University.

Humphreys, K. (2004). *Circles of Recovery: Self-Help Organizations for Addictions*. New York: Cambridge University Press.

Humphreys, K., Wing, S., et al. (2004). Self-help organizations for alcohol and drug problems: Toward evidence-based practice and policy. *Journal of Substance Abuse Treatment*, 26(3):151-158, discussion 159-165.

Hyams, G., Cartwright, A., & Spratley, T. (1996). Engagement in alcohol treatment: The client's experience of, and satisfaction with, the assessment interview. *Addiction Research*, 4(2): 105-123.

Imhof, J. (1991). Countertransference issues in alcoholism and drug addiction. *Psychiatric Annals*, 21:292-306.

Ingersoll, K.S., Wagner, C.C., et al. (2002). *Motivational Groups for Community Substance Abuse Programs*. Richmond, VA: Mid-Atlantic Addiction Technology Transfer Center.

Institute of Medicine (1990). *Broadening the Base of Treatment for Alcohol Problems*. Washington, DC: National Academy Press.

Institute of Medicine (1990). *Treating Drug Problems, Volume 1: The Report*. Washington, DC: National Academy Press.

Ivey, A.E., Simek-Morgan, L., et al. (2001). *Theories of Counseling and Psychotherapy: A Multicultural Perspective* (5th ed.). Boston: Allyn & Bacon.

Ja, D., & Aoki, B. (1993). Substance abuse treatment: Cultural barriers in the Asian-American community. *Journal of Psychoactive Drugs*, 25(1):61-71.

Jacka, D., Clode, D., et al. (1999). Attitudes and practices of general practitioners training to work with drug-using patients. *Drug and Alcohol Review*, 18(3):287-291.

Jaffe, J. (Ed.) (1995). *Encyclopedia of Drugs and Alcohol*. New York: Macmillan.

Jandt, F.E. (Ed.) (2003). *Intercultural Communication: A Global Reader*. Thousand Oaks, CA: Sage Publications.

Janikowski, T.P., & Glover-Graf, N.M. (2003). Qualifications, training, and perceptions of substance abuse counselors who work with victims of incest. *Addictive Behaviors*, 28(6):1193-1201.

Jensen, J. (1992). Treatment planning in the 90's: Part 1. *Addiction and Recovery*, 12(7):48-50.

Jensen, J. (1993). Treatment planning in the 90's: Part 2. *Addiction and Recovery*, 13(3):50-52.

Joanning, H., Thomas, F., et al. (1992). Treating adolescent drug abuse: A comparison of family systems therapy, group therapy, and family drug education. *Journal of Marital & Family Therapy*, 18(4):345-356.

Joe, G.W., Simpson, D.D., & Broome, K.M. (1998). Effects of readiness for drug abuse treatment on client retention and assessment of process. *Addiction*, 93(8):1177-1190.

Joe, G.W., Simpson, D.D., et al. (2001). Relationships between counseling rapport and drug abuse treatment outcomes. *Psychiatric Services*, 52(9):1223-1229.

Johnson, N.P., & Chappel, J.N. (1994). Using AA and other 12-Step programs more effectively. *Journal of Substance Abuse Treatment*, 11(2):137-142.

Johnson, S.L. (2004). *Therapist's Guide to Clinical Intervention* (2nd ed.). San Diego, CA: Elsevier, Inc.

Joint Commission on Accreditation of Healthcare Organizations (JCAHO) (2002). *A Practical Guide to Documentation in Behavioral Health Care* (2nd ed.). Oakbrook Terrace, IL: JCAHO.

Joint Commission on Accreditation of Healthcare Organizations (JCAHO) (2005). *2006-2007 Comprehensive Accreditation Manual for Behavioral Health Care*. Oakbrook Terrace, IL: JCAHO.

Joint Commission on Accreditation of Healthcare Organizations (JCAHO) (2005). *2006-2007 Standards for Behavioral Health Care*. Oakbrook Terrace, IL: JCAHO.

Jonnes, J. (1999). *Hep-Cats, Narcs, and Pipe Dreams: A History of America's Romance With Illegal Drugs*. Baltimore: Johns Hopkins University Press.

Kaczmarek, P., Barclay, D., & Smith, M. (1996). Systematic training in client documentation: Strategies for counselor educators. *Counselor Education and Supervision*, 36(September):77-84.

Kadden, R.M., & Skerker, P.M. (1999). Treatment decision making and goal setting. In B.S. McCrady & E.E. Epstein (Eds.) *Addictions: A Comprehensive Guidebook*. New York: Oxford University Press, 216-231.

Kaminer, Y. (2004). Dually diagnosed teens: Challenges for assessment and treatment. *Counselor*, 5(2):62-68.

Kasarabada, N.D., Hser, Y.I., et al. (2002). Do patients' perceptions of their counselors influence outcomes of drug treatment? *Journal of Substance Abuse Treatment*, 23(4):327-334.

Kaskutas, L.A., Marsh, D., & Kohn, A. (1998). Didactic and experiential education in substance abuse programs. *Journal of Substance Abuse Treatment*, 15(1):43-53.

Kauffman, E., Dore, M.M., & Nelson-Zlupko, L. (1995). The role of women's therapy groups in the treatment of chemical dependence. *American Journal of Orthopsychiatry*, 65:355-363.

Kaughman, E. (1991). The family in drug and alcohol addiction. In N.S. Miller (Ed.) *Comprehensive Handbook of Drug and Alcohol Addiction*. New York: Marcel Dekker, 851-876.

Kent, C. (1997). Ending with clients: Closure in counseling. In S. Harrison & V. Carver (Eds.) *Alcohol and Drug Problems: A Practical Guide for Counselors* (2nd ed.). Toronto, Canada: Addiction Research Foundation, 203-215.

Kerr, S.D. (1992). A comparison of four nursing documentation systems. *Journal of Nursing Staff Development*, 8(January/February):276-331.

Khantzian, E.J., Golden, S.J., & McAuliffe, W.E. (1999). Group therapy. In M. Galanter & H.D. Kleber (Eds.) *Textbook of Substance Abuse Treatment* (2nd ed.). Washington DC: American Psychiatric Association, 367-377.

Kinney, J. (2000). Treatment techniques and approaches. In *Loosening the Grip: A Handbook of Alcohol Information* (6th ed.). New York: McGraw-Hill, 558.

Kinney, J. (2003). *Loosening the Grip: A Handbook of Alcohol Information* (7th ed.). New York: McGraw-Hill.

Kirby, M.W. (2004). Self-help organizations for alcohol and drug problems: Toward evidence-based practice and policy. *Journal of Substance Abuse Treatment*, 26(3):161-162.

Kiresuk, T.J., Smith, A., & Cardillo, J.E. (1994). *Goal Attainment Scaling: Applications, Theory, and Measurement*. Mahwah, NJ: Lawrence Erlbaum Associates.

Knight, D.K., & Simpson, D.D. (1999). Family assessment. In P.J. Ott, R.E. Tarter, & R.T. Ammerman (Eds.) *Sourcebook on Substance Abuse: Etiology, Epidemiology, Assessment, and Treatment*. Boston: Allyn & Bacon, 236-247.

Knight, J.R., Sherritt, L., et al. (2002). Validity of the CRAFFT substance abuse screening test among adolescent clinic patients. *Archives of Pediatrics and Adolescent Medicine*, 156(6):607-614.

Knight, J.R., Sherritt, L., et al. (2003). Validity of brief alcohol screening tests among adolescents: A comparison of the AUDIT, POSIT, CAGE, and CRAFFT. *Alcohol, Clinical and Experimental Research*, 27(1):67-73.

Kosten, T.R., Rounsaville, B.J., & Kleber, H.D. (1987). Multidimensionality and prediction and treatment outcome in opioid addicts: 2.5-year follow-up. *Comprehensive Psychiatry*, 28(1):3-13.

Kozier, B., Erb, G., & Oliveri, R. (1991). *Fundamentals of Nursing: Concepts, Process and Practice* (4th ed.). Redwood City, CA: Addison-Wesley.

Kramer, K.L., Robbins, J.M., et al. (2003). Detection and outcomes of substance use disorders in adolescents seeking mental health treatment. *Journal of the American Academy of Child and Adolescent Psychiatry*, 42(11):1318-1326.

L'Abate, L., Farrar, J.L., & Serritella, D. (1991). *Handbook of Differential Treatments for Addictions*. Boston: Allyn & Bacon.

Latimer, W.W., Winters, K.C., et al. (2003). Integrated family and cognitive-behavioral therapy for adolescent substance abusers: A Stage I efficacy study. *Drug and Alcohol Dependence*, 71:303-317.

Laudet, A.B. (2003). Attitudes and beliefs about 12-step groups among addiction treatment clients and clinicians: Toward identifying obstacles to participation. *Substance Use & Misuse*, 38(14):2017-2047.

Laudet, A.B. (April 2005). Exploring the recovery process: Patterns, supports, challenges and future directions. Presented at the Seminar Series of the Division of Epidemiology, Services and Prevention Research, conducted at the National Institute on Drug Abuse, Center for the Study of Addiction and Recovery.

Laudet, A.B., Magura, S., et al. (2000). Recovery challenges among dually diagnosed individuals. *Journal of Substance Abuse Treatment*, 18(4):321-329.

Lawson, A.W., & Lawson, G.W. (1998). *Alcoholism and the Family: A Guide to Treatment and Prevention* (2nd ed.). Gaithersburg, MD: Aspen Publishers.

Lawson, A.W., & Lawson, G.W. (2005). Families and drugs. In R.H. Coombs (Ed.) *Addiction Counseling Review: Preparing for Comprehensive, Certification and Licensing Examinations*. Mahwah, NJ: Lawrence Erlbaum Associates, 175-199.

Lawson, A.W., Lawson, G.W., & Rivers, P.C. (1996). *Essentials of Chemical Dependency Counseling* (2nd ed.). Gaithersburg, MD: Aspen Publishers.

Lawson, G.W., & Lawson, A.W. (1992). *Adolescent Substance Abuse: Etiology, Treatment, and Prevention*. Gaithersburg, MD: Aspen Publishers.

Lawson, G.W., Lawson, A.W., & Rivers, P.C. (1996). Group counseling in the treatment of chemical dependency. In *Essentials of Chemical Dependency Counseling*. Gaithersburg, MD: Aspen Publishers, 141-177.

Lawson, K.A., Wilcox, R.E., et al. (2004). Educating treatment professionals about addiction science research: Demographics of knowledge and belief changes. *Substance Use & Misuse*, 39(8):1235-1258.

Leal, A. (1990). Hispanics and substance abuse: Implications for rehabilitation counselors. *Journal of Applied Rehabilitation Counseling*, 21(3):52-54.

Legal Action Center (2003). *Confidentiality and Communication: A Guide to the Federal Drug and Alcohol Confidentiality Law and HIPAA*. New York: Legal Action Center.

Lemieux, C.M. (2002). Social support among offenders with substance abuse problems: Overlooked and underused? *Journal of Addictions & Offender Counseling*, 23:41-57.

Levin, J.D. (1995). *Introduction to Alcoholism Counseling: A Bio-Psycho-Social Approach* (2nd ed.). New York: Taylor & Francis.

Levin, J.D. (2004). Counseling and therapy techniques in substance abuse treatment. *Issues in Psychoanalytic Psychology*, 26(2):145-162.

Lewis, J.A. (Ed.) (1994). *Addictions: Concepts and Strategies for Treatment*. Gaithersburg, MD: Aspen Publishers.

Lewis, J.A. (2005). Assessment, diagnosis, and treatment planning. In R.H. Coombs (Ed.) *Addiction Counseling Review: Preparing for Comprehensive, Certification, and Licensing Examinations*. Mahwah, NJ: Lawrence Erlbaum Associates, 357-379.

Lewis, J.A., Dana, R.Q., & Blevins, G.A. (2001). *Substance Abuse Counseling* (3rd ed.). Pacific Grove, CA: Brooks/Cole.

Lewis, V., Allen-Byrd, M., et al. (2004). Understanding successful family recovery in treating alcoholism. *Journal of Systemic Therapies*, 23:39-51.

Liddle, H.A. (2002) *Multidimensional Family Therapy for Adolescent Cannabis Users*. Cannabis Youth Treatment Series, Volume 5. DHHS Publication No. (SMA) 02-3660. Rockville, MD: Center for Substance Abuse Treatment, Substance Abuse and Mental Health Services Administration.

Liddle, H.A. (2003). *Multidimensional Family Therapy for Early Adolescent Substance Abuse Treatment Manual*. Bloomington, IL: Chestnut Health Systems.

Lipton, H., & Lee, P. (1998). *Drugs and the Elderly: Clinical, Social, and Policy Perspectives*. Stanford, CA: Stanford University Press.

Litt, M.D., Kadden, R.M., et al. (2003). Coping skills and treatment outcomes in cognitive-behavioral and interactional group therapy for alcoholism. *Journal of Consulting and Clinical Psychology*, 71(1):118-128.

Loganbill, C., & Stoltenberg, C. (1983). The case conceptualization format: A training device for practicum. *Counselor Education and Supervision*, 22: 235-241.

Longabaugh, R. (2003). Involvement of support networks in treatment. *Recent Developments in Alcoholism*, 16:133-147.

Lopez, F. (1994). *Confidentiality of Patient Records for Alcohol and Other Drug Treatment*. Technical Assistance Publication (TAP) Series 13. DHHS Publication No. (SMA) 95-3018. Rockville, MD: Center for Substance Abuse Treatment, Substance Abuse and Mental Health Services Administration.

Lordan, E.J., Kelley, J.M., et al. (1997). Treatment placement decisions: How substance abuse professionals assess and place clients. *Evaluation and Program Planning*, 20(2):137-149.

Lowinson, J.H., Ruiz, P., et al. (Eds.) (1997). *Substance Abuse: A Comprehensive Textbook* (3rd ed.). Baltimore: Lippincott Williams & Wilkins.

Luborsky, L., Crits-Christoph, P., et al. (1986). Do therapists vary much in their success? Findings from four outcome studies. *American Journal of Orthopsychiatry*, 56(4):501-512.

Luborsky, L., Diguer, L., et al. (1996). Factors in outcomes of short-term dynamic psychotherapy for chronic vs. nonchronic major depression. *Journal of Psychotherapy Practice and Research*, 5(2):152-159.

Lyter, S.C., & Lyter, L.L. (2000). Intervention with groups. In A.A. Abbott (Ed.) *Alcohol, Tobacco, and Other Drugs: Challenging Myths, Assessing Theories, Individualizing Interventions*. Washington, DC: National Association of Social Workers Press, 247-304.

Maisto, S.A., & McKay, J.R. (1995). Diagnosis. In J.P. Allen & M. Columbus (Eds.) *Assessing Alcohol Problems: A Guide for Clinicians and Researchers*. NIAAA Treatment Handbook Series, No. 4. Bethesda, MD: National Institute on Alcohol Abuse and Alcoholism, 41-54.

Maisto, S.A., & Saitz, R. (2003). Alcohol use disorders: Screening and diagnosis. *American Journal on Addictions*, 12:S12-S25.

Makover, R.B. (2004). *Treatment Planning for Psychotherapists: A Practical Guide to Better Outcomes*. Arlington, VA: American Psychiatric Publishing, Inc.

Manhal-Baugus, M. (1996). Confidentiality: The legal and ethical issues for chemical dependency counselors. *Journal of Addictions and Offender Counseling*, 17(1):3-11.

Manhal-Baugus, M. (1996). Reducing the risk of malpractice in chemical dependency counseling. *Journal of Addictions and Offender Counseling*, 17(1):35-42.

Maracle, B. (1994). *Crazywater: Native Voices on Addiction and Recovery*. New York: Penguin Books.

Mark, T.L., Kranzler, H.R., et al. (2003). Physicians' opinions about medications to treat alcoholism. *Addiction*, 98(5):617-626.

Marlatt, G.A., Barrett, K., & Daley, D.C. (1999). Relapse prevention. In M. Galanter & H.D. Kleber (Eds.) *Textbook of Substance Abuse Treatment* (2nd ed.). Washington, DC: American Psychiatric Association, 353-366.

Marlatt, G.A., & Donovan, D.M. (Eds.) (2005). *Relapse Prevention: Maintenance Strategies in the Treatment of Addictive Behaviors*. New York: Guilford Press.

Marrelli, T.M. (2000). *Nursing Documentation Handbook* (3rd ed.). St. Louis, MO: Mosby.

Martin, S.S., & Inciardi, J.A. (1993). A case management treatment program for drug-involved prison releases. *Prison Journal*, 73:319-331.

Martino, S., Carroll, K., et al. (2002). Dual diagnosis motivational interviewing: A modification of motivational interviewing for substance-abusing patients with psychotic disorders. *Journal of Substance Abuse Treatment*, (23)4:297-308.

Matano, R.A., & Yalom, I.D. (1991). Approaches to chemical dependency: Chemical dependency and interactive group therapy—A synthesis. *International Journal of Group Psychotherapy*, 41:269-293.

McCaughrin, W.C., & Price, R.H. (1992). Effective outpatient drug treatment organizations: Program features and selection effects. *International Journal of the Addictions*, 27:1335-1358.

McCollum, E.E., & Trepper, T.S. (2001). *Family Solutions for Substance Abuse: Clinical and Counseling Approaches*. New York: Haworth Press.

McCollum, E.E., Trepper, T.S., et al. (2004). Solution-focused group therapy for substance abuse: Extending competency-based models. *Journal of Family Psychotherapy*, 14(4):27-42.

McCrady, B.S., & Epstein, E.E. (1996). Theoretical bases of family approaches to substance abuse treatment. In F. Rotgers, D.S. Keller, & J. Morgenstern (Eds.) *Treating Substance Abuse: Theory and Technique*. New York: Guilford Press, 117-142.

McCrady, B.S., & Epstein, E.E. (Eds.) (1999). *Addictions: A Comprehensive Guidebook*. New York: Oxford University Press.

McCrady, B.S., & Miller, W.R. (Eds.) (1993). *Research on Alcoholics Anonymous: Opportunities and Alternatives*. New Brunswick, NJ: Rutgers Center of Alcohol Studies.

McIntosh, J., & McKeganey, N. (2000). The recovery from dependent drug use: Addicts' strategies for reducing the risk of relapse. *Drugs: Education, Prevention & Policy*, 7(2):179-192.

McIntyre, J.R. (2004). Family treatment of substance abuse. In. S.L.A. Straussner (Ed.) *Clinical Work With Substance-Abusing Clients* (2nd ed.). New York: Guilford Press, 237-263.

McKay, J.R. (1996). Family therapy techniques. In F. Rotgers, D.S. Keller, & J. Morgenstern (Eds.) *Treating Substance Abuse: Theory and Technique*. New York: Guilford Press, 143-173.

McKay, J.R., Lynch, K.G., et al. (2005). Do patient characteristics and initial progress in treatment moderate the effectiveness of telephone-based continuing care for substance use disorders? *Addiction*, 100(2):216-226.

McKay, J.R., Lynch, K.G., et al. (2005). The effectiveness of telephone-based continuing care for alcohol and cocaine dependence: 24-month outcomes. *Archives of General Psychiatry*, 62(2):199-207.

McKim, W.A. (2002). *Drugs and Behavior: An Introduction to Behavioral Pharmacology* (5th ed.). Upper Saddle River, NJ: Prentice Hall.

McLellan, A.T., Carise, D., & Kleber, H.D. (2003). Can the national addiction treatment infrastructure support the public's demand for quality care? *Journal of Substance Abuse Treatment*, 25(2):117-121.

McLellan, A.T., Grissom, G.R., et al. (1993). Private substance abuse treatments: Are some programs more effective than others? *Journal of Substance Abuse Treatment*, 10(3):243-254.

McLellan, A.T., Grissom, G.R., et al. (1997). Problem-service "matching" in addiction treatment: A prospective study in 4 programs. *Archives of General Psychiatry*, 54(8):730-735.

McLellan, A.T., Hagan, T.A., et al. (1999). Does clinical case management improve outpatient addiction treatment? *Drug & Alcohol Dependence*, 55(1-2):91-103.

McLellan, A.T., Kushner, H., et al. (1992). The fifth edition of the Addiction Severity Index. *Journal of Substance Abuse Treatment*, 9(3):199-213.

McLellan, A.T., Luborsky, L., et al. (1980). An improved diagnostic evaluation instrument for substance abuse patients: The Addiction Severity Index. *Journal of Nervous and Mental Disease*, 168(1):26-33.

McLellan, A.T., Luborsky, L., et al. (1985). New data from the Addiction Severity Index: Reliability and validity in three centers. *Journal of Nervous and Mental Disease*, 173(7):412-423.

McLellan, A.T., & McKay, J.R. (1998). Components of successful treatment programs: Lessons from the research literature. In A.W. Graham, T.K. Schultz, & B.B. Wilford (Eds.) *Principles of Addiction Medicine* (2nd ed.). Chevy Chase, MD: American Society of Addiction Medicine, 327-343.

McLellan, A., McKay, J., et al. (2005). Reconsidering the evaluation of addiction treatment: From retrospective follow-up to concurrent recovery monitoring. *Addiction*, 100(4):447-458.

McLellan, A.T., Woody, G.E., et al. (1988). Is the counselor an "active ingredient" in substance abuse rehabilitation? An examination of treatment success among four counselors. *Journal of Nervous and Mental Disease*, 176:430-432.

Mee-Lee, D. (1998). Use of patient placement criteria in the selection of treatment. In A.W. Graham, T.K. Schultz, & B.B. Wilford (Eds.) *Principles of Addiction Medicine* (2nd ed.). Chevy Chase, MD: American Society of Addiction Medicine, 363-370.

Mee-Lee, D., Miller, M.M., & Shulman, G.D (1996). *Patient Placement Criteria for the Treatment of Substance-Related Disorders* (2nd ed.). Chevy Chase, MD: American Society of Addiction Medicine.

Meier, P.S., Barrowclough, C., et al. (2005). The role of the therapeutic alliance in the treatment of substance misuse: A critical review of the literature. *Addiction*, 100(3):304-316.

Mejta, C.L., Bokos, P.J., et al. (1997). Improving substance abuse treatment access and retention using a case management approach. *Journal of Drug Issues*, 27:329-340.

Mercado, M.M. (2000). The invisible family: Counseling Asian American substance abusers and their families. *Family Journal: Counseling and Therapy for Couples and Families*, 8(3): 267-272.

Meyers, K., Hagan, T.A., et al. (1999). Critical issues in adolescent substance use assessment. *Drug and Alcohol Dependence*, 55(3):235-246.

Meyers, R.J., Apodaca, T.R., et al. (2002). Evidence-based approaches for the treatment of substance abusers by involving family members. *Family Journal: Counseling and Therapy for Couples and Families*, 10(3):281-288.

Meyers, R.J., & Smith, J.E. (1995). *Clinical Guide to Alcohol Treatment: The Community Reinforcement Approach*. New York: Guilford Press.

Meyers, R.J., Smith, J.E., & Miller, E.J. (1998). Working through the concerned significant other. In W.R. Miller & N. Heather (Eds.) *Treating Addictive Behaviors* (2nd ed.). New York: Plenum Press, 149-161.

Miller, G. (2002). *Incorporating Spirituality in Counseling and Psychotherapy: Theory and Technique*. Hoboken, NJ: John Wiley & Sons.

Miller, G. (2004). *Learning the Language of Addiction Counseling* (2nd ed.). Hoboken, NJ: John Wiley & Sons.

Miller, N.S., Gold, M.S., & Smith, D.E. (Eds.) (1997). *Manual of Therapeutics for Addictions*. New York: Wiley-Liss.

Miller, W.R., & Heather, N. (Eds.) (1998). *Treating Addictive Behaviors: Processes of Change* (2nd ed.). New York: Plenum Press.

Miller, W.R., & Rollnick, S. (1991). *Motivational Interviewing: Preparing People To Change Addictive Behavior*. New York: Guilford Press.

Miller, W.R., & Rollnick, S. (2002). *Motivational Interviewing: Preparing People To Change Addictive Behavior* (2nd ed.). New York: Guilford Press.

Mirabeau, F. (1997). Evaluation outcome study of family education in the treatment of alcoholic patients. *Journal of Addictions Nursing*, 9(2):77-80.

Mitchell, R. (2001). *Documentation in Counseling Records* (2nd ed.). Alexandria, VA: American Counseling Association.

Moline, M.E., Williams, G.T., & Austin, K.M. (1997). *Documenting Psychotherapy: Essentials for Mental Health Practitioners*. Thousand Oaks, CA: Sage Publications.

Montemuro, M. (1988). CORE: Documentation: A complete system for documenting nursing care. *Nursing Management*, 19(August):28-32.

Monti, P.M., Kadden, R.M., et al. (2002). *Treating Alcohol Dependence: A Coping Skills Training Guide* (2nd ed.). New York: Guilford Press.

Moos, R.H., Finney, J.W., & Cronkite, R.C. (1990). *Alcoholism Treatment: Context, Process, and Outcome*. New York: Oxford University Press.

Moos, R.H., & Moos, B.S. (2004). Help-seeking careers: Connections between participation in professional treatment and Alcoholics Anonymous. *Journal of Substance Abuse Treatment*, 26(3):167.

Mora, J. (1998). The treatment of alcohol dependency among Latinas: A feminist, cultural and community perspective. *Alcoholism Treatment Quarterly*, 16:163-177.

Morehouse, E.R. (2000). Matching services and the needs of children of alcoholic parents: A spectrum of help. In S. Abbott (Ed.) *Children of Alcoholics: Selected Readings, Volume II*. Rockville, MD: National Association for Children of Alcoholics, 95-117.

Moxley, D.P., & Washington, O.G. (2001). Strengths-based recovery practice in chemical dependency: A transpersonal perspective. *Families in Society: The Journal of Contemporary Human Services*, 82(3):251-262.

Mueser, K.T., Noordsy, D.L., et al. (2003). *Integrated Treatment of Dual Disorders: A Guide to Effective Practice*. New York: Guilford Press.

Murphy, L.L., & Impara, J.C. (Eds.) (1996). *Buros Desk Reference: Assessment of Substance Abuse*. Lincoln, NE: Buros Institute of Mental Measurements.

Musto, D.F. (1999). *The American Disease: Origins of Narcotic Control* (3rd ed.). New York: Oxford University Press.

NAADAC–The Association for Addiction Professionals (2004). *NAADAC Code of Ethics*. Alexandria, VA: NAADAC.

Najavits, L. (2002). *Seeking Safety: A Treatment Manual for PTSD and Substance Abuse*. New York: Guilford Press.

Najavits, L.M., Crits-Christoph, P., et al. (2000). Clinicians' impact on the quality of substance use disorder treatment. *Substance Use & Misuse*, 35(12-14):2161-2190.

Najavits, L.M., & Weiss, R.D. (1994). Variations in therapist effectiveness in the treatment of patients with substance use disorder: An empirical review. *Addictions*, 89:679-688.

Nathan, P.E., & Gorman, J.M. (Eds.) (2002). *A Guide to Treatments That Work* (2nd ed.). New York: Oxford University Press.

National Association of Social Workers (NASW) (1999). *Code of Ethics*. Washington, DC: NASW.

National Institute on Drug Abuse (NIDA) (1994). *Assessing Drug Abuse Among Adolescents and Adults: Standardized Instruments*. Clinical Report Series. Rockville, MD: NIDA.

National Institute on Drug Abuse (NIDA) (1999). *Principles of Drug Addiction Treatment: A Research-Based Guide*. NIH Publication No. 00-4180. Rockville, MD: NIDA.

National Institute on Drug Abuse (NIDA), Szapocznik, J., et al. (2003). *Brief Strategic Family Therapy for Adolescent Drug Abuse*. Therapy Manuals for Drug Addiction, Manual 5. Rockville, MD: NIDA, 87.

Nebelkopf, E., & Phillips, M. (2003). Morning star rising: Healing in Native American communities. *Journal of Psychoactive Drugs*, 35(1):1-5.

Negreiros, J. (1994). Theoretical orientations in drug abuse prevention research. *Drugs: Education, Prevention and Policy*, 1(2):135-142.

Niemann, S.H. (2001). Guidance/psychoeducational groups. In D. Capuzzi & D.R. Gross (Eds.) *Introduction to Group Counseling* (3rd ed.). Denver, CO: Love Publishing Company, 265-290.

Nowinski, J. (1990). *Substance Abuse in Adolescents and Young Adults: A Guide to Treatment*. New York: W.W. Norton.

Nowinski, J. (1999). Self-help groups for addictions. In B.S. McCrady & E.E. Epstein (Eds.) *Addictions: A Comprehensive Guidebook*. New York: Oxford University Press, 328-346.

Nowinski, J. (2003). Self-help groups. In J.L. Sorensen, R.A. Rawson, et al. (Eds.) *Drug Abuse Treatment Through Collaboration: Practice and Research Partnerships That Work*. Washington DC: American Psychological Association, 55-70.

O'Connell, D., & Beyer, E. (Eds.) (2002). *Managing the Dually Diagnosed Patient: Current Issues and Clinical Approaches* (2nd ed.). New York: Haworth Press.

O'Farrell, T.J. (Ed.) (1993). *Treating Alcohol Problems: Marital and Family Interventions*. New York: Guilford Press.

O'Farrell, T.J., Choquette, K.A., et al. (1993). Behavioral marital therapy with and without additional couples relapse prevention sessions for alcoholics and their wives. *Journal of Studies on Alcohol*, 54:652-666.

O'Farrell, T.J., & Fals-Stewart, W. (1999). Treatment models and methods: Family models. In B.S. McCrady & E.E. Epstein (Eds.) *Addictions: A Comprehensive Guidebook*. New York: Oxford University Press, 287-305.

O'Farrell, T.J., & Fals-Stewart, W. (2000). Behavioral couples therapy for alcoholism and drug abuse. *Behavior Therapist*, 23(3):49-54, 70.

O'Farrell, T.J., & Murphy, C.M. (2002). Behavioral couples therapy for alcoholism and drug abuse: Encountering the problem of domestic violence. In C. Wekerle & A.-M. Wall (Eds.) *Violence and Addiction Equation: Theoretical and Clinical Issues in Substance Abuse and Relationship Violence*. New York: Brunner-Routledge, 293-303.

Ogborne, A.C., Wild, T.C., et al. (1998). Measuring treatment process beliefs among staff of specialized addiction treatment services. *Journal of Substance Abuse Treatment*, 15(4):301-312.

O'Hara, P., Parris, D., et al. (1998). Influence of alcohol and drug use on AIDS risk behavior among youth in dropout prevention. *Journal of Drug Education*, 28(2):159-168.

O'Leary, T.A., Brown, S., et al. (2002). Treating adolescents together or individually? Issues in adolescent substance abuse interventions. *Alcoholism: Clinical and Experimental Research*, 26(6):890-899.

O'Leary, T.A., & Monti, P.M. (2002). Cognitive-behavioral therapy for alcohol addiction. In S.G. Hofmann & M.C. Tompson (Eds.) *Treating Chronic and Severe Mental Disorders: A Handbook of Empirically Supported Interventions*. New York: Guilford Press, 234-257.

Orenstein, A., & Ullman, A. (1996). Characteristics of alcoholic families and adolescent substance use. *Journal of Alcohol and Drug Education*, 41(3):86-101.

Oslin, D.W., & Holden, R. (2002). Recognition and assessment of alcohol and drug dependence in the elderly. In A.M. Gurnack, R. Atkinson, & N. Osgood (Eds.) *Treating Alcohol and Drug Abuse in the Elderly*. New York: Springer Publishing, 11-31.

Pagani-Tousignant, C. (1992). *Breaking the Rules: Counseling Ethnic Minorities*. Minneapolis, MN: Johnson Institute.

Palm, J. (2004). The nature of and responsibility for alcohol and drug problems: Views among treatment staff. *Addiction Research & Theory*, 12(5):413-431.

Paniagua, F.A. (2005). *Assessing and Treating Culturally Diverse Clients: A Practical Guide* (3rd ed.). Thousand Oaks, CA: Sage Publications.

Paul, J.P., Stall, R., & Bloomfield, K.A. (1991). Gay and alcoholic: Epidemiologic and clinical issues. *Alcohol Health and Research World*, 15:151-160.

Pedersen, P.B. (1997). *Culture-Centered Counseling Interventions: Striving for Accuracy*. Thousand Oaks, CA: Sage Publications.

Pedersen, P.B. (1997). *Decisional Dialogues in a Cultural Context: Structured Exercises*. Thousand Oaks, CA: Sage Publications.

Pedersen, P.B., Draguns, J.G., et al. (Eds.) (2002). *Counseling Across Cultures* (5th ed.). Thousand Oaks: Sage Publications.

Perkinson, R.R. (1997). *Chemical Dependency Counseling: A Practical Guide*. Thousand Oaks, CA: Sage Publications.

Perkinson, R.R. (1997). Group therapy. In *Chemical Dependency Counseling: A Practical Guide*. Thousand Oaks, CA: Sage Publications, 69-87.

Petrila, J. (1998). *Ethical Issues for Behavioral Health Care Practitioners and Organizations in a Managed Care Environment*. Managed Care Technical Assistance Series 5. Rockville, MD: Substance Abuse and Mental Health Services Administration.

Petry, N.M., Petrakis, I., et al. (2001). Contingency management interventions: From research to practice. *American Journal of Psychiatry*, 158(5):694-702.

Petry, N.M., & Simcic, F., Jr. (2002). Recent advances in the dissemination of contingency management techniques: Clinical and research perspectives. *Journal of Substance Abuse Treatment*, 23(2):81-86.

Pilgrim, C., Abbey, A., et al. (1998). Implementation and impact of a family-based substance abuse prevention program in rural communities. *Journal of Primary Prevention*, 18(3): 341-361.

Pita, D.D. (2004). *Addictions Counseling: A Practical and Comprehensive Guide to Counseling People With Addictions*. New York: Crossroad Publishing.

Platt, J., & Husband, S. (1993). An overview of problem solving and social skills approaches in substance abuse treatment. *Psychotherapy*, 30:276-278.

Pope-Davis, D.B., & Coleman, H.L.K. (1997). *Multicultural Counseling Competencies, Assessment, Education and Training, and Supervision*. Thousand Oaks, CA: Sage Publications.

Powell, D.J., & Brodsky, A. (2004). *Clinical Supervision in Alcohol and Drug Abuse Counseling: Principles, Models, Methods* (Revised ed.). San Francisco: Jossey-Bass.

Presser, N.R., & Pfost, K.S. (1985). A format for individual psychotherapy session notes. *Professional Psychology Research and Practice*, 16:11-16.

Prochaska, J.O., & DiClemente, C.C. (1982). Transtheoretical therapy: Toward a more integrative model of change. *Psychotherapy: Theory, Research, and Practice*, 19:276-288.

Prochaska, J.O., & DiClemente, C.C. (1986). Toward a comprehensive model of change. In W.R. Miller & N. Heather (Eds.) *Treating Addictive Behaviors: Processes of Change*. New York: Plenum Press, 3-27.

Prochaska, J.O., DiClemente, C.C., & Norcross, J.C. (1992). In search of how people change: Applications to addictive behaviors. *American Psychologist*, 47:1102-1114.

Prochaska, J.O., DiClemente, C.C., & Norcross, J.C. (1997). In search of how people change: Applications to addictive behaviors. In G.A. Marlett & G.R. Vandenbos (Eds.) *Addictive Behaviors*. Washington, DC: American Psychological Association, 671-695.

Project MATCH Research Group (1998). Therapist effects in three treatments for alcohol problems. *Psychotherapy Research*, 8(4):455-474.

Ramsay, J.R., & Newman, C.F. (2000). Substance abuse. In F.M. Dattilio & A. Freeman (Eds.) *Cognitive-Behavioral Strategies in Crisis Intervention* (2nd ed.). New York: Guilford Press, 126-149.

Rapp, R.C., Siegal, H.A., & Fisher, J.H. (1992). A strengths-based model of case management/advocacy: Adapting a mental health model to practice work with persons who have substance abuse problems. In R.S. Ashery (Ed.) *Progress and Issues in Case Management*. NIDA Research Monograph No. 127. DHHS Publication No. (ADM) 92-19467. Rockville, MD: National Institute on Drug Abuse, 79-91.

Rawson, R.A., Obert, J.L., et al. (1993). Relapse prevention models for substance abuse treatment. *Psychotherapy*, 30:284-298.

Rassool, G.H., & Lind, J.E. (2000). Perception of addiction nurses toward clinical supervision: An exploratory study. *Journal of Addictions Nursing*, 12(1):23-29.

Read, J.P., Bollinger, A.R., & Sharkansky, E. (2003). Assessment of comorbid substance use disorder and posttraumatic stress disorder. In P. Ouimette & P.J. Brown (Eds.) *Trauma and Substance Abuse: Causes, Consequences, and Treatment of Comorbid Disorders*. Washington, DC: American Psychological Association.

Rehabilitation Accreditation Commission (RAC) (1998). *Introduction to Outcomes Management in Behavioral Health*. Tucson, AZ: RAC.

Rehabilitation Accreditation Commission (RAC) (1999). *Opioid Treatment Program Accreditation Standards*. Tucson, AZ: RAC.

Rehabilitation Accreditation Commission (RAC) (1999). *2000 Behavioral Health Standards Manual*. Tucson, AZ: RAC.

Reilly, P.M., & Shopshire, M.S. (2002). *Anger Management for Substance Abuse and Mental Health Clients: A Cognitive Behavioral Therapy Manual*. DHHS Publication No. (SMA) 02-3661. Rockville, MD: Center for Substance Abuse Treatment, Substance Abuse and Mental Health Services Administration.

Ridley, M.S. (1994). Practical issues in the application of case management to substance abuse treatment. *Journal of Case Management*, 3:132-138.

Riordan, R.J., & Walsh, L. (1994). Guidelines for professional referral to Alcoholics Anonymous and other twelve step groups. *Journal of Counseling & Development*, 72:351-355.

Robbins, M.S., Bachrach, K., et al. (2002). Bridging the research gap in adolescent substance abuse treatment: The case of brief strategic family therapy. *Journal of Substance Abuse Treatment*, 23(3):123-132.

Roget, N., & Johnson, M. (1995). *Pre- and Post-Treatment Planning in the Substance Abuse Treatment Case Management Process*. Carson City, NV: Nevada Bureau of Alcohol and Drug Abuse.

Rollnick, S. (1998). Readiness, importance, and confidence: Critical conditions of change in treatment. In W.R. Miller & N. Heather (Eds.) *Treating Addictive Behaviors* (2nd ed.). New York: Plenum Press, 49-60.

Rotgers, F. (2002). Clinically useful, research validated assessment of persons with alcohol problems. *Behaviour Research & Therapy*, 40:1425.

Rotgers, F., Keller, D.S., & Morgenstern, J. (Eds.) (2003). *Treating Substance Abuse: Theory and Technique*. New York: Guilford Press, 117-142.

Rotunda, R.J., West, L., et al. (2004). Enabling behavior in a clinical sample of alcohol-dependent clients and their partners. *Journal of Substance Abuse Treatment*, 26(4):269-276.

Rounsaville, B.J., & Carroll, K.M. (1997). Individual psychotherapy. In J.H. Lowinson, P. Ruiz, et al. (Eds.) *Substance Abuse: A Comprehensive Textbook*. Baltimore: Lippincott Williams & Wilkins, 430-439.

Rowe, C., Liddle, H.A., et al. (2002). Integrative treatment development: Multidimensional family therapy for adolescent substance abuse. In F.W. Kaslow (Ed.) *Comprehensive Handbook of Psychotherapy: Integrative/Eclectic*, Volume 4. New York: John Wiley & Sons, 133-161.

Rowe, C., Parker-Sloat, E., et al. (2003). Family therapy for early adolescent substance abuse. In S.J. Stevens & A.R. Morral (Eds.) *Adolescent Substance Abuse Treatment in the United States: Exemplary Models From a National Evaluation Study*. New York: Haworth Press, 105-132.

Rugel, R.P. (1991). Addiction treatment in groups: A review of therapeutic factors. *Small Group Research*, 22:475-491.

Rutzky, J. (1998). *Coyote Speaks: Creative Strategies for Psychotherapists Treating Alcoholics and Addicts*. Northvale, NJ: Jason Aronson.

Rydz, D., Shevell, M.I., et al. (2005). Developmental screening. *Journal of Child Neurology*, 20(1):4-21.

Sabin, C., Benally, H., et al. (n.d.). *Walking in Beauty on the Red Road: A Holistic Cultural Treatment Model for American Indian and Alaska Native Adolescents and Families*. Bloomington, IL: Chestnut Health Systems.

Sampl, S., & Kadden, R. (2001). *Motivational Enhancement Therapy and Cognitive Behavioral Therapy for Adolescent Cannabis Users: 5 Sessions*. Cannabis Youth Treatment Series, Volume 1. DHHS Publication No. (SMA) 01-3486. Rockville, MD: Center for Substance Abuse Treatment, Substance Abuse and Mental Health Services Administration.

Sanchez-Craig, M., & Wilkinson, D.A. (1997). Guidelines for advising on treatment goals. In S. Harrison & V. Carver (Eds.) *Alcohol and Drug Problems: A Practical Guide for Counselors* (2nd ed.). Toronto, Canada: Addiction Research Foundation, 125-139.

Santisteban, D.A., & Szapocznik, J. (1994). Bridging theory, research and practice to more successfully engage substance abusing youth and their families into therapy. *Journal of Child and Adolescent Substance Abuse*, 3:9-24.

Schafer, J., & Cherpitel, C.J. (1998). Differential item functioning of the CAGE, TWEAK, BMAST, and AUDIT by gender and ethnicity. *Contemporary Drug Problems*, 25(2):399-409.

Scharf, L. (1997). Revising nursing documentation to meet patient outcomes. *Nursing Management*, 28(April):38-39.

Schorling, J.B., & Buchsbaum, D.G. (1997). Screening for alcohol and drug abuse. *Medical Clinics of North America*, 81(4):845-865.

Schuckit, M.A. (1999). Goals of treatment. In M. Galanter & H.D. Kleber (Eds.) *American Psychiatric Press Textbook of Substance Abuse Treatment* (2nd ed.). Washington, DC: American Psychiatric Press, 89-95.

Schultz, J.E., & Parran, T., Jr. (1998). Principles of identification and intervention. In A.W. Graham, T.K. Schultz, & B.B. Wilford (Eds.) *Principles of Addiction Medicine* (2nd ed.). Chevy Chase, MD: American Society of Addiction Medicine, 249-261.

Schwartz, R.C., & Smith, S.D. (2003). Screening and assessing adolescent substance abuse: A primer for counselors. *Journal of Addictions & Offender Counseling*, 24:23-34.

Schwebel, R. (2004). *The Seven Challenges Manual*. Tucson, AZ: Viva Press.

Scoates, G.H., Fishman, M., & McAdam, B. (1997). Health Care Focus Documentation— More Efficient Charting. *Nursing Management*, 27(April):30-32.

Scott, C.G. (2000). Ethical issues in addiction counseling. *Rehabilitation Counseling Bulletin*, 43(4):209-214.

Semlitz, L. (2001). Treatment planning and case management. In T.W. Estroff (Ed.) *Manual of Adolescent Substance Abuse Treatment*. Arlington, VA: American Psychiatric Publishing, Inc.

Senior, M., Smith, M., & Taylor, S. *EMPACT–Suicide Prevention Center Teen Substance Abuse Treatment Program Treatment Manual*. Bloomington, IL: Chestnut Health Systems.

Shaw, S. (1999). Group therapy with adolescents. In G.W. Lawson & A.W. Lawson (Eds.) *Adolescent Substance Abuse: Etiology, Treatment, and Prevention*. Gaithersburg, MD: Aspen Publishers, 121-131.

Sheehan, M.F. (1991). Dual diagnosis. *Psychiatric Quarterly*, 62:107-134.

Sheridan, M.J., & Green, R.G. (1993). Family dynamics and individual characteristics of adult children of alcoholics: An empirical analysis. *Journal of Social Service Research*, 17(1-2): 73-97.

Sholevar, G.P., & Schwoeri, L.D. (2003). Alcoholic and substance-abusing families. In G.P. Sholevar (Ed.) *Textbook of Family and Couples Therapy: Clinical Applications*. Washington, DC: American Psychiatric Association, 671-694.

Shoptaw, S., Stein, J.A., & Rawson, R.A. (2000). Burnout in substance abuse counselors: Impact of environment, attitudes, and clients with HIV. *Journal of Substance Abuse Treatment*, 19(2):117-126.

Shulman, L.H., Shapira, S.R., et al. (2000). Outreach developmental services to children of patients in treatment for substance abuse. *American Journal of Public Health*, 90(12): 1930-1933.

Siegal, H.A. (2005). Case management. In R.H. Coombs (Ed.) *Addiction Counseling Review: Preparing for Comprehensive, Certification and Licensing Examinations*. Mahwah, NJ: Lawrence Erlbaum Associates, 381-399.

Siegal, H.A., Rapp, R.C., et al. (1995). The strengths perspective of case management: A promising inpatient substance abuse treatment enhancement. *Journal of Psychoactive Drugs*, 27:67-72.

Siegal, H.A., Rapp, R.C., et al. (1997). The role of case management in retaining clients in substance abuse treatment: An exploratory analysis. *Journal of Drug Issues*, 27:821-832.

Singelis, T.M. (Ed.) (1998). *Teaching About Culture, Ethnicity, and Diversity: Exercises and Planned Activities*. Thousand Oaks, CA: Sage Publications.

Slaght, E., Lyman, S., et al. (2004). Promoting healthy lifestyles as a biopsychosocial approach to addictions counseling. *Journal of Alcohol and Drug Education*, 48(2):5-16.

Smith, J.E., Milford, J.C., & Meyers, R.J. (2004). CRA and CRAFT: Behavioral approaches to treating substance-abusing individuals. *Behavior Analyst Today*, 5(4):391-403.

Snow, D.L., Tebes, J.K., & Ayers, T.S. (1997). Impact of two social-cognitive interventions to prevent adolescent substance use: Test of an amenability to treatment model. *Journal of Drug Education*, 27(1):1-17.

Snow, M.G., Prochaska, J.O., & Rossi, J.S. (1994). Processes of change in Alcoholics Anonymous: Maintenance factors in long term sobriety. *Journal of Studies on Alcohol*, 55(3):362-371.

Snyder, C.M., Kaempfer, S.H., & Reis, K. (1996). An interdisciplinary, interagency, primary care approach to case management of the dually diagnosed patient with HIV disease. *Journal of the Association of Nurses in AIDS Care*, 7(5):72-82.

Sobell, M.B., & Sobell, L.C. (1999). Stepped care for alcohol problems: An efficient method for planning and delivering clinical services. In J.A. Tucker, D.M. Donovan, & G.A. Marlatt (Eds.) *Changing Addictive Behavior: Bridging Clinical and Public Health Strategies*. New York: Guilford Press, 331-343.

Soden, T., & Murray, R. (1997). Motivational interviewing techniques. In S. Harrison & V. Carver (Eds.) *Alcohol and Drug Problems: A Practical Guide for Counselors* (2nd ed.). Toronto, Canada: Addiction Research Foundation, 19-59.

Spencer, J.W. (1993). Making "suitable referrals": Social workers' construction and use of informal referral networks. *Sociological Perspectives*, 36(3):271-285.

Springer, D.W., McNeece, C.A., & Arnold, E.M. (2003). Group intervention. In D.W. Springer, C.A. McNeece, & E.M. Arnold (Eds.) *Substance Abuse Treatment for Criminal Offenders: An Evidence-Based Guide for Practitioners*. Washington, DC: American Psychological Association.

Springer, D.W., McNeece, C.A., et al. (2003). Individual treatment. In D.W. Springer, C.A. McNeece, & E.M. Arnold (Eds.) *Substance Abuse Treatment for Criminal Offenders: An Evidence-Based Guide for Practitioners*. Washington, DC: American Psychological Association.

Springer, D.W., & Orsbon, S.H. (2002). Families Helping Families: Implementing a multifamily therapy group with substance-abusing adolescents. *Health & Social Work*, 27(3):204-207.

Springhouse Corporation (1994). *Nursing Fundamentals*. Springhouse, PA: Springhouse Corporation.

Springhouse Corporation (2002). *Illustrated Manual of Nursing Practice* (3rd ed.). Philadelphia: Lippincott Williams & Wilkins.

Stanton, M. (2005). Couples and addiction. In M. Harway (Ed.) *Handbook of Couples Therapy*. New York: John Wiley & Sons, 313-336.

Stanton, M.D., & Heath, A.W. (1997). Family and marital therapy. In J.H. Lowinson, P. Ruiz, et al. (Eds.) *Substance Abuse: A Comprehensive Textbook*. Baltimore: Lippincott Williams & Wilkins, 448-454.

Stasiewicz, P.R., & Bradizza, C.M. (2002). Alcohol use disorders. In M. Hersen & L.K. Porzelius (Eds.) *Diagnosis, Conceptualization, and Treatment Planning for Adults: A Step-by-Step Guide*. Mahwah, NJ: Lawrence Erlbaum Associates, 271-290.

Stellato-Kabat, D., Stellato-Kabat, J., & Garrett, J. (1995). Treating chemical-dependent couples and families. In A.M. Washton (Ed.) *Psychotherapy and Substance Abuse: A Practitioner's Handbook*. New York: Guilford Press, 314-336.

Stevens, P., & Smith, R.L. (2004). *Substance Abuse Counseling: Theory and Practice* (3rd ed.). Old Tappan, NJ: Prentice Hall.

Storti, S.A. (1997). *Alcohol, Disabilities, and Rehabilitation*. San Diego, CA: Singular Publishing Group.

Straussner, S.L. (1997). Group treatment with substance abusing clients. *Journal of Chemical Dependency Treatment*, 7:67-80.

Substance Abuse and Mental Health Services Administration (SAMHSA) (2004). *The Confidentiality of Alcohol and Drug Abuse Patient Records Regulation and the HIPAA Privacy Rule: Implications for Alcohol and Substance Abuse Programs*. Rockville, MD: SAMHSA.

Sue, D.W., & Sue, D. (2002). *Counseling the Culturally Different: Theory and Practice* (4th ed.). New York: John Wiley & Sons.

Sullivan, E., Mino, M., et al. (2002). *Families as a Resource in Recovery From Drug Abuse: An Evaluation of la Bodega de la Familia*. New York, NY: Vera Institute of Justice.

Sullivan, G. (1996). Is your documentation all it should be? RN, 59(October):59-61.

Summers, R.F., & Barber, J.P. (2003). Therapeutic alliance as a measurable psychotherapy skill. *Academic Psychiatry*, 27(3):160-165.

Sylvestre, D.L., Loftis, J.M., et al. (2004). Co-occurring hepatitis C, substance use, and psychiatric illness: Treatment issues and developing integrated models of care. *Journal of Urban Health*, 81(4):719-734.

Szapocznik, J., Hervis, O., et al. (2003). *Brief Strategic Family Therapy for Adolescent Drug Abuse*. Therapy Manuals for Drug Addiction, Manual 5. NIH Publication No. 03-4751. Rockville, MD: National Institute on Drug Abuse.

Szapocznik, J., & Williams, R.A. (2000). Brief strategic family therapy: Twenty-five years of interplay among theory, research and practice in adolescent behavior problems and drug abuse. *Clinical Child & Family Psychology Review*, 3(2):117-134.

Thomas, C., & Corcoran, J. (2001). Empirically based marital and family interventions for alcohol abuse: A review. *Research on Social Work Practice*, 11(5):549-575.

Thombs, D.L. (1999). *Introduction to Addictive Behaviors* (2nd ed.). New York: Guilford Press.

Tickle-Degnen, L. (1998). Communication with clients about treatment outcomes: The use of meta-analytic evidence in collaborative treatment planning. *American Journal of Occupational Therapy*, 52(7):526-530.

Tickle-Degnen, L. (1998). Using research evidence in planning treatment for the individual client. *Canadian Journal of Occupational Therapy*, 65(3):152-159.

Tims, F.M., Leukefeld, C.G., & Platt, J.J. (Eds.) (2001). *Relapse and Recovery in Addictions*. New Haven, CT: Yale University Press.

Trimble, J.E., Bolek, C.S., & Niemcryk, S.J. (Eds.) (1992). *Ethnic and Multicultural Drug Abuse: Perspectives on Current Research*. New York: Harrington Park Press.

Tuchman, E., Gregory, C., et al. (2005). Office-based opioid treatment (OBOT): Practitioner's knowledge, attitudes, and expectations in New Mexico. *Addictive Disorders and Their Treatment*, 4(1):11-19.

Vannicelli, M. (1992). *Removing the Roadblocks: Group Psychotherapy With Substance Abusers and Family Members*. New York: Guilford Press.

Vannicelli, M. (2002). A dualistic model for group treatment of alcohol problems: Abstinence-based treatment for alcoholics, moderation training for problem drinkers. *International Journal of Group Psychotherapy*, 52(2):189-213.

Vaughn, M.G., & Howard, M.O. (2004). Adolescent substance abuse treatment: A synthesis of controlled evaluations. *Research on Social Work Practice*, 14(5):325-335.

Vedel, E., & Emmelkamp, P.M.G. (2004). Behavioral couple therapy in the treatment of a female alcohol-dependent patient with comorbid depression, anxiety, and personality disorders. *Clinical Case Studies*, 3(3):187-205.

Velasquez, M.M. (2001). *Group Treatment for Substance Abuse: A Stages of Change Therapy Manual*. New York: Guilford Press.

Velleman, R. (2001). *Counseling for Alcohol Problems* (2nd ed.). Thousand Oaks, CA: Sage Publications.

Velleman, R., & Templeton, L. (2002). Family interventions in substance misuse. In T. Petersen & A. McBride (Eds.) *Working With Substance Misusers*. New York: Routledge, 145-153.

Venturelli, P. (Ed.) (1994). *Drug Use in America: Social, Cultural, and Political Perspectives*. Boston: Jones and Bartlett Publishers.

Wakefield, P.J., Williams, R.E., et al. (1996). *Couple Therapy for Alcoholism: A Cognitive-Behavioral Treatment Manual*. New York: Guilford Press.

Waldron, H.B., & Slesnick, N. (1998). Treating the family. In W.R. Miller & N. Heather (Eds.) *Treating Addictive Behaviors* (2nd ed.). New York: Plenum Press, 271-283.

Wallen, J. (1993). *Addiction in Human Development: Developmental Perspectives on Addiction and Recovery*. New York: Haworth Press.

Waltman, D. (1995). Key ingredients to effective addictions treatment. *Journal of Substance Abuse Treatment*, 12(6):429-439.

Walton, M.A., Blow, F.C., & Booth, B.M. (2000). A comparison of substance abuse patients' and counselors' perceptions of relapse risk: Relationship to actual relapse. *Journal of Substance Abuse Treatment*, 19(2):161-169.

Ward, K. (2002). Confidentiality in substance abuse counseling. *Journal of Social Work Practice in the Addictions*, 2(2):39-52.

Washton, A.M. (1995). *Psychotherapy and Substance Abuse: A Practitioner's Handbook*. New York: Guilford Press.

Washton, A.M. (1997). Structured outpatient group therapy. In J.H. Lowinson, P. Ruiz, et al. (Eds.) *Substance Abuse: A Comprehensive Textbook* (3rd ed.). Baltimore: Lippincott Williams & Wilkins, 440-448.

Appendix D – Complete Bibliography

Washton, A.M. (2002). Outpatient groups at different stages of substance abuse treatment: Preparation, initial abstinence, and relapse prevention. In D.W. Brook & H.I. Spitz (Eds.) *Group Therapy of Substance Abuse*. New York: Haworth Press, 99-121.

Webb, C., Scudder, M., et al. (2002). *The Motivational Enhancement Therapy and Cognitive Behavioral Therapy Supplement: 7 Sessions of Cognitive Behavioral Therapy for Adolescent Cannabis Users*. Cannabis Youth Treatment Series, Volume 2. DHHS Publication No. (SMA) 02-3659. Rockville, MD: Center for Substance Abuse Treatment, Substance Abuse and Mental Health Services Administration.

Weed, L.L. (1968). Medical records that guide and teach. *New England Journal of Medicine*, 278:593-600.

Weinstein, D.L. (Ed.) (1993). *Lesbians and Gay Men: Chemical Dependency Treatment Issues*. New York: Haworth Press.

White, W. (1996). *Pathways From the Culture of Addiction to the Culture of Recovery: A Travel Guide for Addiction Professionals*. Center City, MN: Hazelden.

White, W. (2002). *An Addiction Recovery Glossary: The Languages of American Communities of Recovery*. Behavioral Health Recovery Management Project. Peoria, IL: Fayette Companies; Bloomington, IL: Chestnut Health Systems.

White, W. (2004). Recovery: The new frontier. *Counselor*, 5(1):18-21.

White, W. (2004). *Recovery Rising: Radical Recovery in America*. Behavioral Health Recovery Management Project. Peoria, IL: Fayette Companies; Bloomington, IL: Chestnut Health Systems.

White, W., Boyle, M., & Loveland, D. (2003). A model to transcend the limitations of addiction treatment. *Behavioral Health Management*, 23(3):38-44.

White, W., Boyle, M., et al. (2004). *What Is Behavioral Health Recovery Management? A Brief Primer*. Behavioral Health Recovery Management Project. Peoria, IL: Fayette Companies; Bloomington, IL: Chestnut Health Systems.

White, W., & Sanders, M. (2004). *Recovery Management and People of Color: Redesigning Addiction Treatment for Historically Disempowered Communities*. Behavioral Health Recovery Management Project. Peoria, IL: Fayette Companies; Bloomington, IL: Chestnut Health Systems.

White, W.L. (1998). *Slaying the Dragon: The History of Addiction Treatment and Recovery in America*. Bloomington, IL: Chestnut Health Systems.

White, W.L., & Popovitz, R.E. (2001). *Critical Incidents: Ethical Issues in the Prevention and Treatment of Addictions* (2nd ed.). Bloomington, IL: Chestnut Health Systems.

White Bison, Inc. (2002). *The Red Road to Wellbriety: In the Native American Way*. Colorado Springs, CO: White Bison, Inc.

Whittinghill, D. (2002). Ethical considerations for the use of family therapy in substance abuse treatment. *Family Journal: Counseling and Therapy for Couples and Families*, 10(1):75-78.

Wiger, D.E. (2005). *The Clinical Documentation Sourcebook: The Complete Paperwork Resource for Your Mental Health Practice* (3rd ed.). New York: John Wiley & Sons.

Wiger, D.E. (2005). *The Psychotherapy Documentation Primer*. New York: John Wiley & Sons.

Wiger, D.E., & Solberg, K.B. (2001). *Tracking Mental Health Outcomes: A Therapist's Guide to Measuring Client Progress, Analyzing Data, and Improving Your Practice*. New York: John Wiley & Sons.

Wild, T.C., Newton-Taylor, B., et al. (2001). Attitudes toward compulsory substance abuse treatment: A comparison of the public, counselors, probationers and judges' views. *Drugs: Education, Prevention & Policy*, 8(1):33-45.

Williams, R., & Gorski, T.T. (1997). *Relapse Prevention Counseling for African Americans: A Culturally Specific Model*. Independence, MO: Herald House/Independence Press.

Williams, R., & Gorski, T.T. (1997). *Relapse Warning Signs for African Americans: A Culturally Specific Model*. Independence, MO: Herald House/Independence Press.

Winters, K.C. (2001). Assessing adolescent substance use problems and other areas of functioning: State of the art. In P.M. Monti, S.M. Colby, & T.A. O'Leary (Eds.) *Adolescents, Alcohol, and Substance Abuse: Reaching Teens Through Brief Interventions*. New York: Guilford Press, 80-108.

Winters, K.C., Latimer, W.W., & Stinchfield, R. (2002). Clinical issues in the assessment of adolescent alcohol and other drug use. *Behaviour Research & Therapy*, 40(12):1443-1456.

Witkiewitz, K., & Marlatt, G.A. (2004). Relapse prevention for alcohol and drug problems: That was Zen, this is Tao. *American Psychologist*, 59(4):224-235.

Woody, G.E. (2003). Research findings on psychotherapy of addictive disorders. *American Journal on Addictions*, 12(3):S19.

Zelvin, E. (1993). Treating the partners of substance abusers. In S.L. Straussner (Ed.) *Clinical Work With Substance-Abusing Clients*. New York: Guilford Press, 196-213.

Ziedonis, D., Krejci, J., et al. (2001). Integrated treatment of alcohol, tobacco, and other drug addictions. In J. Kay (Ed.) *Integrated Treatment of Psychiatric Disorders*. Washington, DC: American Psychiatric Association, 79-111.

Zimmerman, M., Sheeran, T., et al. (2004). Screening for psychiatric disorders in outpatients with DSM-IV substance use disorders. *Journal of Substance Abuse Treatment*, 26(3): 181-188.

Zuckerman, E.L. (2003). *The Paper Office: Forms, Guidelines, and Resources To Make Your Practice Work Ethically, Legally, and Profitably* (3rd ed.). New York: Guilford Press.

Zweben, A., & Fleming, M.F. (1999). Brief interventions for alcohol and drug problems. In J.A. Tucker, D.M. Donovan, & G.A. Marlatt (Eds.) *Changing Addictive Behavior: Bridging Clinical and Public Health Strategies*. New York: Guilford Press, 251-282.

Zweben, J.E. (Ed.) (1990). Understanding and preventing relapse. *Journal of Psychoactive Drugs*, 22(2).

Zweben, J.E. (1995). Integrating psychotherapy and 12-Step approaches. In A.M. Washton (Ed.) *Psychotherapy and Substance Abuse: A Practitioner's Handbook*. New York: Guilford Press, 124-140.

Zweben, J.E. (2001). Hepatitis C: Education and counseling issues. *Journal of Addictive Diseases*, 20(1):33-42.

Appendix E – Other Contributors

Research assistance was provided by the following individuals:

Christopher Anderson, Ph.D. Candidate
Michelle Burgener, M.A.
Charlotte M. Chapman, LPC, CAC
Deborah Cruze
Claire Imholtz, M.L.S.
Nancy J. Kendall
Michael Mancini, Ph.D. Candidate
Pamela Miles
Andrea Mitchell
Mary O'Malia
Virgie Paul, M.L.S.
Substance Abuse Librarians and Information Specialists (SALIS)
Nancy Sutherland
Joycelyn Tucker Burgo, M.A.
Jan Wrolstad, M.Div.

The following individuals served as consultants or field reviewers or contributed in other ways to the revisions:

Holly M. Anderson, M.S.
Sandra C. Anderson, Ph.D.
Steve Applegate, M.Ed.
Carolyn S. Barrett-Ballinger
Janice S. Bennett, M.S., CSAC
Digna Betancourt-Swingle, M.S.W.
Greg Blevins, Ph.D.
Sandra Brown, Ph.D.
Remi J. Cadoret, M.D.
Donald V. Cline, M.Ed., M.A.
Evadne Cox-McCleary
Thomas M. Delegatto
George De Leon, Ph.D.
Maria Del Mar Garcia, M.S.W., M.H.S.
Dallas M. Dolan, M.S., CCDC, CPC
Catherine Dubé, Ed.D.
Arthur C. Evans, Ph.D.
Linda Foley
Terence T. Gorski, M.S.W.
Paul Grace, M.S.
Rick Gressard, Ph.D., LPC, MAC
Richard Hayton, M.A.
Lorraine K. Hill, M.P.S, MAC, CAAC
Jerome H. Jaffe, M.D.
Steve Jaggers, M.S.
Karen Kelly, Ph.D., MAC, CRPS, CCS, CCJS
Roxanne Kibben, M.A., NCAC I
Gary Lawson, Ph.D.
Judy Lewis, Ph.D.
Bruce Lorenz, NCAC II
Janet Mann
Peter Manoleas, LCSW
Neal McGarry
David Miller, M.A., CSAC II
Merlene Miller, M.A.
Peter Myers, Ph.D.
Peter E. Nathan, Ph.D.
Angie Olson, M.S.
Eileen McCabe O'Mara, Ed.D., MAC
Peter Palanca, M.A., CADC
Jeff Pearcy, M.P.A., CADC III
Paul D. Potter, M.S.W., MAC
Anthony R. Quintiliani, Ph.D., CDAS/HCHS, NCAC II
Nereida Diaz Rodriguez, Ph.D.
Mark Sanders, LCSW, CADC
Kevin R. Scheel, M.S., MAC, LMFT
Arthur J. Schut, M.A.
Howard J. Shaffer, Ph.D.
William L. Shilley, M.A.
Michael Taleff, Ph.D., CAC, MAC
Tom TenEyck, M.A.
Kevin Wadalavage, M.A., CASAC, MCAC
Alicia Wendler, M.A.
Richard Wilson, M.A.
Joan E. Zweben, Ph.D.
Janet Zwick